Paddy 'Scoop' Reynolds was born ages ago in east Belfast. He attended the Christian Brothers secondary school in Barrack Street, before joining the local *Daily Mail* in the 1940s as an office-boy-cum-reporter. He is a retired Northern news editor for the *Irish Press* group and a reformed alcoholic, off the booze for so long that he feels he could swim in it — provided he keeps his mouth shut.

THE LATE PADDY MURPHY

To Willie

With Best Wishes

Paddy Reynolds

THE LATE PADDY MURPHY

Memoirs of an Irish Journalist

PADDY REYNOLDS

THE BREHON PRESS
BELFAST

First published 2004 by
The Brehon Press Ltd
1A Bryson Street,
Belfast BT5 4ES
Northern Ireland

ISBN 0 9544867 3 0

Cover design: The Valkyrie
Printed by Cox & Wyman Ltd

ACKNOWLEDGEMENTS

Thanks first and foremost to my journalist daughter Pauline, who press-ganged me into this, typed every word, dot and comma at my stuttering dictation, and researched and sub-edited the entire book from beginning to end.

Thanks also to Brendan Anderson and Damian Keenan, my ever helpful, risk-taking publishers.

Acknowledgement is due to all those living and dead (RIP) who provided much anecdotal material, including, above all, my own wee Ma. It was she who, in my cub-reporting days, was so prolific in her newsgathering sorties that practically every other house in our neighbourhood at one time or another featured in my stories, setting what must have been a record for national newspapers.

Thanks also to John Parker, James A (Peter) Robinson, Henry Millar, Tom Samways, Jack Murdoch, Charlie Fennell, Seamus Brady, Mick O'Kane, Michael Keane, Bill Redmond, Gerry Fox, Matt Farrell, George Kerr, Colonel Matt Feehan, Vincent Browne, Eamon de Valera, Dáil Deputies Seán Dunne and Maureen O'Carroll, Senator Michael Ahern, Malachy McAlister, Ciaran McKeown, Donal O'Donnell, Alan Murray, Declan (The Digger) Fay, Colin Brady, James and Eileen Kelly, Paddy Scott, Paddy Topping, Oscar Carolan, Eddie Dineen, Brendan Murphy, Billy Simpson, Cecil Deeney and Johnny Nesbitt. Not forgetting Lord (Gerry) Fitt, the Reverend Dr Ian K Paisley, Lord and Lady Donegall, Brendan Behan, Myles na Gopaleen and Paddy Kavanagh.

to my darling wife Enda and four gorgeous daughters:
Anne, Pauline, Joanie and Colette

PART ONE

one

THE OMENS FOR A CAREER IN journalism were not promising. As a timorous, wide-eyed office boy with the *Daily Mail* in Belfast I might have claimed, with some justification perhaps, that I had reached the first rung of the ladder. But when the big chance of a breakthrough that could have brought me up a step or two presented itself, I fell off my perch. I bungled an exclusive story that could well have been the making of me.

On the morning of Wednesday 14 April 1943 my boss, the chief reporter, called me in for a showdown. James A (Peter) Robinson was rated as one of the best journalists in the country. I trembled in the presence of the great man as he launched his post-mortem interrogation, poking my left shoulder with the index finger of his right hand, punctuating every word with a piston-like jab.

'And where,' he demanded ominously, 'did you say you lived?'

I gave him no credit for his memory as I'd told him only a few days earlier. But I said again that I lived at number 15 Albert Drive.

'And is that anywhere near Bell's Bridge?' he asked in a tone which suggested he already knew the answer. Indeed, it was only a stone's throw away, I assured him.

'And tell me,' he went on as if he had something up his sleeve. 'Did anything happen last night at Bell's Bridge?'

Of course something had happened. Had he not heard? 'A man was murdered,' I said.

'A man was murdered? A man was murdered?' he slowly repeated, savouring every measured word. 'And how the hell do you know?'

Of course I knew. Didn't I see them carrying the body from the stream wrapped in a sheet? Better than that, I had all the salient facts. The victim was Hugh Craig. He was aged 35, a butcher by trade from Ballygowan, County Down. And how did I know all that? The man who found the body told me. He had picked up the victim's identity card, which was lying near the corpse and read the details before the police arrived.

And what else did I know? Well, only what this man and other bystanders told me. The victim was lying naked near the edge of the stream, face upwards and head slightly to the side, showing a bullet hole above the right ear. He was wearing only socks, collar and tie. His shirt was missing but his jacket and overcoat were thrown carelessly over the body. There was a rumour that his balls had been cut off, but I withheld this information, not because it was unconfirmed, but because I was afraid the Boss would think I was in the habit of using bad language.

'And pray tell me,' Robinson persisted sarcastically. 'What else do you know?'

'The victim was engaged to Mina Hill and they were to be married next June,' I replied.

'And how the hell did you know that?' the Boss retorted.

I explained that the man who found the body worked in Belfast's aircraft factory and he recognised the girl's photograph, which was with the victim's identity card. In fact, she was a secretary in the factory and he knew her well.

'Don't tell me you've any more details?' said the Boss, showing symptoms of burgeoning apoplexy.

I went on to recount that, according to police District Inspector Moffat, who arrived at the scene to lead the murder inquiry, the theory was that Craig was shot elsewhere and his body dumped near the stream, which was less than one hundred yards off the main Cregagh Road.

'A murder on your doorstep and you bloody well missed it!' the Boss exploded. 'The *Daily Mail* hadn't a line of it this morning. We could have had a scoop if only you'd phoned me. And why the hell didn't you, you stupid little bugger?'

Now, that was the unkindest cut of all. I may have been a 14-year-old greenhorn, but I wasn't stupid. Of course I knew it was a big story and I ought to have phoned him about it, even though I was only the office boy. But there was a cruel twist to it all and I hadn't the heart to explain it, even by way of mitigation.

I was already in tears that the Boss should think me such a fool. The simple truth was I just hadn't the money to phone, nor could I get it. I was too ashamed to tell him I couldn't raise the two pennies to make the call in case he would think we were poverty-stricken in our house. After all, a single penny in those days was a week's pocket money.

When I got home on the night of the murder I was in high spirits and anxious to tell the family all I knew. But when I announced that I had to phone the Boss, my sister Molly and two brothers, Joe and Willie, began to tease me.

'Listen to him. He's only the office boy and already he thinks he's a reporter.'

It knocked the heart out of me. They weren't being deliberately cruel, as children can be. I suspect it was their way of trying to hide the sad fact that we didn't have a penny between us.

I confided none of this to the Boss, who concluded his verbal onslaught with the edict: 'In future boy, if you see two dogs shagging in the street, or a man spitting in a public place, bloody well phone me.'

I felt I had kissed goodbye to any prospect I ever had of becoming a reporter and concluded that being an office boy was a dead end job anyway. Why I'd bothered to join the newspaper in the first place was now a matter of profound regret. Initially, it was an escapist bolthole for me. Faced with the prospect of another year in the same class at school, I had decided to look for a job. The setback was due to my being hospitalised for appendicitis.

My father had planned a university education for me, a first in the ancestral family, though he could ill afford the money from his postman's pay. So I made my first and only call to the Labour Exchange Bureau in Corporation Street, known colloquially in Belfast as the 'Brew'. I reckoned that if I got work I could forget about further education.

The clerk behind the counter somehow assumed I was after a white-collar job. An innocent abroad, I wasn't quite sure what he meant when he said there was a vacancy for a clerk in the *Daily Mail*. It sounded promising.

Where I came from in east Belfast, clerks were a bit of a status symbol. I had never even heard of the *Daily Mail*, which sounded more like a post office than a newspaper, so I decided the least I could do was see what it was like in case I was asked about it at the interview.

I made for the nearest newspaper stand and, having glimpsed the front page, my heart sank. Alongside the masthead was the paper's slogan: 'For King and Empire'. I immediately ruled myself out.

I was no monarchist and was brought up to believe that, as far as jobs were concerned in my divided city, a Catholic had no chance with an employer who 'kicked with the wrong foot'. The consensus was that Catholics were deemed to be republicans and thus anti-'King and Empire'. The feeling that my journey to the *Daily Mail* in Rosemary Street was not really necessary was compounded by the fact that the clerk in the 'Brew' had warned that there were about six other candidates already ahead of me for the job.

There were two doors at either end of the *Daily Mail* offices and I didn't know which one to enter. The door on the left said 'Circulation' in gold lettering with a black border and the one on the right said 'Editorial'. Not knowing exactly what each word meant, I took a chance and went through the door on the left only to be told I was in the wrong place and it was the editorial department I wanted.

This wasn't a good start and I thought of beating a retreat but before I could, I was led into what can only be described as a euphemism for an office. I would have been ashamed to admit that my place of work was so dilapidated. The floor was covered with linoleum, much of it worn down to the bare floorboards. The front windows, which afforded a display of newspaper pictures for public scrutiny, were screened off by heavy, dust-laden, wartime blackout curtains. These were drawn at night to frustrate German bombers. The chocolate brown coloured wooden walls were plastered with myriad old newspaper clippings, long past their sell-by date. Interspersed on the borders of these was a bewildering riot of telephone numbers, scribbled it seemed at random and some written almost up as far as ceiling level. It was as if every time a phone call was made it was obligatory to scrawl the number on the wall.

The only furniture was four rickety chairs and two old tables, which could have passed as collectors' items if they were not so disfigured by the burns made by God knows how many cigarette ends. One of the chairs was a swivel type, but because the gyration coil was broken it was permanently stuck and completely lopsided. This seat, nevertheless, served the news desk, another the sports desk. There was only one chair for visitors. The fourth was at a teleprinter, which seemed completely out of place in this Dickensian setting.

The only heating was provided by a small electric, dirt encrusted fire with an exposed element, which mysteriously still burned red despite being broken in two. A man in a trilby was leaning over it with a long strip of torn newspaper when I arrived for the job interview. As he thrust the paper onto the bare element, a huge flame shot up with imminent danger of setting his hat alight. Thus, he lit his cigarette, carelessly allowing the ash from the paper to fall into the fire.

Then he turned to face me, this man with a renowned reputation as the doyen of local journalists. He was universally known as Peter Robinson whose byline, however, always appeared inexplicably in the *Daily Mail* as James A Robinson. I eventually put this down to affectation.

I was not aware of it then, but I was later to learn that the *Daily Mail* was such an establishment newspaper in those days that its hierarchy regarded its Belfast office as something of a consulate outpost of the British Empire. It referred to its chief correspondent as 'Our Man in Ulster'. It supported the Orange Order and eulogised the Orange Lambeg Drum in occasional leading articles as symbolising, in its thunderous rhythmic beat, 'Ulster's throbbing loyalty to the Crown'. I felt decidedly out of place.

When James A Robinson was poached from the *Belfast Telegraph* to become the *Mail's* special correspondent in Belfast, it was as if a diplomatic post was being filled. I was later to see photographs of 'his nibs' taking up his appointment, posing on the steps of Northcliffe House in London, wearing a top hat and tails like some Ulster Raj and sporting a gold topped walking stick, as befitting an important sense of occasion.

One of the first questions the great man asked was when could I start work, as if I had already accepted the job. It made me wonder why the six or so rivals ahead of me for the post had not been successful. Perhaps they did a 'bunk' as soon as they saw the dump they were to work in. No mention was made about salary or prospects, so I asked him.

'Ten shillings a week,' he said, and almost in the same breath changed it to 'twelve and sixpence' when he saw the look on my face.

Fair dues to him. He didn't ask my religion, but it was obvious he had a good idea already when I told him I went to the Christian Brothers school.

On the subject of work prospects he really floored me by his bland assurance 'there's not a boy has left this office who hasn't landed a good job', which left me speculating if any boy had ever actually stayed.

'You need sharpened up,' he said, stubbing me in the shoulder with his index finger as was his wont. 'We'll soon take the corners off you, boy.' He always called me 'boy' in the manner of someone from the Deep South of Alabama.

There's no denying I had a lot to learn. Painfully shy, self-conscious in the extreme, introverted, insecure and timid to a fault, I felt deficient in all the qualities that were surely the stuff of ace reporters. Such was my personality, make-up and social background that I held in awe people in high places — people who lived in big houses, people with posh or educated accents, people in uniform, moneyed people and generally people endowed with all the attributes I lacked.

Unaccountably as a youngster I had, on the other hand, grandiose ideas despite my glaring lack of assets. I certainly would not have liked too many people to know that our family of six lived in a house for which the rent was only six shillings and fourpence a week (the equivalent of thirty-two pence nowadays), which was a damning status symbol in my eyes.

And why hadn't my father the decency to hold down a better job than a mere postman, knowing how sensitive was his son, his second born? Although there was plenty of love in our home and no real deprivation, subconsciously I felt deserving of a much better lot in life.

However, after a few days in my first job, I began to feel it might not be all that bad. The office was a sort of magnet for some very interesting people — well-known journalists and politicians I would never otherwise have encountered. A frequent visitor was the Reverend Ian Paisley, long before he gained notoriety. He used to arrive at the office on a heavy roadster bicycle, which was apparently his only mode of transport at the time. He would remove his bicycle clips before engaging the Boss in conversation with seemingly interminable dire warnings about Ulster being sold up the river at every twist and turn, a predilection that was to be his concern for the rest of his life.

A flattering highlight of my first few days as office boy — clerk is too grand a job description — was my being deemed eligible to be introduced to a real-life peer of the Realm, and me from a back street. Reporting for duty I was about to hang up my coat, but there was no place to hang it and I had to settle for the back of a chair when the Boss said there were a couple of people who wanted to meet me. Fancy that.

When I entered the office I noticed a man, about whom there was nothing really striking, and a woman who struck a most remarkable figure indeed. While he spurned a chair, which was no doubt far too dirty for him to use, she sat on top of one of the tables with her knees tucked tightly under her chin, stretching her skirt almost to splitting point. From my level, I could see up her clothes and blushed accordingly. But she seemed quite at ease, a truly beautiful woman who was immaculately dressed. But like her husband she obviously thought the *Daily Mail* chairs were not fit for elitist bums.

'This is the office boy,' said the Boss as I shook their hands. 'And this, boy, is Lady Donegall; and this, the Marquis of Donegall.'

Wow, wait until my pals heard when I got home that not only had I met a Lord and a Lady, but I also knew the colour of Her Ladyship's knickers.

'And what is your name?' His Lordship politely inquired.

'Pat,' I gulped. 'Paddy if you like.'

'Nice to meet you, Patrick,' he said warmly, elevating him in my eyes.

For over two centuries the fortunes of Belfast had been closely bound up with Lord Donegall's ancestors. They practically owned the place. The final act of the family's patronage was the presentation by his father — the 9th Earl, Lord Donegall — of Belfast Castle and its extensive grounds to the City Council in 1934 for the use of the public.

The contemporary Lord Donegall was writing a weekly social column called 'Almost in Confidence' in the *Sunday Dispatch*, a now defunct sister paper of the *Daily Mail.* Soon, I was to feature briefly in His Lordship's jottings.

During one of his fleeting visits to Belfast, I had bought a dog ferret in Smithfield market, just a short distance from the *Daily Mail* office, in pursuance of a sporting hobby. I belonged to a gang in our street, which was typical of those times. We specialised in rabbit hunting in the Cregagh Hills. I had also purchased a muzzle for our new ferret to stop it gorging its prey and a little bell to monitor its meanderings in the burrows.

His Lordship was intrigued by this and, as I explained to him the finer points of rabbit hunting and was showing him how to muzzle the animal, it slipped from my grasp onto the floor and scooted away. It disappeared under a six feet high stack of newspaper files in a dark corner of the room. These files dated back for years and were left to moulder and accumulate dust. There was enough grime about the office as it was, so we left well enough alone and were content to wait for 'Snookie' to come out when he was ready.

He had been christened 'Snookie' by Bill Norris, the circulation manager. The name, by the way, was later to be transferred to the Boss. It stuck with him for the rest of his life.

Lady Donegall, in particular, evinced special interest in the missing ferret and at times was close to tears, worrying about its welfare. Miss Bingham, the circulation department secretary, brought a saucer of milk and some chopped liver to try and coax Snookie out, as no one seemed inclined to dismantle the extremely heavy pile of papers.

Finally after three days, during which time strict orders were given to keep all doors shut in case Snookie escaped and was run over in Rosemary Street, the chastened little creature emerged, clearly in need of some tender loving care.

This epic was to inspire Lord Donegall to write in his column the following Sunday how he had gone on safari in deepest Belfast in search of the elusive Snookie.

I also had my moments when Lord and Lady Donegall invited me to join them on a shopping trip. He wanted to buy a cigarette lighter designed in the shape of a Guinness bottle. As I was leading the way to Leahy, Kelly and Leahy's store at the corner of Cornmarket I felt vicariously important as we were smartly saluted by every passing sailor, soldier and airman. There were a lot of them about at the time.

Lord Donegall wore an army officer's uniform, though it occurred to me he must have been a non-combatant as he displayed no military distinctions, simply a shoulder flash bearing the legend 'War Correspondent'. It seemed to be somewhat at variance with the flash on his other shoulder which read 'Home Guard'.

In my quest for career advancement, the most demoralising chore

I had to perform was helping to feed the Boss's cats. At least three or four times a week in the line of duty, I was sent to Sawyers, an upmarket delicatessen shop in Castle Street, to buy a quarter of fish. It cost the Boss only a few pennies, but I paid a high price in terms of humiliation. I would try to be served by the same shop assistant each time I called as the fewer members of staff who knew about my predicament the better.

When I was first sent on this errand, I was going to rebel as a conscientious objector. Was a quarter of fish a weight or a measure? One way or another it was a big embarrassment. The Boss meant a quarter pound in weight — a lousy four ounces. Were the cats on a diet or what, I often asked myself.

He didn't even tell me what kind of fish to get. 'Just tell them it's for my wife's cats,' came the Boss's curt reply. Easier said than done. Such was my shame — what would the neighbours think? — that I used to place my order in a whisper in case anyone overheard me. I never failed to assure the shop assistant that it didn't matter what kind of fish it was as it was only for the Boss's cats.

As I made my journey by bus with the cat food to the Robinson family home in the posh Knock area of Belfast, I would reflect that if only I had the money I could order half a pound of fish to take the bad look off it and save my blushes.

two

SECURITY OF TENURE IN MY HUMBLE post with the *Daily Mail* was precarious from the beginning for two very good reasons.

Not only had I got off to an inglorious start by missing the scoop of a lifetime — a murder on my own doorstep — but the words of the Boss at my interview were now sounding more and more ominous. Stressing the powerful merits of the job, his logic somehow escaped me as he seemed to make a virtue of the fact that there was not one of my predecessors who had left who had not gone on to better themselves in other walks of life. This, he boasted, was due to the invaluable experience they gained in their sojourn with the *Daily Mail.*

Naturally, this left me wondering why none of them remained with that illustrious newspaper. It certainly didn't say much for any prospects of promotion.

Finding another job, however, was not going to be easy. The only work experience I had gained in my young lifetime was down on a farm in the Cregagh environs, an area long since transformed into a sprawling housing estate.

The farm was run by Johnny Nesbitt, known throughout the neighbourhood as Johnny the Milkman, who lived to be one hundred years old. A bigger skinflint I had never encountered, but as a schoolboy I dearly loved life on the farm. I spent many happy hours rambling through the fields, playing in the hayloft, horse riding and milking the cows. I even enjoyed mucking out the stables and byres, relishing the country smells, which made it feel good to be alive.

Johnny the Milkman and his money were not easily parted. In the generosity of his heart, he could only afford to pay me one shilling a week. But as I have said, work on the farm was a labour of love, though I could have been doing with a few bob. This was recognised by Johnny's father, an extremely portly man of over twenty stone about whom it was said he was worth his weight in gold — a man made of money.

Unknown to his son, he would slip me an extra shilling every Friday night without fail, and always with the admonition: 'Don't say a word.'

Such was his enormous girth that he had difficulty delving into his cavernous trouser pocket to extract a fistful of money, which left me marvelling at how anyone could amass such a hoard of shillings and pence.

Johnny's father clearly regarded his shilling as hush money, a sweetener not to be divulged to his son in case he would think I was being overpaid. I also had a sneaking suspicion that Johnny's father recognised I was worth an added inducement to retain my services.

As a farmer's boy, I usually clocked in at six in the morning before going to school and would milk four or five cows until my wee wrists ached. There was only one drawback to my milking ability. I could extract enough milk from a cow to fill a bucket, but it was too heavy for me to carry, so someone always had to take it to the creamery for me.

After my farm chores, I had to walk a good two miles in all weathers to St Anthony's Primary School in Willowfield. This saved me the ha'penny tram fare, which I couldn't afford.

My pocket money was three pennies a week and nothing gave me more pleasure every Friday night than to present my mother with the two shillings, a whole florin, I had earned during the week down on the farm. Every penny counted in our spartan household budget.

After school, I helped Johnny the Milkman on his rounds. The cart was drawn by Pickles, a piebald and a dearly loved horse if ever there was one. I was convinced the 'oul horse' knew every word I said. I was forever slipping him tidbits.

Johnny was dour and set in his ways: a creature born of habit, as they say in the country.

Every weekday, for example, when we came to number 8 on our round in Downshire Park, he would say without fail, 'Only a pint for Mrs Turk t'day.' It was always 'only a pint' for Mrs Turk, except on Sundays.

On the Sabbath day, again without fail, he changed his tune to add a codicil to his normal injunction: 'A pint and a half for Mrs Turk — she's making custard t'day.'

These were his exact words every single Sunday in life when we got to Mrs Turk's house. It was never tapioca or rice pudding she was making. It was always custard. How Johnny the Milkman knew what she was having for pudding every Sunday that God sent, and why she never varied the menu, remained one of the great imponderables of my boyhood.

On Saturday evenings he always made a point of issuing the stern order to his farmer boys: 'Don't be feeding Pickles any corn tonight. I don't want her shitting in the street when the folk are going to church tomorrow.'

Of course, we never heeded him and instead would shovel the corn into Pickles for maximum effect.

Now Johnny always dressed up for his Sunday round. He wore his best suit, a severe black serge with matching bowler, a stiff starched white butterfly collar and a neat, black bow tie. While Pickles jogged along, Johnny stood up with the reins held high and his elbows resting on the lids of the two big milk churns on the float in front of him. The milk all came in cans in those days. The era of bottle or carton had not yet arrived.

As the horse progressed, *clippity-clop*, worshippers in their Sunday best were making their way to St Finian's Church of Ireland. Nearly everyone in those days, it seems, went to church as a matter of course. The pavements were actually thronged with people, all sedately dressed. Not a suitable time for Pickles to start manuring the King's highway and farting like a trooper.

While Johnny the Milkman was doffing his hat to his customers going to church, his acute discomfiture was palpable, as the horse's indiscretion seemed to know no bounds.

Between clenched teeth he would emit a soft, nervous and embarrassed whistle while he seethed: 'Ye wee bastards; after what I told you ye've fed Pickles corn. I can see it in her shite.'

Such was our malicious intent to upset poor Johnny, we reckoned our joy would have been complete if only we had devised a way of making Pickles stop and have a good pee into the bargain, precisely at church-going time.

Alas, one awful morning I was to find Pickles dead in her stable. The vet pronounced that the poor horse had died of colic. I was heartbroken and prayed fervently that we hadn't killed her with kindness or hastened her end by force-feeding her oats.

One of the highlights of Sunday observance where I lived would now be regarded as something of a phenomenon. In those pre-television days people of all ages, but mostly teenagers showing off their Sunday best, would take to the streets in droves to promenade up and down on opposite sides of the road as if they meant business. For the boys and girls, eyeing each other up while exchanging aimless pleasantries was an afternoon and evening exercise in potential matchmaking. The not so young at heart were content to take the air and stretch their legs to work up an appetite.

But for members of our boys' street gang, Sundays were marked by an extraordinary ritual. Our promenading would stretch to the outer reaches of Belfast, which we dubbed 'toffs' territory'. After exhaustive treks to such affluent leafy suburbs as Gilnahirk, Knock and Cherryvalley, we would randomly target the big houses for a spot of unashamed begging.

First we would ask for a drink of water as if we were dying of thirst, and then up the ante with a plea for bread. I still cringe to think of it: 'Missus, could you spare us a piece?' Add a silent prayer for jam on it and the picture is complete.

In our vernacular a 'piece' was a slice of loaf, normally garnished with margarine or, on rare occasions as a special treat, spread with butter. A 'piece' could also mean the sandwich content of a working man's lunch box.

Seldom, if ever, were we turned away, in compliance with the Biblical injunction: 'Hungry and you gave us to eat, thirsty and you gave us to drink.'

Shy and sensitive as I was, I found the role of a starveling from the back streets utterly humiliating, but as a loyal gang member I had to swallow my pride. The origin of our begging ritual remains a mystery.

On a lighter side, the story is told of one of our gang who, on being given a small, hard-baked buttered oatmeal biscuit, which he had neither sampled nor seen before, licked it clean and returned it saying: 'Thanks for the butter, missus. Here's your bit of cardboard back.'

three

HAVING DECIDED TO MAKE THE BEST of my day job as office boy with the *Daily Mail*, a source of encouragement was my frequent encounters with local reporters, who made a habit of dropping into Rosemary Street. Two in particular were to play an important part in the advancement of my career: Jimmy Kelly of the *Irish Independent* and Paddy Scott of the *Irish Press*.

They were both Northern Ireland editors of their respective papers, which were based in Dublin. On every weekday like clockwork, they wrote up their copy in the late afternoon in the *Daily Mail* premises, apparently preferring it to their own local newsrooms. Invariably, I would deliver their stories to the General Post Office, just around the corner in Royal Avenue, for transmission by teleprinter to their offices in Dublin. Thus, I availed of the opportunity of gaining some insight into the day-to-day slogging of a reporter, avidly reading through their copy and enjoying the privilege as I saw it of a sneak preview of what hundreds of thousands of people would read in print the following day.

But more to the point, Jimmy and Paddy jointly produced a magazine on the side for the liquor trade. They encouraged me to contribute to it on a professional basis. In search of material, I trawled through every newspaper and magazine I could lay my hands on in search of any items with the remotest reference to alcohol. Plagiarism it might have been, but at least I always rewrote what I 'lifted'. I don't know what gave me more pleasure — seeing my words in print at last or pocketing the spoils. There was no danger, however, of me striking it rich. The pay was a penny a line in old money, but it was worth it.

At the time, Jimmy was courting and it was his practice to pick up his fiancée, Eileen Shanahan, when she finished work as a secretary in a cinema office and take her along to the *Daily Mail* to wait for him until he had written up his copy.

To pass the time, Eileen and I used the back circulation office when it was vacant to play football with an old discarded gent's hat stuffed with newspapers and tied with string. This went on for hours on end, day after day for months. I think I spent more time with Eileen than Jimmy did. For some reason our sports correspondent, the ever-resourceful John Parker, finally reclaimed the hat, which was originally a miniature sample from a local millinery shop. He got his wife to wash, stretch and dye it and, as far as I know, he wore it for the rest of his life.

Printers' ink was now beginning to get into my blood. With so little work to do as an office boy and out of sheer boredom I took up typing as nothing more than a hobby. With only two fingers I eventually managed to work up a speed that would do justice to any touch typist. Such was my proficiency that my status began to rise.

I was increasingly being called upon to type, not only for the Boss, but also for Mr Parker. All news and sports copy — indeed most communications — were sent by teleprinter to the *Daily Mail* office in Manchester, where the Irish edition was printed.

Soon I was working as a full time unpaid teleprinter operator and occasionally, when I was thus employed, the thought occurred to me — at the risk of flattering myself — that perhaps I could do just as well as some of these writers.

Finally, I decided to have a go at creative writing, acting on the old adage that you won't plough a field turning it over in your mind. At school the only subject I was ever good at was English. It was once my modest boast that I won a school's essay competition, sponsored by the Royal National Lifeboat Institution, for which I received a certificate signed by the Duke of Gloucester.

Our English teacher at St Anthony's Primary, Paddy 'Macker' McManus, was also the school choir master and it was in this role that he was personally best remembered, if only for his slight eccentricities. It must be said, old Macker put as much into his music teaching as he did into his English lessons and was known at times to get a bit carried away. There was certainly a rush of blood to the head on the occasion of our choir attaining stardom status when invited to perform in public for the first time at St Mary's Hall, the hub of Belfast's Catholic community entertainment. It was as if we had reached Carnegie Hall or the London Palladium, although St Mary's was almost the pits in the eyes of most of the faithful.

Blissfully oblivious of political correctness as we know it today, poor Macker formed a grand 'Black and White Minstrel Show' in our school to celebrate St Patrick's Day, however incongruous, and our choir was the showcase. We all had to dress up as if we were going to bed in identical red-and-white striped pyjamas and matching polka dot jackets. Our little faces were blackened with chimney soot and Macker kept admonishing us not to forget our ears and hands with a reminder that boys from Dixieland were black all over. It might not be politically correct nowadays, but that's how it was in my school days. No doubt we would have been shocked to be branded racist.

The star roles of Mr Sambo, Mr Bones and Mr Interlocutor, who exclusively remained all white for some inexplicable reason, were decided not on merit but favouritism. This privileged trio had speaking parts between songs about 'Ole Man River' and 'Poor Ole Joe'.

The choice of soloist for the part of 'Poor Ole Joe' was a downright miscast if ever there was one. The role called for someone with as deep a voice as you could find among boyish vocalists. Danny Graham, though excellent otherwise, had a very thin voice indeed — so thin, in fact, that some of his begrudgers said you couldn't hear it behind a tramway ticket. Nevertheless, he became

Poor Ole Joe because he was top of the pecking order on the list of Macker's favourites.

On stage, we ordinary minstrels formed a horseshoe shape in three tiers, one above the other. Mr Sambo sat at one end of the horseshoe, Mr Bones at the other and Mr Interlocutor in the middle. An accomplished violinist, Macker the maestro provided our sole musical score, feverishly playing his fiddle out of sight behind our elevated horseshoe.

Macker also wrote the script and comedy was definitely not one of his fortes. When Mr Interlocutor asked Mr Sambo what a joke was, Mr Sambo made what was supposed to be the sidesplitting reply, that it was '*de inside ob an egg*'. Similes were certainly not one of Mr Bones' strong points. When Mr Interlocutor asked him what a conundrum was, he thought the question was about ammunition and replied, '*a conundrum, Massah, is wot ah put in mah gun to shoot*'.

This strange sense of humour certainly raised a laugh on our big night debut in St Mary's, but for all the wrong reasons.

Cometh the hour, cometh the man. When Mr Interlocutor, on cue, asked Mr Sambo what a joke was, poor Mr Sambo let his first night nerves get the better of him and said it was '*wot ah put in mah gun to shoot*'.

Macker nearly took the head staggers. He got so excited that he tried to correct the mistake by prompting, almost aloud so that the audience must have heard him, and adopting for reasons best known to himself the Dixieland vernacular: '*de inside ob an egg ... de inside ob an egg*'.

To make matters worse, when Mr Interlocutor asked Mr Bones what a conundrum was, Mr Bones insisted it was '*de inside ob an egg*'. 'No, no,' Macker prompted desperately, nearly screaming, '*it's wot ah put in mah gun to shoot.*'

The audience was further bemused when we launched into our rendition of 'Poor Ole Joe'. It was our custom during school performances to hum the tune, swinging slowly from side to side in unison, our eyes firmly fixed to our right awaiting the torturously slow arrival from the wings of Poor Ole rheumatic Joe.

Because of the layout of St Mary's stage, it was not possible for Poor Ole Joe to make his entrance from the right as we expected. But nobody told us. While we hummed, '*he's ah comin'* ... ' and swayed, as usual, with all heads rigidly directed to our right, Poor Ole Joe was making his painful way from our left, meekly warbling, '*ah's a comin' ... an mah head am bended low ...*'

Poor Macker nearly had a fit. Out of sight, behind our horseshoe formation, he stopped playing the fiddle. In a desperate attempt to redeem the situation, he began darting up and down, wielding his bow as a weapon, prodding each of us in the backside and frantically crying out, '*he am comin' de udder way ... he am comin' de udder way ...* '

Each of us in the back row at the receiving end of Macker's bow popped up in turn like Jack-in-the-boxes and swiftly switched our longing gaze for Poor Ole Joe from right to left. The rest of the Minstrels, denied any such alert, continued to look lovingly right, so that we were all at sixes-and-sevens and in complete disarray.

From then on, it was all downhill and the public debut of the St Anthony's Minstrel Show proved to be its swansong.

While Macker's skill as a music teacher left a lot to be desired, his literary prowess seemed to have rubbed off on me and, from an early age, English was to be my strongest subject at school.

The initial inspiration for my first short story came from the football pools, which had then come into vogue. It was about a husband who left his wife and faked his death, but came back from the dead when he heard that his widow had won the pools. She welcomed him home with open arms and, reunited, they lived happily ever after.

I agonised over every word and it took me ages to write the story, which I called 'The Return of the Prodigal Husband'. I sent it to the *Ireland's Saturday Night*, a sporting magazine-type newspaper, which was a sister paper of the evening *Belfast Telegraph* and known locally as 'The Ulster'.

I kept it a secret in case of rejection and bought the paper Saturday after Saturday with unabated expectation of seeing my epic in print, only to be disappointed each time. Finally, with self-righteous indignation and boyish naïvety, I wrote to the editor, demanding that he publish my story forthwith or return it so I could market it elsewhere.

In despair, I eventually stopped buying 'The Ulster' as a protest. But one Saturday night I was, as usual, in the local Ambassador cinema with my pals when I visited the toilet during an interval. A man next to me was having a pee while reading a paper, which he had clamped against the wall. It was the *Ireland's Saturday Night*. Marvel of marvels, I glanced over to the front page and noticed beside the masthead a small panel which in the trade we call a 'box'. It said in bold print: READ 'THE RETURN OF THE PRODIGAL HUSBAND'. BACK PAGE.

Overjoyed, I grabbed the paper from the bemused man, spinning him around while he was still peeing. 'It's mine, it's mine!' I almost screamed.

He must have misunderstood, for he said I could keep the paper as he had finished with it anyway and, quickly buttoning his flies, he fled.

Although I got paid more than the equivalent of a week's wage for the story, the fifteen shillings I received was nothing compared to the tremendous thrill I experienced with my journalistic baptism. With a new found confidence, I began writing bits and pieces for Billy Irwin, a reporter with the *Belfast News Letter*, who was moonlighting occasionally for the *Sunday Chronicle* and the *Sunday Empire News*. But more than anyone else, it was our sports reporter in the *Daily Mail*, John Parker, who really helped me along the road to the Fourth Estate.

A loveable man in many ways, John had a weakness, characterised by the Irish in their charity as being 'fond of a drop', a euphemism for an ability to drink a lot. It was a weakness I was to experience myself in later life, a weakness that almost destroyed me. In hindsight, I can see a mirror image of myself in John Parker.

Irritable and restless, he would come into the office of a morning, nervously pacing up and down watching the clock. I was not to know it then, but he was waiting for the pubs to open at 10am. An hour or two later he would come back, all lit up, a new man ready for the fray.

At his dictation, I would regularly type his copy, correcting him when I thought he had used wrong grammar or a sentence didn't read properly. 'Write it yourself,' he would often say impatiently.

And so it was that I was occasionally overwhelmed to see in the next day's *Daily Mail*, under his byline, a word here and there — should it be a 'but' or an 'and' — or a sentence or two which was all my own work, though he got credit for it.

As time went on, old John began to depend on me more and more to do simple things for him, just as in my later career I would come to depend on colleagues to do things for me.

Being a binge drinker, John had long periods of sobriety and was well able to look after himself. Still, I was eventually writing entire articles for him under his pseudonym, Patrick Walker. Though he never paid me as such, the delight of seeing my efforts in print under his name was reward enough.

More than anyone else, he encouraged me in many ways and, as a former news editor for the *Northern Whig* newspaper, he was a good teacher. Though a full time freelance for the *Daily Mail*, he was also what is termed a 'stringer', contributing to the *Irish Independent* in Dublin and its sister paper, the *Evening Herald*.

I loved covering amateur boxing for him at the Ulster Hall in Belfast and sending the results to the Dublin newspapers. These papers had a practice of paying contributors on the basis of receiving claims for payment from them. John never really bothered submitting his claims, trusting he would be paid eventually *in lieu*. Consequently, fees due to him over months, if not years, continued to mount.

Once, during a drinking spree when he needed extra money, he phoned the *Independent* in a moment of pique. Not wanting to give the impression that he was hard up and, at the same time, wanting to make sure that they realised they owed him, he recklessly implied that he didn't mind one way or another about the money.

'For all I care you can give it to the *Herald* Boot Fund,' he told them and slammed down the receiver.

In those days, the *Evening Herald* helped the deprived children of Dublin to buy footwear through donations to what they called their Boot Fund and it was to this that John had alluded during his phone call.

Reading a copy of the *Herald* some time later, the pipe John was smoking fell out of his mouth in astonishment when he got to the Acknowledgements section of the paper. There, at the top of the list of donors to the Boot Fund, was 'John Parker Esq., Clanbrassil, Marino, County Down — £175', which was a fortune then. Next on the list with a meagre ten guineas was the Lord Mayor of Dublin, who traditionally topped it.

'They took me at my word, the silly bastards,' said John, adding philosophically: 'Ah well, at least people will see I'm a hell of a sight more generous than the first citizen of Dublin.'

On one occasion, the Boss confronted John about not paying me for all the help I was giving him. After all, I was still only the office boy. Poor John, who was drinking at the time, took this greatly to heart and full of remorse arrived at work the next day well under the weather.

'So you think I let you down, son?' he asked, as tears streamed down his flushed cheeks. 'I would never let you down. Never.'

And with that, he emptied his pockets, scattering money all over the floor. 'Pick it up, pick it up,' urged the Boss. 'You've earned it.'

Next morning, I handed the money back to John, letting him know as politely as I could that I preferred to be paid when he 'was himself'.

He had the shakes at the time, but insisted on me holding on to the money — after he deducted a few bob for a drink. In days ahead, I was to know all about how much the price of a 'cure' meant to the alcoholic.

four

THE TIME CAME WHEN THE *DAILY MAIL* editor in Manchester, a Mr Balderson — I never got to know his Christian name — arrived in Belfast on one of his periodic visits. As it turned out, this was the chance John Parker had been waiting for. He had long promised to 'put a word in' for me to become a cub reporter. I had no illusions about this, however, knowing perfectly well that as a national newspaper the *Daily Mail* didn't employ juniors and only recruited staff who were already fully trained.

Mr Balderson, whom I didn't know by sight, arrived at the office unannounced. He let himself in after knocking at the door and took a seat without revealing who he was. I was the only one there and was busy at the typewriter. What a cheek, I thought, when he asked me what I was doing. In fact, I was writing a story for John Parker.

The visitor persisted in looking over my shoulder while I continued to type and I felt like telling him off, only he looked like someone important. He even had the temerity to ask my job description, to which I grudgingly conceded the truth, that I was only the office boy. At this stage, John Parker and the Boss arrived and, after a round of handshakes, all three of them went off without me being formally introduced, not even as 'the boy'.

Next morning, I knew John had been on a drinking spree, but he told me to make sure I would be in the office at seven o'clock that evening as he had set up my interview with Mr Balderson. The fateful hour arrived ... but not the editor, nor John Parker. Bitterly disappointed, I felt completely gutted, utterly devastated. Before the night was out, however, I was to have the editor literally and most unexpectedly at my very feet. Alas, this is not to say he was actually eating out of my hand. Far from it: the poor man was so pissed when he finally arrived that he wasn't even able to bite his tongue.

It was long past locking up time and I decided to call it a day. I phoned the Boss, who was at home. He wasn't even aware that an interview had been arranged which could send his office boy up the journalistic ladder. Nor did he seem to have much interest in the prospect. He simply told me to pack it in and go home.

The premises were secured by a metal gate blocking the hallway entrance and constructed on a concertina principle. I had just slotted the bottom bar in place and was about to lower the top bar to slide across the gate when the towering figure of a man emerged out of the gloom. It was a foggy evening and the man didn't see the bottom bar, over which he tripped and collapsed in a heap in the hallway, almost knocking me over. He was a jovial character and obviously in high spirits as he lay at my feet. He was giggling and laughing as only the inebriated can. But it was only when I detected, in his maudlin muttering, a reference to 'that awful man Parker' and what a great day they'd had that I realised who it was.

Now Mr Balderson was heavily built and it took all my boyish strength to help get him on his feet and into the office. He slumped into the Boss's rickety chair and fell fast asleep without betraying any recognition of me.

After waiting in the vain hope of Mr Parker turning up, I phoned the Boss at his home to inform him that the editor had arrived in the office. I tried to be as diplomatic as I could, without saying outright that he was plastered. I simply said he was asleep, after taking a fall and wasn't looking too well. The Boss told me he would come in and I could go home.

So much for the enchanted evening I had been looking forward to for so long with such high hopes. At the end of the day, I was still the office boy. I thought I'd never forgive John, the archetypal alcoholic — one drink and all appointments cancelled.

Next morning, he staggered into the office with the mother of a hangover. He tried to explain how he and Mr Balderson had had 'one too many', but told me not to worry.

'You think I've let you down,' he said, collapsing into a chair. 'Just listen to this.'

He picked up the phone and made a call that was to change the course of my life. In total disbelief, I heard him speak to the operator.

'This is Belfast 24383. I want to send a telegram. It's to Mr Balderson, care of the Shelbourne Hotel, Dublin. The message reads: "Don't forget wee Paddy, signed John Parker".'

He beamed at me as if to say, 'a job well done, you've arrived.'

'Is that it?' I asked incredulously. 'Is that supposed to get me a job? Four words. Don't forget wee Paddy?'

'Trust me,' was all he said as he went off to get a cure.

Three days later, I received a letter from the *Daily Mail*, Deansgate, Manchester. It was from the news editor, Eldred Reeve. He was pleased to inform me that I was herewith appointed a junior reporter for Associated Newspapers Limited (the *Daily Mail*, *Sunday Dispatch* and *London Evening News*) at a salary of three guineas a week, with kindest regards and all best wishes for the future.

Thus, I was appointed to a job I had never applied for, and for which I was never formally interviewed. I never met, nor had I even spoken to Eldred Reeve. To my knowledge John Parker, God bless him, was the only one to intercede for me.

I might have expected the Boss, as the *Daily Mail*'s number one man in Northern Ireland, to mediate. But if he ever put in a word for me, or was ever consulted about my promotion, he never mentioned it then or thereafter. I don't recall even a word of congratulations about the appointment, which was unprecedented insofar as I was the first and only junior reporter I knew of on the editorial staff of Associated Newspapers.

It was not their policy, as I have already indicated, to recruit greenhorns like myself with no academic qualifications or the benefit of a course or training in journalism. And though I suspected I was starting at the wrong end of the ladder — most cub reporters begin not at national newspaper level but with local or provincial papers — I thank God and dear old John Parker for the breakthrough.

Even an office boy in the *Daily Mail* enjoyed the occasional perk and my last one in that capacity before my shock promotion came in the wake of the launch in Belfast of the whale factory ship, the *SS Balena*, built by Harland and Wolff. It was memorable as a time capsule, telling as much about me as I was then and the hard times in which we lived.

After its successful trials, the Norwegian owners threw a party to end all parties in those austere wartime days as the *Balena* lay at anchor far out in Belfast Lough. The *Daily Mail* assigned Sam Edgar, their special correspondent, to cover the VIP event. Sam, who later became Ireland Correspondent for the *Sunday Empire News*, was a caring, generous-spirited journalist, anxious to give me a leg up in the world.

I was present when the dinner party invitation card 'for two' arrived. He promptly asked me to join him, and what an Epicurean dream break it turned out to be.

We were ferried from Belfast Harbour to the magnificent *Balena*, lying off the Bangor coast. It was my first time on a boat and I thought it a great adventure. I was too young to drink at the grand champagne reception and too nervous even to avail of a fruit juice. I felt completely out of place and heartbreakingly self-conscious, never having mixed in such prestigious company before, and was constantly expecting someone at any moment to challenge my boyish presence.

To put me at my ease, Sam took me aside as a diversion to scrutinise the seating accommodation on a display board outside the great Banqueting Room. I noted the name A N Other beside S Edgar and began to panic. Why was my name omitted? Who was this person 'Other'? Had he or she superseded me at the last minute? And if there was no place for me, where would I go and what would I do when everybody else was eating? Perhaps I should have brought my own lunch.

Sam, acknowledging the plight written all over my face, hastened to explain what A N Other meant. He assured me my name would have been displayed had he not forgotten to advise our hosts in advance. Even then I could not help suspecting Sam was inventing this just to please me. To put me finally at ease he suggested a preview of the magnificent and spacious dining room while the champagne reception was still going on.

What struck me most about the vast spread of tables, apart from the dazzling white linen which bedecked them and the bewildering array of cutlery, was the preponderance everywhere of a wide variety of tempting fruit in huge bowls. I had never before seen anything like it. I knew what a banana looked like, but couldn't recall its taste. Now I was counting them in great bunches. Apples, pears and oranges I had sampled, but rarely grapes. These were beyond my family's purse and regarded as a luxury, reserved for hospital patients. Now they were draping lusciously, green and black, over every bowl. Other fruits I couldn't identify, never having seen and therefore never having tasted any of them.

It seemed too good to be true, especially when Sam in an aside dismissed the gorgeous display as simply 'table decorations'. There were so many wartime substitutes it wouldn't have surprised me if the fruit were made of wax after all. No one was looking, so I put it to the test and started sampling the display with wild abandon like a child let loose in a sweet shop, so that Sam had to restrain me from gorging myself before we sat down to eat.

The banquet, which went on for hours, was the greatest feast of my young life. Until then I was unaware that meals came in courses. In our house, with wartime food rationing still in force, we were lucky to get meat once or twice a week. Here, there was enough prime roast beef on my plate to feed our entire family for a fortnight.

By the time the guests sat down the pre-dinner cocktails were doing their stuff and there was an air of relaxed informality. My initial inhibitions about what knives, forks and spoons to use and how to tackle the lobster began to subside. I only had to follow the lead of my inebriated neighbours to mask my dearth of table etiquette.

As the wine continued to flow no one seemed to mind how anyone behaved, so I got stuck in regardless. If only our street gang could see me now.

The Governor of Northern Ireland, Cabinet Ministers, captains of industry, moguls of commerce, the great and the good were making merry all around me. In such exalted company, I realised I should have worn my Sunday best, such as it was, of a family hand-me-down. I wasn't to know, however, that I would be hob-nobbing with the high and mighty. I had to be content, in a state of excruciating self-consciousness, with my extant dinner dress of an open necked white shirt, short patched trousers (my hour had not yet come for long ones), down-at-heel shoes and socks around my ankles.

Doggy bags were unheard of in those days, otherwise I would have shared the Epicurean delights on offer with my nearest and dearest subsisting on rations at home. While no one was looking, I was tempted to stuff my pockets with the leftovers, being only dissuaded at the prospect of lobster thermidor not travelling well.

Our waiter, joining in the merriment, was so tipsy that he began taking liberties himself. At one stage, while serving the vegetables, I had the temerity to ask if those were boiled potatoes or wee onions on the platter.

'I'd go easy on them if I were you son,' he giggled. 'They're bulls' balls.'

In this rarefied atmosphere, I didn't question whether such delicacies existed or if the waiter was pulling my leg. Anyway, slightly shocked, I decided in my state of puberty to decline the offer.

The interminable dinner speeches produced at least one gem that was to find lasting favour with our street gang. The speaker was one of the ship's officers, a Norwegian top brass, who proposed a toast in his own tongue, which had a certain ring about it and instantly appealed to me. Unaccountably, I found myself repeating it over and over again. Translated, I believe it meant: 'My health, your health, every beautiful woman's health.' Phonetically it tripped off my tongue: '*mim-skol-dim-skol-ala-flacker-flicker-skol.*'

Before that night was out, I had introduced it to our street gang. From then on it was to become our rallying call, our battle cry as we engaged our rival gangs in combat, a catchphrase that was to be heard for many a day hence all over the neighbourhood.

As our unforgettable ship's *soiree* was drawing to a close, Sam slipped me half a crown to give to the inebriated waiter. That was a quarter of my week's wages and I was tempted by the thought that charity began at home. It was such a splendid banquet, however, that I finally parted with my magnanimous tip. It was the first time in my life I had been in a position to do so.

My gesture must have touched the waiter for, when he was passing round the cigars at the end of dinner, he invited me to have one for my old dad. My dad didn't smoke cigars, but our street gang was known to enjoy the odd surreptitious Woodbine. With my pals in mind, I tentatively extracted a single cigar from the proffered box.

'Go on son, have another,' I was persuaded by the giggling waiter. And I did. With another nudge and a wink he invited me to 'go on son' and have as many cigars as I wanted. I stuffed a fistful into my right pocket and a fistful into my left, and that night I passed them round our street gang. I regaled them with a blow-by-blow account of the feast and we rehearsed our new anthem: '*mim-skol-dim-skol-ala-flacker-flicker-skol.*'

Later, in the Ambassador cinema on the Woodstock Road, we were split into pairs as the cheapest seats near the screen fell vacant in doubles. We kept in occasional touch with our new Norwegian chant and as the cowboy film began we started to light up our foot long Havanas. Usherettes with flashing torches demanded to know who was smoking so much and spoiling the view.

The front stalls were now permeated with the rich aroma of rising clouds of cigar smoke, so dense as they converged from various parts of the cinema close to the screen that they almost obliterated the film. As the cowboys performed their roles to frequent whoops in the Norwegian tongue, there was soon a perceptible change in the atmosphere.

The initial exultant hurrahs of '*mim-skol-dim-skol ...* ' began to fade and peter out entirely, only to give way to the harrowing sounds of involuntary puking, coughing, choking, spluttering and other symptoms of digestive distress and respiratory troubles.

This was succeeded by a spontaneous exodus of the collective street gang. On the pavement outside, still throwing up while gulping for air, we clung to each other or the nearest lamppost, our eyes rolling in our heads and our faces the colour of death. Groaning and clutching our stomachs we vowed never to smoke again as long as we all lived.

It had been a glorious day for me. Pity it had to end on such a sick note.

five

THE FIRST ENTRY IN MY WRITER'S SCRAPBOOK reads: 'Appointed Junior Reporter, April 8 1945.' The second states: 'First Story, April 9 1945.'

Not only had I struck oil within twenty-four hours of taking up the new post, but I had only to cross the road from my home to get my first big scoop. And I owe it all to my dear wee Ma, who was to become one of my best contacts for local news. It was she who told me when I announced my promotion, 'Well son, I've got a good story for you already.'

We lived, as I mentioned earlier, at 15 Albert Drive. Evelyn Vance lived opposite at number 14 and my Ma was able to fill me in with all the relevant details for my first *bona fide* published article.

Evelyn was about to become a GI bride. She could hardly believe that the young lad from across the road was now a reporter and was interviewing her about being married that very day. Her husband-to-be was 23-year-old Milton Taylor, a corporal in the United States army from Baltimore in Maryland. Evelyn was also a serving soldier in the Army Technical Service and the couple had met at a dance in the American Red Cross Club in Belfast. What made the story, apart from the fact that GI brides were then hitting the headlines, was that the groom had been given seven days leave, straight from the fighting front in Germany, to marry his bride by special licence.

Some time later, when I switched to sports reporting for a short spell, my first story was provided by Evelyn's next door neighbour, William Sheppard, who lived at number 16. The tip-off came from the usual reliable source — my Ma. She heard that William, an ex-schoolboy soccer international and now middleweight weightlifting champion of all Ireland, was aspiring to Olympic Games glory. Like Evelyn Vance he found himself being interviewed by the young lad across the road, who was now a sports reporter.

However, back as a cub news reporter, the Boss appeared to be at a loss to find a working agenda for me. The *Daily Mail* was only keen on human interest or 'offbeat' stories. Rarely did any article from Northern Ireland make the headlines in Britain.

World War Two was drawing to a close. The devastating Blitz stories had all been written. The Yanks had come and gone. Postwar Belfast found Catholics and Protestants living in relative peace and harmony. There was nothing to presage almost thirty years of mayhem that was to be the lot of a deeply divided community with bombs, shootings, murders and sectarian strife on an endemic scale. In the main, local newspapers had to rely on parish-pump and run-of-the-mill stories to fill their pages. The courts consistently provided a happy hunting ground with drunk-in-charge drivers often making the headlines.

Faced with the dilemma of giving me something to do, and to mark the launch of my apprenticeship, the Boss introduced me to the Petty Sessions Court in Belfast's old Town Hall. By introduction, I mean he simply dumped me at the Press Desk, whispered something to the reporters already present and left me to get on with it. Clearly, I was to learn the hard way.

I was still trying to find my bearings on the first day when the clerk of the court, Frank Caldbeck, leaned over from his seat below the magistrate and told me His Worship would like to meet me in his chambers at the end of the court session. How civilised, I thought, that a man so eminent as John H Campbell KC, RM should condescend to welcome a lowly junior reporter on his day of baptism in the courts. Rising from his desk to meet me, I entered his inner sanctum with some trepidation. As he cordially shook my hand, he said, 'I think we have already met.' Then he floored me completely.

'I once caught you red-handed raiding my orchard, did I not?' I might have pleaded 'guilty as charged, your Worship', but kept my counsel. 'You were a St Anthony's boy,' he recalled.

Indeed, as a pupil at St Anthony's Primary School, I had taken part in that audacious raid. His Worship attended Mass in St Anthony's Church, where I sang in the school choir and it was there that our paths first crossed.

As King's Counsel and Resident Magistrate, we boys held him in such awe that he was known only as 'Judge' Campbell. He was the sole member of the congregation who could speak out loud in chapel and get away with it. Often he would tick us off for not paying attention.

His Worship lived in the 'big house', as we knew it, at Hillfoot Road, Cregagh, not far from the colony of ex-servicemen's cottages where I lived.

Ours was a vastly different world, of course. In my boyish eyes our abodes did not even rank as houses, but were officially classed 'cottages', which I equated with the homes of mere labourers and consequently at the bottom of the league. Because they were allocated solely to ex-soldiers, sailors and airmen from World War One, our locality was colloquially christened 'the camp' or 'the colony'.

My father, a scrupulously honest person, was bitter that this was to be his lot after fighting for 'King and Empire in the freedom of small nations'. He had joined up in the first place, not out of any love for His Britannic Majesty or the Empire on which the sun never set. He did so because he was an Irish nationalist naïve enough to fall for the promise that, after the war, every Ulster ex-serviceman would be given a home 'fit for heroes to live in'. This meant free rent for each house, an acre of land and a cow as a reward for answering the call: 'Your Country Needs You.'

Not only was there a rent of six shillings and four pence a week, which most families could ill afford, there was certainly not a cow to be seen in the camp. That didn't bother my father, nor did the fact that his plot of land was only a fraction of an acre. What really made him bitter was the blatant discrimination against Catholic ex-servicemen in the allocation of the cottages, a seminal curse of future generations in our divided society.

My father used to say a German bullet or shell made no distinction between Catholic and Protestant on the battlefield. A bullet in the Battle of the Somme shattered his left kneecap, leaving him with a permanently stiff leg. Yet when the war was over and there was a 'Protestant parliament for a Protestant people' in Northern Ireland, the bias against Catholics in housing allocation was universal and undeniable. In our street, only three of the twenty houses were rented to Catholics, a ratio that permeated the other streets in the area.

The camp was built in a tree-like shape and each street was named after a World War One battlefront. The camp's trunk was Thiepval Avenue; its branches Somme Drive, Albert Drive and Hamil Drive; its roots the two pronged Picardy Avenue and Bapaume Avenue.

Located in the backwater of east Belfast, there were no streetlights as the gas lamp era was drawing to an end and the age of electric lighting had not yet reached our area. When it did, it was greeted like the Second Coming. The camp was *en fête* for the great switch-on. Families took to the streets. There were open-air tea parties and boxcar races for the children.

The end of the momentous countdown to the big switch-on was marked by the eruption of a frenzy of wild cheering. I recall standing wide-eyed at my garden gate as the lamppost across the street was suddenly crowned with a bright arc of light. We were no longer in darkness, yet one wondered that blood should have been spilled that night.

Inconceivably, at least to a youngster like me, the highlight of the festivities was a series of bare knuckle fights between pairs of grown men, each one nominated for his known pugilist prowess by rival factions in our community. To rousing cheers they fought, round by round from street to street, followed by cheering crowds until one or other of the contestants was knocked out or surrendered. So much for the fighting spirit of our beloved camp.

But back to the big house on the hill: the home, in palatial grandeur, of Judge Campbell. His magnificent walled-in orchard had been written off as a no-go area until our street gang decided otherwise.

The magistrate, who was noted for his fine sense of humour, joked lamely that he thought the statute of limitations applied to my orchard raiding crime and I deserved to be let off with a caution. But I knew something he didn't as I left his august presence.

There was a sequel to the orchard raid, which formed the basis of a short story I was to write while practising my typing skills as an office boy. I called it 'Forbidden Fruit' and sent it to the *Ireland's Saturday Night*, but it was never published. I kept a copy of it and now let it speak for itself, except to say that I agonised over every single word.

FORBIDDEN FRUIT
By Patrick Reynolds

In the library of his stately home surrounded by ponderous legal tomes the learned judge struck terror into our pulsating young hearts. He had caught us in the orchard at the bottom of his garden and here we were now at his mercy in his private legal den.

Reclining in his baggy flannels and tweeds in an easy chair, the judge might as well have been in wig and robes and we in the dock on a capital charge in any Court of Justice in the land, such was the awe in which we held him. A huge portrait of an ancient legal luminary frowned down on us from its place above the ornate marble fireplace.

It had all been Hendy's fault. Hendy was the leader of our gang and had led Bunty, Mo and I in the successful forays on every orchard in the neighbourhood, bar one.

Hendy sought to appease any moral scruples we had by claiming it was not a mortal sin to steal from orchards, provided we did not steal too much and told it in Confession.

The judge's orchard was regarded by all as impregnable and strictly out of bounds. All that is, except for Hendy. It was flanked on all sides by a towering stone wall, decked by ugly spikes of broken glass. It represented to Hendy the outstanding challenge of his young life. He had made a solo reconnaissance and boldly assured us, 'The job can be done, judge or no judge.'

We first had to negotiate a stream that flowed along one side of the orchard. Hendy had discovered, near the base of a corner wall, a small dried up drain that had once served as an overflow from a spring well inside the orchard and which we christened Charlie Chan's Well. The aperture was choked with slime and dead leaves. With commendable foresight, Hendy brought along his younger brother's sand spade. After scooping the way clear we slithered through. The orchard was between us and His Lordship's mansion.

'We'll only take one melon,' Hendy ordered, pointing to a bed of vegetable marrows, 'and only two apples, two pears and two plums each.' He spoke as someone who knew where to draw the line when it came to committing a venial sin.

Hendy, Bunty and Mo were already in the branches of a pear tree and I was preparing to climb a low hanging branch when a hefty kick in the pants sent me sprawling.

'Hold it there!' It was the booming voice of the dreaded judge. The same voice that had sent men to the gallows.

Hendy, Bunty and Mo thudded from the trees like over-ripe fruit. The judge caught me by the scruff of the neck and yanked me to my feet. I thought it superfluous when he boomed again, 'Stand your ground.' We had all taken root anyway.

'You little brats,' he snorted. 'I'll show you ... I'll show you.' Then he ordered us to 'March!' At that moment Hendy shed all the qualities that had stamped him as a future leader of men. He had completely gone to pieces like the rest of us.

'March!' boomed the judge again, as he prodded us on with Judas digs in the back in the direction of the big house. Into a spotless kitchen he shepherded us, made us wipe our feet, wash our hands and brush down our clothes. Then he ushered us along a lofty panelled corridor hung with brooding portraits, across a marble hall, under a brilliant chandelier and into the library.

From the depths of his easy chair, he launched a homily on our waywardness and a full-blooded tirade that went on and on. When he mentioned the police, poor Mo began to bawl. Soon we were all sobbing and the venerable judge decided we'd had enough.

'Now that you've learned your lesson,' he relented, 'I have something for you.' His Lordship shuffled from the room.

'He's gone for the cops,' wailed poor Mo. 'We're done for.'

'*Whisht*,' said Hendy our noble leader.

Outside there was a tinkle of glasses and the benevolent judge, now beaming, emerged with a tray laden with biscuits and buns. He was actually smiling; a feat of which we thought him incapable.

'Sorry. I have only milk,' he said and politely handed each of us a glass. 'It's the maid's day off. I'm afraid I'm quite alone and am rather a bad hand at making tea. But do help yourselves, gentlemen, to the goodies.' We gingerly began to find our appetites.

'And now, gentlemen, I think I shall join you,' the judge beamed and from a magnificent glass cabinet he took out a big bottle. It had a white horse on the label.

'My medicine, gentlemen,' he said with some relish. He poured out a stiff dose and it seemed to be very agreeable, for he filled up his glass again and I thought he must be quite ill indeed, for he filled it up a third time.

He was smacking his lips after four doses of the medicine and I was relieved that it appeared to have done him good for now he was quite chatty and in the best of spirits.

He asked us to have another drink and hastened to add, 'More milk, of course.' Again our good host was on his feet and was leaving the room, only this time I noticed he tried to find the handle on the wrong side of the door. He arrived back with more milk and in a most unbecoming fashion he spilled as he poured into our glasses. Then he asked us lots of questions, but we had to be cagey about answering some of them in relation to our addresses. As he encouraged us to 'eat up now, gentlemen, eat and be merry', he had another draught and by now the medicine bottle was nearly empty.

From the glass cabinet the judge took out a box of cigars and was about to pass them around when he caught himself on. He lit a cigar, nestled back in the easy chair and asked us all how we got our nicknames.

'When I was a boy like you,' he mused, 'they used to call me "lanky" at school.' He emptied the last of the bottle into his glass and started to giggle.

Then he confided with obvious delight: 'And do you know something? I also raided orchards. Ah, but I was never caught. By Jove. No sir. Never caught.'

For the next hour the jolly old judge went on talking and talking. He began to yawn and rub his eyes. Finally, rising shakily to his feet, he said: 'It's time, gentlemen, I had my nap. It's been a most exhilarating day ... '

He nearly fell over a chair and almost upset the empty tray as he showed us out and told us to be good boys in future. As we slowly walked down the broad, winding driveway to the Hillfoot Road, freed at last, Bunty remarked: 'If you ask me, I think that old judge is drunk.'

Hendy was deep in thought. 'You heard what the judge said. He's all on his own and he's going to have a nap. Now's our chance.'

He pointed to a gate, which led to the orchard at the bottom of the judge's garden. The gate was open ...

'Now remember what I said. One melon, two apples, two pears and two plums and no cheating. Go! Go! Go!'

It was the end of a perfect raid.

During my fledgling days at the courts, I must have got into His Worship's good books. Perhaps, if he had been aware that I had raided his orchard not once but twice on the same day, it might have been different.

As it was, this man, who I used to look up to as some kind of god, had now become not only a personal friend but also my daily chauffeur.

It began when he spotted me one morning as I waited for a bus at the stop on the Cregagh Road, just around the corner from Albert Drive. This was on his way to the courts from his home. The Boss had by now detailed me to cover the courts as a matter of daily routine, which meant I was there every day instead of checking in at the *Daily Mail* office first. As I stood at the bus stop I didn't notice the RM drive past, but he clearly recognised me. He pulled up and beckoned me impatiently. Having so little in common, it was extremely difficult at first to make conversation. But as time went on we became voluble, though unlikely, friends.

Every morning from then on he gave me a lift into work, he to take his seat on the Bench and me to sit at the Press Desk. He would even wait when I was occasionally late.

I often thought His Worship would have made a good reporter given his remarkable news sense. Many court cases, I feel sure, would never have seen the light of day in local newspapers if it hadn't been for his highly quotable quips. At times, in the course of case hearings, it seemed he was directing his comments more towards the press that anyone else, thus ensuring eye-catching headlines and a lot of self-publicity on an almost daily basis in both the morning and evening papers.

There were quite a few characters around and they made such regular court appearances that I sometimes wondered if they were only breaking the law to get their names in the paper. Some even pleaded to be sent to jail for offences trumped up by themselves in the expectation of free board and lodgings for a spell. Of such trivia were headlines made in those pre-Troubles days.

One of the best known characters was poor old Bella Holly of no fixed abode. She seemed to revel in her notoriety and went out of her way to attract the limelight. A veteran of two hundred or so court appearances, mostly on simple drunken charges, she made the most of it. Formal proceedings were often dispensed with in the absence of even the charge being read out or any evidence produced.

On one occasion the magistrate, shaking his head in mock bemusement, asked: 'Bella, dear. What am I going to do with you?'

Clasping her hands as in prayer, Bella replied: 'Just sentence me to death, Your Majesty.'

'Very well,' said His Royal Highness. 'Take her away, and throw her to the lions.' A very grateful Bella left the dock with a blessing on her benefactor.

The RM's penchant for publicity was strikingly illustrated one morning when he invited the court's press corps to his chambers. They included Jimmy Boyd (*News Letter*) who was later to become an editorial executive with the BBC in Northern Ireland; Joe Sherlock, full time court reporter for the *Belfast Telegraph*; Hugh Young (*Irish News*), later to become news editor of that paper, and yours truly.

'I've a novel sort of story for you, gentlemen,' said Mr Campbell, with a hint of the melodramatic. 'My chambers have been burgled.' There was clearly a break-in but nothing seemed to be missing.

I felt that the publicity-conscious RM was sure to put a spin on it and he did just that. He drew our attention to a photograph on his desk of his daughter, Beatrice Campbell. He held it up.

'As you can see, the intruder has left a message,' he went on, pointing to a scribble written in lipstick across the picture, which read: 'Forgive me, you are so beautiful.'

Of course, the inference we were invited to draw was that here was a woman whose beauty so touched a burglar's wayward heart that he couldn't bring himself to rob her dear father.

Be that as it may, the subsequent publicity was massive. The original story was followed up by all the Fleet Street papers and Beatrice's photograph was on practically every front page. Typical headlines ran 'Beauty Melts Burglar's Heart' and 'Burglar Falls For Beauty'. Beatrice was a little-known actress prior to this, but now her film career really took off and she literally became a star overnight.

Incidentally, she went on to marry a leading actor at the time, Nigel Patrick, and the wedding took place in our church, St Anthony's — a red-letter day in the history of our neighbourhood.

six

WRITING FOR AN ENGLISH NEWSPAPER, ALBEIT mainly for its Irish edition, I realised of course that court reporting had its limitations. Belfast's local papers, the evening *Telegraph* and the three morning dailies, the *Irish News*, *News Letter* and *Northern Whig* published most of the hearings, however innocuous, as a matter of record.

In being more discerning, the *Daily Mail* was correspondingly more demanding. But full of juvenile enthusiasm I was determined to milk the courts for all they were worth.

I would sit there tenaciously to the bitter end while my colleagues on the local papers were generally inclined to call it a day before adjournment, after consulting with the clerk on the merits of the cases still to be heard. They would file whatever copy they had to their newsrooms and then adjourn to the Ulster Tavern across the road. My hour for the drink had not yet come.

Like Macawber, I was forever expecting something to turn up in the courts and I must say my constancy quite often paid off handsomely. I began to earn the dubious reputation of being a bit of a 'scoop merchant', meaning something of a specialist in landing exclusives. This might not have done my ego any harm, but I'm afraid it did not endear me to some of my colleagues who were carpeted for missing my scoops. While I wished at times it could have been otherwise, I stuck to the principle of all being fair in love and war.

Laughter in court cases was a popular diversion in local journalism. Sometimes, however, there was a word other than 'funny' for some of the episodes reported. The word 'lavatorial' comes to mind as I recall a case which I'm sure would never have seen the light of day but for the high profile of the person involved.

It centred on the wife of the then Northern Ireland Minister of Education in the Stormont Government, Colonel S H Hall-Thompson. As it turned out, she must have regretted to her dying day ever taking her case to court, such was her acute embarrassment and the guffaws the case in its progress engendered among what she might have deemed to be the lower classes in the public gallery.

Her Ladyship arrived in style at Belfast Petty Sessions Court. A policeman stood guard at her limousine, while her chauffeur, in full uniform and with his shiny peaked cap tucked under his arm, sat discreetly behind her at the back of the court.

The magistrate, Mr Campbell, and the court clerk, Mr Caldbeck, were at pains to defer at all times to Her Ladyship.

It transpired she had instigated legal proceedings by phoning the police when she observed two men behaving suspiciously in the bushes near her palatial home. The court sergeant, who was a bit of a wag, was overheard in a facetious aside to characterise the two defendants as they entered the dock as 'gormless geeks'. They were charged under summary jurisdiction with loitering with intent to commit a felony.

In a quivering, cultured voice Her Ladyship, decked in rich furs and jewels, gave evidence which was brief and to the point. The defendants were trespassing and simply up to no good when she observed them acting suspiciously at the back of her house.

Conscious of the fact that the men had no solicitor to represent them and aware, no doubt, that they were entitled to pit their wits against the spouse of the man foremost in the field of education in Northern Ireland, Mr Campbell was scrupulously careful to explain their rights.

'Either of you, or both, may ask the witness any questions, but may not make any statements since you have not yet been sworn. Understand?'

The men gave the distinct impression they did not understand a word of it. They remained stolidly silent as the magistrate, in exasperation, said: 'Have you any questions to ask this witness? Remember, only questions.'

Still looking blankly around them the first defendant ventured to speak. 'I was only having a pump, yer Honour,' he muttered.

'You were only what?' exploded the magistrate.

'Having a piss,' rejoined the defendant.

'That's not a question,' said the magistrate.

'I'm telling you. I was only making my water,' the defendant persisted.

Turning to Her Ladyship, Mr Campbell asked, 'Do you understand the defendant?'

'Gracious, no,' she gasped.

'He implies he was urinating. Did you see him in the act of doing that?'

'Heavens above, no.'

Skipping quickly to the second defendant, he was duly asked if he had any questions.

'I was only having a keek,' he replied limply.

'I keep telling you that type of statement is not a question.'

'I was caught short, yer Worship.'

Mr Campbell turned again to the esteemed witness. 'Did you see the defendant in the act of defecating?' he asked.

'Dear me, no ... this is getting too much.'

Whereupon, Her Ladyship lapsed into a swoon, was revived with a glass of water and assisted from the witness box by her chauffeur. The magistrate threatened to clear the court if he heard any more guffaws.

The only other witness, a passer-by at the time of the alleged offence, was equally reticent. Asked to take the 'Book' in his right hand and repeat the oath in front of him he just stood there, his mouth agape.

'Are you deaf?' asked the court clerk, rather peremptorily.

'No,' came the reply.

'Then take the Book in your right hand,' repeated the clerk.

'What Book?'

'The Bible. Or do you not want to be sworn on the Word of God?'

'I don't see no Book.'

The witness looked all around him. The clerk looked all around him. In the Press Box we stood up in mock concern and looked all around us.

'Who would want to steal the Bible?' asked the clerk, rhetorically. He was known to have a facetious streak.

Then, from the back of the court came a plaintive voice.

'Heavens above!' uttered Her Ladyship. 'I thought it was my handbag.'

In her confusion after giving evidence, she had sauntered off with the Bible under her arm. The poor woman had to run the gauntlet, or rather stagger as best she could, of the highly amused hangers-on in the public gallery to return the Good Book to its rightful place.

Finally sworn in, the only other witness simply attested that at no time had he seen either of the defendants perform any bodily functions at the relevant time, though he could not say what they were up to in the bushes.

The case was dismissed 'on its merits', whatever that meant. Sweating profusely, cheeks crimson, Her Ladyship was assisted by her chauffeur from the court to her limousine in a state of collapse.

Sometimes it was the story behind the story that made court reporting so rewarding. One such example came up in the Summons Court, when a man was charged with the crime of playing pitch and toss. On the face of it, this type of case would not even merit a mention in the local papers.

The wife of the accused, Elizabeth Toner, appeared on his behalf and was fined half a crown, which she could ill afford. She was crying and in a very distressed state. As she left the court, she mumbled something about keeping a 'death vigil' for her baby. I wondered what she meant, but some days elapsed before I decided to try and find out. I called at her address, which was on the court's summons charge sheet.

The house was in a side street on the Ormeau Road, opposite the Gas Works. It had been graded as 'condemned' by the City Corporation. The first thing I noticed when the woman opened the door was the bare floor, which appeared to be made of dried mud. The stench suggested a nearby piggery, which could have accounted for the infestation of flies.

'I was just wondering about the baby I heard you mention in court,' I said.

'Ah, poor wee Elizabeth died last Wednesday.' Then in the same breath she added, 'Would you like to see her? She's doing fine now, thank God.'

I was about to turn away, not quite knowing what to say and thinking the poor woman was demented when she enthused, 'It's a miracle.'

Along the dark hallway was a pram and sitting up inside was a lovely baby, a picture of health, with bright blue eyes and rosy cheeks.

'This is wee Elizabeth,' said the mother, who went on to relate an almost incredible story — one which even impressed my hard-bitten colleague, *Daily Mail* photographer Henry Millar, who came with me on the off-chance of a picture.

The child had been a patient in Purdysburn Fever Hospital, suffering from severe gastro-enteritis, and the mother was sent for. There were complications and Mrs Toner was told that the child's illness was terminal. She took her home to die.

'I prayed to Martin de Porres, the Black Saint, to intercede for a miracle and I put my trust in God,' she told me.

'Day and night I kept a bedside vigil with wee Elizabeth, who was so weak I could only feed her through the tube of a fountain pen, which the hospital had given me. But the fight to live was just too much for the wee thing and she gave up the ghost. All of a sudden, her body went stiff, turned a blue colour and she passed away. She was as cold as marble.

'Dr Kerr from York Street pronounced her dead and wrote me a death certificate. I went to O'Kanes, the undertakers in Donegall Street to make the funeral arrangements. Neighbours drew their blinds in sympathy and we had a wake for Elizabeth. I put her death notice in the paper.

'Then the miracle happened. I was in the kitchen making tea and when I came out Elizabeth was sitting up as happy as Larry, tugging at the white linen, which I had laid her out in as a corpse. I got down on my knees and thanked God and St Martin for his intercession. The poor child was ravenous and after feeding her she never looked back. As you can see she's as right as rain.'

I checked with O'Kane's, who confirmed the funeral arrangements, and contacted Dr Kerr. He was clearly embarrassed, but would not confirm that he had pronounced the child dead. His version was that he had explained to Mrs Toner 'in lay terms' that Elizabeth had lapsed into a 'death-like' coma. He pleaded patient confidentiality to avoid elaborating further, although he did concede he was 'absolutely mystified' at the child's sudden return to health.

The story of the miracle baby, which as I've related had its genesis in a simple court case, was carried in all editions of the *Daily Mail*. People sent letters of goodwill and gifts from all over Britain. A teddy bear arrived from Buckingham Palace in the name of the future Queen of England, Princess Elizabeth.

For months afterwards I wrote many follow-up articles, charting the little girl's progress, and mother and child were frequent visitors to the *Daily Mail* office in Belfast. However, there was a tragic sequel to the story.

The Toner family was eventually moved to a converted old army Nissen hut at Sydenham, where conditions were not much better than the condemned house they had vacated. Mrs Toner complained of persistent cold and damp in the draughty, leaking new home and little Elizabeth, having survived for five years after her return from the dead, finally succumbed to a bout of pneumonia and passed away.

One of the longest running and most dramatic court stories I covered in those days was Robert Taylor's trial for murder. As I listened to him being sentenced at Belfast Commission to be 'hanged by the neck' until he was dead, I could not have known that one day I would come face to face with him after he escaped the hangman's noose.

Taylor was a 21-year-old painter and decorator who was twice tried for a murder committed forty-eight hours before his proposed Easter Monday wedding in 1949. It caused a great sensation, murder in that era being a rarity.

Taylor was accused of the brutal slaying of a 52-year-old housewife, Minnie McGowan, while she was alone in her house at Ponsonby Avenue in north Belfast. Several violent attempts were made to kill her. She suffered severe scalds from a pot of boiling soup poured over her head and shoulders. In addition, her head had been hacked with a carving knife, and her throat was bruised and showed signs of attempted strangulation with a cord. The gas oven, near to where she was struck down in her kitchen, was turned on.

Taylor was tried twice, as the first jury failed to agree on a verdict. It took the second jury, at a hearing three months later, only thirty-five minutes to find him guilty.

The prosecution case was that on the day of the murder, Taylor needed to find just £12 to buy the bridal bouquets and pay for the hire of his wedding cars. He had to have the money, cash in advance, by the afternoon of that day. He went to Mrs McGowan's home, in which he had carried out several painting jobs, expecting to find money there. He was disappointed. There were only a few shillings in the house.

Mrs McGowan lived for fifty-six hours after she was attacked and gasped on her deathbed to people who came to her aid: 'It was Robert the painter who did it. He works for Barrett in Sunnyside Street.'

As the Lord Chief Justice, Sir James Andrews, passed sentence wearing the Black Cap, Taylor stood erect and composed himself in the dock until he heard the words 'hanged by the neck'. Then he bit hard into his quivering lips. The execution was fixed for 16 November.

But the end was not nigh for Taylor, who appealed against the verdict. In the Court of Appeal it was submitted on his behalf that the jury had separated during the second trial. This was in breach of the instructions of the trial judge who had ordered that they must stay together and not discuss the case with outsiders during an outing to relax at a seaside resort. As it happened, the jurors parted company with half of them going to a public house and the other half going to a café.

The Appeal Court ruled that, while there was no evidence that the case was discussed in public by any of the jurors, the accused had been denied certain of his legal rights of protection and accordingly the guilty verdict and sentence were quashed. Taylor was freed and went to ground, having been smuggled out of the court by a back door.

Weeks later I bumped into him in the street, quite by chance, and was surprised that he recognised me.

'You were in the Press Box at my trial,' he said.

He had never been interviewed since his acquittal and appeared to be very pent up. Out of work, he said he didn't even have the price of a fag. I told him I didn't smoke, but if he'd like to drop into the *Daily Mail* office in Rosemary Street, I would get him a cigarette. I also hinted there might be a bob or two in it for him. The days of chequebook journalism had not yet arrived and he was glad to accept the ten shillings I offered him for the story, telling him it was all the money I had.

As he cupped his hands to light the cigarette, I noticed that his fingernails were bitten to the quick. For a chilling moment I reflected that these were the hands that a jury decided had committed murder most foul.

Taylor, with his sharp, piercing, blue eyes was a man with a large chip on his shoulder. He complained that no one would give him a job, although he revealed he had been given work as a part-time table waiter. He claimed piquantly that he had served the top table at a recent Royal banquet at Belfast City Hall in honour of the visiting Princess Elizabeth. He also claimed he had been turned down as an emigrant to Australia.

He was particularly bitter about being drummed out of the

Orange Order and made a point of saying it was an Orangeman on the jury at his first trial who alone held out against finding him guilty. This juror contacted Taylor when he won his appeal, just to let him know that it was he who had saved his skin. He invited Taylor to his café on the Newtownards Road to celebrate and Taylor told me he gorged himself on free ice cream.

But what was it like in the death cell? Apparently the ordeal did not affect his appetite, for he said, 'The food was great.' Not for a moment did he really believe he was going to die.

From the death cell, he could see a tall cabinet, which he knew was fronting a false anteroom off the corridor. The cabinet, he explained, opened onto the gallows and, although he had a fascination for it, he said, 'Something told me I would never swing.' He added coldly, 'I didn't lose much sleep over it.'

His fiancée, Lily Jones, a 21-year-old weaver from Lilliput Street, stood by him and a short time after the interview the couple were secretly married.

I was peeved that my scoop didn't earn what we in the trade call a 'byline' with my name appended instead of the anonymous 'By *Daily Mail* Reporter'.

Taylor subsequently fled to Canada, where he died peacefully in his sleep in July 2000.

seven

IT WAS A MUCH MORE MUNDANE story that provided my first byline after a year as a cub reporter. What a tremendous thrill it gave me to see, on an inside page of the paper, a single column story, which proclaimed to the world that it was 'By Patrick Reynolds, *Daily Mail* Reporter'. The date was 21 February 1946.

I was walking on air. To see my name in print for the first time proved that I had at last arrived. Yet it was a very simple story and again it was my dear wee Ma, God bless her, who had made it possible. When she told me that she had 'a great story', I could not have doubted her news sense.

Somebody had told her of a man who had been smoking a pipe since he was four years old. It was hardly the makings of a bylined story. I was not even going to bother about it, only our photographer Henry Millar said he was desperate for a picture, any picture.

The eventual story so impressed me that I can still recall, word for word, the opening paragraphs:

> Seventy-one years ago, in a little white-washed cottage near Ballyclare, County Antrim, a mother caught her four-year-old, curly haired son smoking a clay pipe. His name was William J McKeen. He was taken by the ear and spanked.

But William J had another puff of the pipe and again he was caught. So Mrs McKeen went into town and brought back an ounce of the strongest tobacco and William J was encouraged to smoke it. He did — and without losing colour!

Every week she bought William J an ounce of tobacco in the hope of sickening him. It never did. He was well and truly hooked, but his mother continued to keep him in smokes until he was able to earn his own money ...

William J was 75 when I interviewed him at his home at Cherryville Street, Belfast. The Chancellor of the Exchequer, Mr Hugh Dalton, was presenting his budget that day. Since William J reckoned, after he did his sums, that he had smoked something like an incredible half a ton of tobacco in his lifetime, I suggested he should write to the Chancellor, pleading exemption from tobacco tax. William J did just that and it was this turn of events which made the story. Old William J received an official reply of refusal, signed by the Chancellor, that looked so important he had it framed and hung over the mantelpiece.

Another unpromising story resulted in yours truly making the news and getting my own picture in the paper for the first time. The setting was an international ploughing match at Mallusk near Belfast, which was hardly the stuff bylines were made of.

To cope with the mud, glorious mud, I brought along a pair of gumboots, which I charged up to the *Daily Mail* on expenses. But I never counted on becoming a competitor. This happened, out of the blue, when the Swiss team dropped out. They had developed language problems with the horses they had borrowed from local farmer Sam Houston. The horses dug their hooves in because they couldn't understand the foreign tongue.

Henry Millar egged me on to have a go because I'd been saying that ploughing looked so boring, I wondered why anyone bothered.

This is how my story appeared in the following day's edition, under my byline:

I was the odd man out in yesterday's international ploughing match at

Mallusk near Belfast. I had no sooner remarked that it looked easy than I was given two horses and a plough and told to try it.

The greenhorn in lounge suit and gumboots drew quite a gathering as competitor number 111 — unofficially. There were 10,000 spectators watching the 110 men and women competitors who represented 11 countries. There were Irish, English, Scots, Manx, Welsh, Swiss, Canadians, Dutch, Kenyans, Arabs, Egyptians, and then there was me.

In the 26-acre field, I had a plot of my own, 60 yards long. Sam Houston supplied my horses, Barney the black one and Sammy the bay. Both were shaggy nine-year-olds with a lot of horse sense. I had never spoken to a horse before, but Sam told me that '*tcht, tcht*' meant go, 'hup off' meant to the right and 'come 'ere', to the left.

My plough had already been set to make a seven-inch furrow and I took up the reins. It took a lot of 'tcht, tchting' to start and a lot of 'whoa, whoaing' to stop.

I nearly broke my arm, trying to keep the plough straight and I found it hard to hold the plough handles and double reins at the same time, but at the end of ten minutes I had ploughed my first furrow.

By this time, quite a large gallery of spectators had gathered around to watch me at work. I overheard one of them say it would be harvest time before I ploughed an acre, but for the most part I enjoyed a charitable silence as the bemused spectators looked on in disbelief.

Barney and Sammy were puzzling at times. Once they stopped, when I hadn't said 'whoa' and then they started without 'tcht, tcht'. A judge, with a blunt Ulster accent, advised me not to give up the day job ...

A double column, nine-inch deep photograph of me looking like an idiot in a pin stripe suit with collar and tie, ploughing rickety furrows in an international championship, appeared on page three of the *Daily Mail*, consigning me to live down a new found notoriety as the farmer's boy.

My biggest scoop as a junior came, once again, courtesy of my dear wee Ma. A friend of hers heard a rumour while out attending a church service at Clonard Monastery in west Belfast that the Chief of Staff of the IRA, Hugh McAteer, was secretly engaged to a woman in the parish. But she could not discover this woman's identity.

It meant a lot of foot slogging and knocking on doors in Clonard for me to track down Miss X. People in this staunchly republican area were clearly suspicious of a stranger inquiring about the love life of a man who was regarded locally more as a freedom fighter than a terrorist leader. Finally, in a small two-up, two-down terrace house in Odessa Street, the woman herself opened the door. I said I was looking for Hugh McAteer's girlfriend and I knew by the way she blushed that I had found her.

'Who told you?' she asked and I couldn't bring myself to confess it was my Ma. She introduced herself as she invited me in. Over a cup of tea, Nora McKearney chatted shyly, but openly. She even supplied the photographs to go with the story, which ran through all editions of the *Daily Mail*.

Under the headline 'Nora waits for the lover she sees four hours a year', it read:

> Miss Nora McKearney, a 26-year-old Belfast factory worker who can only have four hours a year with her lover — and never a minute of privacy — is prepared to wait another eight years for her wedding day. And already she has waited five years.
>
> Hugh McAteer, 34-year-old IRA Chief of Staff, is the man to whom she is engaged. He is serving 15 years in Belfast Jail for treason felony. If he is out before 1958, he will consider himself lucky.
>
> 'I thought our engagement was a secret. We have kept it a long time,' said Nora. 'But we have nothing to hide. I met Hugh in 1941, after he had served five years of a seven-year sentence for possession of arms. We were a happy couple for 11 months. Then in November 1942, he was arrested on a treason felony charge and sentenced to another 15 years. He escaped in January 1943 and was at large for 11 months.
>
> 'Whether there will be any remission for good conduct remains to be seen. But even if he has to serve every single day of the sentence, I will wait. During a visit to Crumlin Road jail Hugh proposed. I went to Derry — that is where he lives — saw his parents, got the ring and brought it to the prison. We became officially engaged.'
>
> Nora displayed the gold, three-stone ring she wears every time she keeps a tryst in the gloomy, unromantic anteroom in the jail, over which a watchful prison officer presides. There is not a moment of privacy in

this strange love affair — never a word that the warder does not hear, no holding hands, no kissing — two lovers separated by a thin, wire mesh.

'I can write as many letters as I like,' she says, 'but Hugh is only allowed to write once a month. Alternately he sends one to his parents and one to me. Then, once every month, I am allowed a 20-minute visit. This is something to look forward to ... '

McAteer was a folk hero in republican areas and while a prisoner he stood as a Sinn Féin candidate in a General Election in his native Derry. Although unsuccessful, more than 20,000 people voted for him.

His daring, over-the-wall escape from the Belfast prison in 1943 caused a sensation, which was compounded by his dramatic appearance before a packed audience in a cinema on Belfast's Falls Road while he was on the run. From the stage, surrounded by IRA bodyguards and cheered on by supporters, he read a copy of the 1916 Proclamation of the Easter Rising before going into hiding again.

After serving eight years of a fifteen-year sentence, McAteer was unexpectedly released from prison and the couple married three years later.

Another 'all editions exclusive', which involved a lot of knocking on doors, was also instigated by my Ma. She'd overheard someone in a queue talking about a girl who was going to marry a man she had never met. All she could find out was that the girl lived at Bread Street in east Belfast.

No one in the Bread Street area could help me in my quest and I was about to give up when a shopkeeper on the Newtownards Road provided a clue. The girl concerned was a customer, but he knew her only as Sylvia. And she had moved out of the district to 'some street off Ravenhill Road, opposite the Ormeau Park'.

No problem, I thought, until I got there. I hadn't realised that the Ormeau Park was half a mile long and 'some street opposite it' could have been any one of many: London Street, Dublin Street, Toronto Street, Delaware Street, Rochester Street, Florida Street, Ravenhill Avenue, Ravenhill Gardens, Ardenlee Avenue, Broughton Park, Broughton Gardens or Ravensdene Park.

Leg weary as I already was, and as much determined as ever to track down Sylvia, the prospect of knocking on so many doors was just too daunting. That's where my pals in the old street gang came in. I talked three of them — Jimmy Robinson, Mo Moran and Jimmy McDowell — into helping me find Sylvia.

Up and down these streets the four of us toiled evening after evening, knocking on doors with commendable patience and some nerve. 'Does Sylvia live here? Sylvia who's going to marry someone she has never met?'

It was getting dark one evening in Rochester Street when a pretty young girl answered the door to me and said, 'I am Sylvia.' She invited me in and over coffee in her parlour, Sylvia Atkinson unfolded the sort of story that papers like the *Daily Mail* relished.

For two years Sylvia, a 22-year-old nurse, and her fiancé, Ernest McBride, a 25-year-old factory foreman from Toronto in Canada, were pen pals and exchanged more than four hundred letters. They got to know each other so intimately by post that they became engaged. He gave up his job in Canada and travelled to Belfast to marry the girl he had never seen. The wedding was set to take place in Ravenhill Road Presbyterian Church three days after I interviewed Sylvia. Then she dropped the bombshell which made it an even better story from a news point of view.

'We decided last night to call the wedding off. We've been thinking it over during these last few days and mutually agreed that we were not made for each other after all,' she confided. Invited guests were alerted at the last minute and, of course, the honeymoon plans were cancelled. The story and photograph of the couple, which Sylvia supplied herself, made the front page of every edition of the *Daily Mail*.

It was literally on my own doorstep that I found, or rather my Ma found, an incredible number of stories. If she'd had her way every family in our small community would have featured in 'our Pat's paper'.

I marvelled at her relentless capacity to unearth stories for me. She always had her ear to the ground and what a nose she had for news.

My Ma was a homely, loving wee woman and very popular in the neighbourhood. She was forever 'running messages' for people in the area who were unable to do their own shopping. They all said she had a heart of corn, this short, droll, roly-poly, wee bundle who was as long as she was broad and gifted with such a healthy attitude to life, always tending to look on the bright side.

She liked to play goalie in our football kickabouts on the garden lawn. Once she was nearly knocked out by my brother Joe for letting in a penalty. 'Get your mitts up, Ma,' he said as he danced, shadow boxing around her, throwing out lefts, rights and upper cuts.

Suddenly we were all aghast when an inadvertent short straight right caught her flush on the nose. Her legs buckled, her eyes started to roll and she was about to sink to the ground when Joe brought her to her senses by lovingly grabbing hold of her, saying: 'Good God Ma, that was some punch. I nearly missed you that time.'

My Ma liked nothing better than shopping for bargains and when she struck gold in a sale, she couldn't resist buying not one, but half a dozen cut price giveaway items. To cheer her up, I used to tell her outrageous fibs about my own shopping conquests when I became a working lad, paying my own way. She was totally elated to learn that the brand new suit I was wearing had cost me only five quid in a sale at the local Markets, a new pair of shoes was half a crown and a new shirt was just a shilling.

'I always knew, son, you were born under a lucky star,' she would say. Then she would chide my two brothers and sister for not getting the bargains I did.

Always neat and tidy, my Ma, nevertheless, had no fashion sense. Buying anything verging on the glamorous was a waste of money. She was even averse to replacing old clothes for new. Once she had a white straw hat adorned with a small bunch of wax grapes, which we siblings couldn't stand the sight of. It was the last straw as far as my taste in hats was concerned. One day when she wasn't looking, I tossed it into the small river, which ran down an old concrete culvert, separating our garden from Johnny the Milkman's field.

For days my poor Ma complained that, though she had searched the house from top to bottom, she couldn't find her good hat. She reasoned it must still be somewhere in there. Then, one day, she announced triumphantly that she had found it.

'It's stuck in the river,' she declared. 'God knows how it got there. It must have been blown away when I wasn't looking.'

The hat was, in fact, trapped in debris by the side of the fast flowing stream. My Ma had spotted it when she went out to feed our goat, Kitty, which grazed in Johnny the Milkman's field. Kitty slept in a shed at the bottom of our garden. A Nubian goat and a great milker, Johnny had given her to us as a pet kid.

Alas, I had to pretend to my Ma that when I went to fetch her hat it broke free before I could reach it and floated away. From that day on she never wore a hat, always insisting she looked better without one.

Kitty was such a prolific provider that she had to be milked three times a day, a chore which usually fell to me because only my brother Willie or I could do the job. The goat had a nasty habit of butting and my Ma seemed to be her favourite target. This made life somewhat hazardous for her as she was the one who had to put Kitty out to graze in the morning and bring her in again at night. This meant negotiating the thick, narrow plank that spanned the stream between our garden and the field.

Consequently, my Ma was in daily imminent danger of being butted overboard and into the water. She always said you had to take the rough with the smooth and so she endured Kitty's fighting spirit, if only because she cherished goat's milk in the firm conviction it contained the cure for tuberculosis. Two neighbours' children who suffered from the disease were gifted a regular free supply.

Johnny the Milkman, who, as I have already indicated, I helped out on his delivery rounds, had appraised me of the facts of life as far as Kitty was concerned. The day would come, he said, when she would be thinking of marriage or 'looking away', as he put it. I would know the time was right when her tail 'would go like a fiddler's elbow and her bleat would waken the dead'.

The only Billy, as far as Johnny knew, was on Bell's farm and the price of his service was a staggering half a crown. When the time came for the nuptials, I felt like an improbable best man. I had not even reached the age of puberty — I was only about nine years old at this point — and sex was never mentioned in our house. How on earth was I to tell my Ma? It took me ages to pluck up the courage.

Kitty was becoming more and more insistent by the hour with her continual bleating. At one time my Ma asked me to check if the goat had fallen into the river and was drowning. Finally, I blurted out, 'Ma, I need half a crown.' Jesus, what was I saying? My weekly pocket money was three pennies and even that was considered a bit over the top, yet here I was asking for ten times that amount, all at once.

'It's for Kitty,' I said and then found myself echoing Johnny the Milkman's words. 'She's looking away.' Without batting an eyelid, my Ma went to her purse, extracted a precious half crown and handed it to me. Not another word was spoken.

Then began a tortuous two mile journey with me leading Kitty on a short rope up Albert Drive, right along Cregagh Road, left by Hillfoot Road to the foot of the Castlereagh hills and wondering, all the way, if everyone I passed knew my secret.

When I arrived at Bell's farm and thought I'd got over the worst of it, I didn't know which way to turn when a woman answered my knock at the front door of the farmhouse. Words failed me. It was bad enough having to broach the subject with my Ma, but how could I put it to a strange woman? I think my guardian angel came to the rescue.

'I have the half crown,' was all I said. The woman led the Billy out of a shed. I looked the other way ... until it was over. None of us spoke. Kitty and I returned home with a lighter step.

What I had not bargained for, subsequently, was becoming a midwife. It was in the middle of a harsh winter's night when Kitty woke us with a distressing sound to her bleating. My elder brother Willie, who was 11 years old, and myself left our warm beds and, by candlelight in the shed at the bottom of the garden, wide-eyed in wonder and mouths agog, we witnessed the miracle of birth.

The kid, a lovely little Nanny and the spit of its mother, had slipped into the world within seconds of showing its head. Kitty feverishly commenced a mop up operation with an urgent, willing tongue. Just when I thought I could go back to bed, Willie exclaimed: 'Hold your horses. It's not over yet!' The words were hardly spoken when, to my astonishment, Kitty effortlessly made it twins.

Then a large membrane slowly emerged in the shape of an opaque balloon and we thought it was going to be triplets until it suddenly burst with a loud plop.

Kitty had given birth to a sturdy young Billy, which was on its spindly legs in no time at all. Alas, the youngster was soon to cause me heartache. By unanimous family consent, and sanctioned by Johnny the Milkman, the young goat was deemed to have no viable future in our domestic husbandry. We had no appetite for goat's meat and had been advised of the malodorous propensities of a buck of this species.

Billy the kid was only a few days old when I was assigned to get rid of him in the only way the folk in our neighbourhood knew to dispose of newly-born pups or kittens superfluous to requirements — death by drowning. The place of execution, known locally as 'the bomb pit', was a few miles away from our house. It was a deep, water-logged crater, left by a huge German missile dropped aimlessly by a Luftwaffe bomber during the war.

I could not bring myself to commit the dire deed. I promptly recruited a less sensitive member of our street gang, who shall remain nameless because of the brutal turn of events that transpired, which might brand him for life as a callous little monster. He placed the poor wee Billy, pathetically bleating for its mother, into a potato sack I provided, which was weighted with stones and fitted with a running noose. He quickly tightened the neck of the bag and, betraying not the slightest trace of emotion, unceremoniously tossed the little bundle of life into the middle of the crater.

Horror-stricken, I stood watching the stream of bubbles rising to the surface. My shock was about to be utterly compounded by a tragic sight that can still haunt me to this day. The wee Billy had broken free from the sack as it sank to the bottom. It managed, somehow, to surface and was now swimming valiantly for its life.

I watched in awe the game little animal striving to keep his head above water. I marvelled too at the strength he was able to summon as he clambered on wobbly feet up the bomb pit's slippery edge. Safely ashore, the kid sneezed several times and, dripping with muddy water, shook itself with surprising vigour.

Just as I was thinking Billy the kid deserved to live, my pal grabbed it by the hind legs and cast it into the deep again. It was just too much. This time there was no stream of bubbles. The fight for life was over.

It immediately diminished my pal in my estimation and left me feeling a moral coward, with pangs of conscience even yet.

eight

POSTWAR LIFE WAS SPARTAN WITH FEW TANGIBLE material signs of the brave new world. We had no car, not even a bicycle between the six of us in our family. That's not to say we were ever deprived, but I often wondered as a youngster why our houses were not as big as the houses on the front of the road.

There was also no telephone in our house, which no doubt accounted for the *faux pas* I once made when I was first asked as an office boy in the *Daily Mail* to answer the phone. I lifted the receiver upside down and timidly spoke into the earpiece while trying to listen to the mouthpiece.

While my Da was more taciturn, my wee Ma was a great social mixer and conceded she could talk the leg off a stool. My Da took a quiet interest in my career, but never an active one. My Ma, on the other hand, made sure everyone in the neighbourhood knew that her Pat was a reporter for the *Daily Mail*, even though he was very much a rookie at the time. That's probably why people would often come to her with all sorts of tittle-tattle, which served to fuel her newsgathering achievements. She was really proud of me and at times would get a bit carried away.

Once, while queuing for bread, which was still being rationed after the war, a woman in front of her was boasting about the great job her son had in the bank. Not to be outdone, my Ma produced a *Daily Mail* from her shopping bag. 'This paper's for my son. He's having a lie-in this morning,' she fibbed. 'He's the editor of the *Daily Mail*, you know.'

My Ma might not have had much of an education — 'no schooling,' she called it — but she certainly knew a good story. I've already related how our neighbours, the Vances at number 14 Albert Drive, provided me with my first news story for the *Daily Mail* and the Sheppards, next door at number 16, provided my first sports story. Well, next door to us at number 13 were the Waterworths, who got into print with a tale about their dog Dinky.

Dinky was a small mongrel who was in the habit of visiting a local factory on Montgomery Road for lunchtime tidbits from the workers. It transpired that one of the men fancied May Waterworth and he used to send her little love notes attached to Dinky's collar, and she replied in kind. The little dog was so fond of the workers and their generosity that he began to spend all day at the factory. One evening he arrived home with a note, advising May that since the factory operated a strict closed shop policy, and since Dinky was now in full time attendance, he would have to join the trade union or there could be a strike. Thus, Dinky was co-opted honorary member number 0001 of the Irish Transport and General Workers' Union and next day the *Daily Mail* proclaimed: 'Woof! Woof! Dinky Joins Trade Union.'

As a footnote to the story, May got her man and Dinky was guest of honour at the wedding.

Of the sixteen houses in Albert Drive, surprisingly no fewer than eight of them produced stories for the paper, some more than one, and all thanks to my Ma. In addition to the four I have already related, the Robinsons at number 1 and the Hutchinsons at number 9 reported individual tragedies. Both Bobby Robinson and Norman Hutchinson endured torturous ordeals at the hands of the Japanese in prisoner of war camps, with both subsequently dying in the line of duty.

'Love Was The Spur', according to the headline for Albert Martin who lived at number 6. He emigrated to Canada to find a job because he couldn't afford to marry his childhood sweetheart, Florence Bain, who was left broken-hearted in her home around the corner at Cregagh Road. But Albert struck it rich in Toronto and Florence flew out to join him at the altar to complete a story with an international flavour.

Next door to the Martins at number 8, Bobby Napier, who was a prisoner of war in Germany, made the news with a message relayed as an SOS by Lord Haw-Haw, the notorious wartime propaganda broadcaster. It was an appeal for a special brand of pipe tobacco, which Bobby sorely missed, called 'War Horse' of all names, and which was manufactured by Gallahers of Belfast. The company duly sent the tobacco to him and derived a lot of publicity in the process.

Albert Drive is intersected by Thiepval Avenue and it too yielded quite a surprising quota of stories in due course — at least seven of them.

Kathleen Robinson, who lived at number 16, married the boy next door at number 14, Thomas Belshaw. Both had been in the army for six years and, although they lived beside each other for twenty years, they had never spoken until the two families started sharing a new double garage at the rear of their houses. This opened up a romance that led to the altar.

Next door to the Robinsons were the Stevensons at number 18. Harold, who was 11, and my younger brother Joe made the news by managing to visit their soccer idol, Jimmy Jones, the Belfast Celtic star centre-forward, in his 'strictly no visitors' private room at the Royal Victoria Hospital. Jimmy had sustained a broken leg during a riot by spectators at a match against arch-rivals Linfield in the Senior Irish League.

I have to admit a vested interest here. I egged on the two boys to visit the player as he had threatened to sue our paper for libel because our report of the riot inadvertently suggested that he had a part in starting it. By writing about the boys' novel hospital visit with a bag of oranges, I availed of the opportunity of putting the record straight. I made it clear that our paper agreed that Jones was a victim and not an instigator of the riot, and that there was no malicious intent in what we originally published. He subsequently dropped his libel suit.

Further along Thiepval Avenue, at number 22, were the McDowells and they hit the headlines when the father Tom and son Jack were rival party election candidates with different shades of socialism.

Next door to the McDowells were the Donalds. Army Private Robert Donald married an Italian wartime heroine, Maria Grassia, from Piacenza near Milan. The couple met in German-occupied Italy, where she fought with the underground resistance movement. She won a Partisan's Commendation medal for bravery, signed by H R Alexander, Commander in Chief of British Forces in Italy.

Babs Douglas, at number 24, was a young singing and dancing star who had to get special War Office permission a month short of her sixteenth birthday to go with her parents, who were both well-known stage performers, to the Korean theatre of war to entertain the troops there. This made a typical propaganda piece.

Vivienne Green, at number 28, featured as the odd girl out in the local boys' soccer team, in which she was the star scorer.

Two streets, which ran parallel and on either side of Albert Drive, provided five more *Daily Mail* stories. At number 2 Somme Drive lived William 'Billy Boy' Firth, a giant at 13 years of age, who kept popping into the news with his amazing feats of strength. He could lift a solid, two-hundredweight blacksmith's anvil chest high and balance heavy cartwheels on his chest. He was trained by John Burke, an all-Ireland weightlifting champion and an ex-RAF pilot who lived at number 21 Somme Drive. While still at school, Billy Boy smashed the country's senior middleweight lifting record.

Billy Boy's next door neighbour, at number 4, was 18-year-old Ena Wilson, who got her picture into the *Daily Mail* for marrying the same man twice. A member of the Belfast Girls Singers, she wed a visiting Danish policeman and opera singer, Gregers Krake, at Belfast Registry Office. Two years later, they had a church wedding in Copenhagen.

Two doors further along, at number 8, Ken 'Plum' Kershaw, the 16-year-old son of a commandant in the police 'B' Special force, made the headlines with an adventure story about running away from home to back-pack around Ireland, starting off with only a half crown in his pocket.

My younger sister Molly came up with a story in Hamil Drive by providing a tilt at bureaucracy. Molly was a shop assistant at Cregagh Stores and had almost as good a news sense as my Ma. The pavement area at the front of the shop was flooded by a burst pipe. The Water Department at Belfast Corporation dispatched a posse to the rescue. It consisted of a plumber and his mate, a tarmac road layer, a cement road layer, a pump operator, two labourers and a supervisor in a shiny black peaked cap.

A large hole was dug through the layers of tarmac and cement and the burst pipe was located. The supervisor looked apprehensive. Out came his tape measure. Slowly and gravely he shook his head, tut-tutting to the shop owner, Mrs Cuthbert, that he and his gang could do nothing about it. The burst pipe was two inches inside her garden and therefore on private property, outside their jurisdiction. So the hole was filled in and sealed with tarmac and cement, leaving the surface as it was and the pipe still leaking.

Off marched the posse: the plumber and his mate, the tarmac road layer, the cement road layer, the pump operator, the two labourers and the supervisor in his shiny black peaked cap.

A private plumber was called and, in no time at all and unaided, he fixed the pipe for Mrs Cuthbert. The *Daily Mail* thought it merited a double column headline.

The courts also produced their quota of stories showing bureaucracy gone mad. One William Maxwell, a 36-year-old grocer, ran a shop in the front parlour of his house in Paxton Street, east Belfast. His crime was selling 'tuppenny' lollipops to children on a Sunday, contrary to the Shops Act (Northern Ireland) 1946, Section 6, Second Schedule. Mr W Smyth, prosecuting, said the City Corporation took an 'extremely serious' view of this breach of the Sabbath laws. The grocer, who was fined twenty shillings with twenty shillings costs, was told by the prosecutor perhaps by way of consolation, that he could 'lawfully sell lollipops on Sundays if he partitioned off his groceries'. This required, in effect, the construction of another shop within the shop. The grocer was informed that, if the partition complied with official requirements, then the Corporation might grant him a certificate to sell sidelines like lollipops on a Sunday.

Another quaint legal rumpus centred on a grocer who was fined for selling a tuppenny cream bun to 13-year-old Walter Henry from Rodney Parade, after hours on a Wednesday, when shops legally closed for a half-day. Henry was the six-stone boxing champion of Ulster and decided to fight the case.

Through his father, he sued the Shops' Inspector, who had caught him with the bun. The Inspector was charged with technical assault for holding Henry's arm, and false imprisonment by restraining him from leaving the shop with the bun allegedly in his pocket. The hearing lasted six hours and involved two barristers, three solicitors and six witnesses. The judge threw the case out with costs against the boy's father. 'A dear bun,' he quipped.

Then again, there was the case of an equally quaint court item involving John McManus, a barber from Servia Street who had lathered a customer's face and had him half shaved when a Shops' Inspector arrived and told him he was breaking the law. It was seven minutes after the legal closing time and the customer had to leave the shop with only one side of his face shaved. The magistrate let the barber off with a caution. And the story's headline? Obvious, really: 'Close Shave!'

Mrs Catherine McCrory was not so lucky. She was charged with serving a loaf of bread and a bottle of milk ninety-five minutes after hours.

'I always do it,' she said. 'I've already been nicked six times for the same thing. My shop is in a working class area and many of the customers get home when the other shops have closed, so they come to me. They need bread and milk for their children. The law is an ass.'

The magistrate admired her candour, but had to fine her one pound, with ten shillings costs.

It's almost inconceivable that such trivia was once the very stuff of day-to-day news reporting. All too soon, the very name of Northern Ireland was to become synonymous with paramilitary and civil violence; the onset of some thirty years of mayhem, which was to earn this land the unwanted attention of the international media.

nine

REPORTING AT SUCH A PAROCHIAL LEVEL, I found life as a journalist a bit of a turn-off. But one day I thought it was all going to change when I was suddenly faced with the prospect of becoming a foreign correspondent.

Our news desk in Manchester, where the Irish edition was published, ordered me to stand by for an emergency overseas assignment. Apparently there was a shortage of reporters in Manchester to cover it. I was in the act of packing my bags when I learned that my date with destiny was no more foreign than the Isle of Man.

I had been reporting for some five years and this was the first big sporting event I had been assigned to — the British Empire Car Trophy Race. It was memorable for two reasons. Firstly, it marked my inaugural flight by airplane and secondly, I was accompanied by another young reporter from Belfast who was destined to reach the top of his profession and gain national fame.

His name was John Cole and he was then a junior reporter with the *Belfast Telegraph*. There was no hint that one day he would be a household name as the BBC's political editor, someone who had the ear of Prime Ministers and was on first-name terms with the country's leading politicians. He spoke then, as now, in his guttural, word-chewing Ulster accent and betrayed no signs of future professional distinction. Like many a young bachelor, he also had an eye for the girls.

We were staying at the Bowling Green Hotel in Douglas, where we dated two girls who were on holiday. John, always the gentleman, did the honours and suggested a night at the theatre. It says something for the two of us that, while John in his grand manner booked and paid for an expensive private box at the theatre, I could only afford penny ice-cream cones for the four of us.

Another local I encountered as an emerging top national journalist was Tom Samways, a natural born newspaperman to whom I am indebted for his great help in my formative years.

With no formal education but a latent flair for writing, his roots were in the back streets of Belfast's Lower Falls. He lived with his mother and great aunt in Raglan Street in a two-up, two-down terrace house with an outside toilet. From the age of 12 he vowed to become a reporter and read every book about and by journalists that he could lay his hands on. He was an avid daily reader in the Falls Road Library. He got into journalism through the back door, so to speak, of the *Daily Mail* in Belfast, as I had done.

His first job, he liked to relate, was as a messenger boy in a corner shop from which he was sacked when he was caught eating chocolate biscuits under the counter. His next move was a concentrated assault on the *Daily Mail* office in Rosemary Street. He plagued the Boss for a job for weeks and, though he never actually got on the payroll, he was eventually employed as a 'gofer'.

He took the opportunity of learning how to type and on several occasions tipped off the Boss about good stories, some of which he got to write himself. Failing to get a staff job, he went to London hoping for an entry into Fleet Street and landed a job as a teleprinter operator in an international news agency, the United Press of America.

Tired of transmitting journalists' stories, he decided by clandestine means to sneak his own work into the news network. As his byline started to pop up in top newspapers serviced by the agency all over the world, editorial bosses began to ask who this Tom Samways was. When the ghostwriter was finally discovered,

Samways was sacked as a teleprinter operator — and given a job as a reporter. He was subsequently headhunted by the *Daily Mirror* and *Sunday Pictorial* in Fleet Street and, after serving as a reporter for a number of years, he became a joint top columnist with the then famous Noel Whitcombe.

After the war, he returned to Belfast, where he spent most of his chequered career with the *Irish News*, alternating as political editor and erstwhile popular columnist. Tom was one of the last of the old school of home grown 'character' journalists for which Belfast was then renowned.

In his early days, before going to London, he was my inspiration during his frequent visits to the *Daily Mail*. He would often discuss, analyse and sub-edit what I had written as a cub reporter and was the first to instill in me the importance of perfecting a story's 'intro'.

His advice was actually the same, word for word, as that given and published years later by the leading Irish author, playwright and columnist Hugh Leonard: 'Always grab the reader by the balls in the first paragraph.'

Early in my career, I also learned that sometimes it paid to be late rather than early on a story. On one occasion, two full days had elapsed after a big story broke before I was assigned to cover it in a remote part of County Donegal. Yet I ended up with a surprise scoop.

Normally our Belfast office didn't deal with events across the border in the Republic. In this instance, however, no other reporter was available at the time.

Five Donegal fishermen, including two brothers, were reported missing, presumed dead, in treacherous waters off the coast. A massive air and sea search had entered its third day. Hope was fading for survivors when I set out so belatedly from Belfast with freelance photographer, Oscar Carolan, to make the most of a follow-up story with next-of-kin interviews.

The five missing men were from an isolated area near Malin Head. After the long drive, slowed drastically by the foul weather, we got completely lost. Somehow, despite assiduous reference to road maps and country signposts, we simply ran out of road. There was no habitation in sight. The last cottage we passed was miles back.

We were lost in a sea of heather, but it was obvious that we were close to the coast. The thunder of Atlantic rollers, crashing against unseen cliffs, was incessant.

Dusk was starting to close when Oscar discerned some sign of life in the shape of a curling plume of smoke to our distant left. Slowly and with great difficulty, we headed towards it by different tracks. Eventually, we came to a derelict shack where some workmen were gathered around a fire. At least we took them to be workmen until we explained we were looking for some missing fishermen in the area. They said they were local fishermen, but had no idea what we were talking about. It was only when I made a roll call and they began to answer it, either with 'that's me' or 'that's him', that it dawned on us. We had found the elusive quintet.

They seemed bemused when we explained that the aircraft we could hear flying overhead and the rescue boats, from as far away as the anti-submarine Naval Base in Derry, were out looking for them. It transpired that their fishing boat had sought shelter in the teeth of a gale and went aground at an isolated location with radio equipment damaged and out of action. Ashore, they found all the telephone lines down, but managed to reach a cottage where they were warmly welcomed. The hospitality was apparently augmented by a poteen still in the vicinity and the party went on longer than expected until the storm began to abate. Oblivious of the massive air and sea rescue operation, which had been launched in the widespread search for them, the men were making the best of their way home when we succeeded, where so many others had failed, and found them.

Without giving the game away about how we slept in on the story in the first place, it took some convoluted explaining in my report to account for our dramatic fluke discovery of the missing men, by getting lost ourselves in the middle of God knows where.

Another unmerited exclusive was also the result of being slow off the mark and making a big mistake into the bargain.

One wintry night in 1946 a former wartime troop carrier, the *Georgetown Victory*, took a wrong turning during foul weather in the Irish Sea. Its bearings should have been to starboard, heading for Glasgow and the scrapyard. Instead, at the mercy of fierce cross winds, it steamed to port side in the opposite direction, towards Ardglass on the County Down coast. Mistaking the runway landing lights at nearby Bishopscourt military air base for approach lights up the Clyde, the huge vessel ran aground at Ballyhornan.

It was three days later before we got wind of it. Our photographer Henry Millar and I set out from Belfast in his tiny vintage Ford boxcar. It was a slow journey, made more difficult by taking a few wrong roads. At times, when we needed to turn back, it meant lifting the car manually and pointing it in the right direction. Poor Henry was not only an inexperienced driver, on his own admission, but he had not yet mastered the art of teasing the car into reverse gear.

The wintry sun was setting by the time we entered the last lap to Ballyhornan, hurtling at a sedate and steady twenty miles an hour. At a turn in the road, heading towards Kallard Point, an astonishing sight suddenly confronted us.

Our way seemed to be completely blocked by a towering ship, lying on its side in a field. If ever a ship was said to be out of its depth, this was it: high and dry with no sign of the sea. The reality, however, was that the *Georgetown Victory* was beached on a rocky stretch of strand some distance from dry land. We were at a dip in the road with a bird's eye ground level perspective, which presented a mirage-like view of the landlocked vessel.

Henry began to panic, complaining about the rapidly fading light. Through a gap in the hedge, he took pictures of the ship as we saw it.

Next day, I was amazed to find one of Henry's photographs had made the front page of the *Daily Mail* and was blown up to cover almost the top half of it. The massive, gaunt-looking ship, lying on its side in the field like a giant, beached whale, looked sensational. Because Henry hadn't used a flashgun, the photograph appeared slightly out of focus, serving only to give it a most dramatic ghost-like effect.

In the foreground the grass in the gap of the hedge, through which Henry had taken the picture of the ship in its prone position, appeared as wild jungle growth. Bushes looked like clumps of trees, growing fore and aft of the vessel. The headline, 'Drama As Gale Lashed Ship Lands In Field', suggested that the *Georgetown Victory* had been lifted clean out of the water by the force of the storm.

As I was late with the story, I had written only a short piece setting out the salient facts, but omitting — prudently, I thought — to mention that the vessel had met her doom three days earlier. The sub editor, who handled the story, must have assumed we had been quick off the mark, if not actually on the spot, when it happened. When Henry took the photographs, crewmembers of the *Georgetown Victory*, who had been shopping in Ballyhornan, were scaling up rope ladders, returning with their supplies. The sub editor, however, presumably thought it was the other way round. According to our story, they were abandoning ship and scaling down rope ladders, fleeing for their lives, not simply reboarding the stricken vessel at their leisure.

All in all, it was a fascinating, enigmatic and dramatic picture, though totally misleading and thoroughly inaccurate. No doubt, however, it would have pleased the old school of cynical reporters who, tongue in cheek, had a catch phrase: 'Why let the facts stand in the way of a good story?' Or picture?

Be that as it may, Henry was given a bonus of fifty guineas by the *Daily Mail* for his scoop, which later also earned him a 'Picture of the Year' award in a Press Photographers competition. Who says the early bird catches the worm?

ten

I NEVER REALISED I WAS SUCH a big cry baby until one day, out of the blue with no prior consultation, I was told I was being transferred to Head Office in Deansgate, Manchester.

The staff in Belfast from the editorial and circulation departments — all six of them — marked the occasion with a farewell presentation ceremony in the back office, which I coped with rather badly and sadly. It struck me as being a very embarrassing and tongue-tied affair for all concerned. Never having experienced a formal get-together before, I was terrified, being completely devoid of all knowledge of the niceties of such events. And even now, as a consequence, I have misgivings about formal occasions.

Bill Norris, the circulation manager, and a man of few words at the best of times had now even fewer words as he self-consciously thrust into my trembling hands a gold nib pen in a presentation case. My first speech in public consisted of but one word: 'Thanks.' Even then, I had to gulp it out. It was also the first time I let anyone see me shed a tear in public and I was simply ashamed of myself for not coping better. The farewell party must have asked themselves what sort of a reporter was this poor lad going to make. Without further ado, I fled the room.

I really should have kept and treasured the token of esteem, but alas the very next day, I lost my lovely gold pen while giving Johnny the Milkman a hand on his farm.

As an old apron string by nature, I was totally unprepared for being the first to break the family mould and leave home. The six of us were closely knit in the extreme and none of us in my young lifetime had ever experienced separation of any kind. Any discussion of my impending exile was studiously avoided, as it was too delicate a subject to be even mentioned. But the anticipated pain of parting was palpable, especially since I had not been told if the move was to be permanent. My bags were packed in virtual silence and we dared not even look at one another in case any of us would break down. The few words spoken were exchanged in whispers.

The Boss had ordered a taxi for me and I was the only one to spot its arrival, having kept an impatient vigil, waiting by our front room window for an hour or so beforehand. Blinded by tears and not even able to announce the taxi's arrival, I grabbed my bags and, without a word to anyone, dashed out of the house.

My emotional state was clearly not the stuff of which hard-bitten reporters-in-waiting are made of, but I was so broken-hearted that my depression left no room for speculation about my future in journalism.

The Boss was standing by the queue of passengers waiting to board the Heysham boat at Queen's Bridge, so I was assured there was at least someone to see me off. I don't recall, however, the Boss saying much to uplift my drooping spirits by way of any wishes of *bon voyage* or any words of reassurance about what lay ahead. Perhaps I am doing him an injustice, but the only thing I can remember is him reminding me to tip the baggage porter aboard ship. My predicament was in not knowing what amount would be appropriate and, given my upbringing, I was even embarrassed asking anyone to carry my bags.

It was an unreal sort of occasion for me, with no farewell handshakes or handkerchief waving as far as I can recall and I was left with an aching, empty feeling once I was alone and aboard ship.

Before I knew what was happening, a porter, unsolicited, relieved me of my luggage, inquired after the number of my cabin and promptly led me there. Instinctively reluctant to pay for such a menial task and anxious not to embarrass the porter, I nevertheless parted with my first ever tip, hoping the half crown was liberal enough, only to learn later that a shilling was the acceptable going rate.

Alone in the cabin and with no travel experience to fall back on, I was unaware of how any of the gadgets worked and stayed up all night, completely bereft of sleep.

The train journey from Heysham to Manchester was fraught with apprehension about what lay in store for me, away from home for the first time. My initial impression of the English people was not favourable, confined as it was to the travelling public. The train was packed, our carriage crammed with grim-faced commuters who never exchanged a single word or a smile during the longer than expected journey.

On arrival at Victoria Station in Manchester, I was met by one of the *Daily Mail*'s top reporters, Harold Pendlebury, an extremely amiable father figure, married to an Irish girl from Clonmel, County Tipperary.

As an innocent abroad, I was still very boyish looking and Harold clearly empathised with my uncertainties. He drove me to the digs arranged for me in advance by the newspaper in Sale Moor, a posh, leafy suburb of Manchester in a lovely rural part of Cheshire. It was a big, rambling, red-bricked Georgian house in genteel decline, set in its own grounds, which we at home would have described as 'a relic of oul dacency'. The branches of a sturdy oak tree rustled the bedroom window of my converted attic flat. Its fascination for me was the owl, which had its home there. Its hooting kept me company during my lonely hours.

The guests were mostly professional people, who struck me as being self-consciously aloof, though not pointedly unfriendly. They also included a coterie of crusty, retired, old military types, who maintained a dignified air, despite being very much down at heel and distinctly alone in the world, subsisting no doubt on their pensions. One in particular, an ex-army colonel who had not a family friend to call his own, befriended me. He was toothless, wore threadbare clothes and had a very cultured accent, at variance with his sartorial inelegance. The poor man seemed to be always hungry and at mealtimes he wolfed down everything in sight, leaving not a crumb.

Those postwar days were hard times and marked by continued strict food rationing. Every week without fail, my dear Ma sent me a food parcel full of goodies, which I shared with the ex-colonel in the privacy of my room. Oddly, he confessed to a weakness for, above all things, stoned pressed dates, which came in small, brick-like blocks. My Ma made sure to include one of these delicacies in every parcel, which I gave unopened to my friend to help feed his peculiar addiction.

As a sign of the times, food shortages were such in those days that every member of our guesthouse was issued with a pot of jam, labelled with our names and room numbers for our individual and exclusive use. It was something of a ritual at mealtimes for the pots of jam to come out of the dining room cabinet and be placed in front of each person, making sure nobody got someone else's ration. To spoon into another's secret jam jar was not cricket, as they say in England, and not to be countenanced, old chap.

One guest, whom I did not regard as a stranger, assuaged the alien feeling I always sensed in the digs. He was none other than the renowned Ulster and Irish rugby international of his day, Jimmy Nelson, a chartered accountant from Belfast who had business in Manchester. We shared the same table at mealtimes and had always something of mutual interest to talk about.

In addition to the food parcels, my Ma always sent me a small weekly laundry bag, which consisted solely of seven detachable collars, starched stiff white as only she could make them — a clean one for every day of the week. She would not trust any English laundry to do them properly. My Ma had a fad for stiff white collars, regarding them as indispensable to setting off any shirt, but I found it a nuisance having to post them back to her every week for renewal.

Even though I was no longer a burden to my family, as a growing boy away from home I persisted in contributing to the household purse, just as I had done as a boy on Johnny the Milkman's farm. Only now my fortune was counted in pounds rather than shillings. Good times or bad, young or old, I always regarded giving my Ma family budget money as a duty, though she never asked for a penny.

The *Daily Mail* office in Manchester was stately compared with the Irish tenement connection in Belfast, a stain I considered on the good name of a great newspaper. The reporters in general, and Harold Pendlebury in particular, took me under their wing as the only junior journalist on the staff.

For reasons best known to the hierarchy, I was assigned mostly to do late shifts. This effectively assured that I missed all the good stories, which more often than not broke during the day. It also meant I was desk-bound most of the time, sifting through shoals of 'hand outs', which inundated the office from myriad sources, especially small local news agencies. Rarely, in my experience, did they yield an item of national newspaper interest.

An exception comes to mind, while I was on night duty for the *Sunday Dispatch*. I was about to spike an item listing results from a gymkhana in Sale, when I noticed it was marked 'more to follow'. When nothing more followed as promised, I put through a call to the gymkhana and caught the secretary just as she was about to lock up. The poor woman could scarcely speak, choking back her sobs. She epitomised the special love for animals for which the English are renowned.

Tearfully, she related how a little girl of 14 was left broken-hearted and inconsolable after her favourite pony Lancs Lass had won the show championship. As her pet trotted round the arena in a glorious victory parade it stumbled and fell, breaking a leg. The poor animal had to be put down on the spot in its moment of triumph. Before the vet performed the dreaded deed, the little girl desperately clung sobbing to her beloved pony, her arms wrapped around its neck. Later, I interviewed the distraught child and we photographed her at home, a forlorn little figure in a now empty stable.

Though I regarded it as no big deal as news items go, it was a classic human interest sob story in English terms, and it says something about the news value pertaining at the time. To my astonishment, it made the off lead, rated the second most important story of the day, on the front page of the *Sunday Dispatch*. The editor, Aubrey Viggers, whom I always regarded as a tough nut, turned out to be an old softie, eulogising profusely about what I had written, almost breaking down as he confessed that having read my epic, he 'simply wept'.

That same editor seemed to have a weakness for judging people by appearances. I must still have retained my office boy looks, for when we first met the weekend after I arrived in Manchester, he mentioned a story of mine about large-scale smuggling across the Irish border, which had made the front page lead in the previous week's *Sunday Dispatch*. But somehow he thought my father had written it and inquired about his well being. I told him my dad was a postman and doing just fine. It left me not knowing if I should be flattered or embarrassed.

My Manchester experience in general could be summed up as both sweet and sour. Sweet because of its brevity and the fact it embraced three summer heatwave months, enabling me to enjoy many tranquil hours exploring the lovely, lush Cheshire countryside; sour because it was the most unproductive spell, thus far, in my essay into journalism. After all, very little of national news interest happened in my patch during the night shift from seven in the evening until three in the morning.

The *Daily Mail* had a fleet of chauffeur driven staff cars, one of which was placed nightly at my disposal to do my exclusive bidding and it made me feel rather important. If the truth were known, however, it was all a futile show-off exercise involving a grand tour of every police station and hospital in the Greater Manchester area during the dead of night. A round of phone calls from the office would have served the purpose equally well. It was always the same answer on these nocturnal missions: 'Nowt doing.'

Not once during my three-month sojourn did any of these grandiose excursions produce a single news item. Still, the ritual continued on the pretext that personal contact always paid off.

These were lonely times, completely bereft of any social highlights and I was miserable and homesick. Parties were non-existent. It was not easy to socialise when I did not even drink or smoke in those days and the people I met were not notably gregarious. My humdrum, desk-bound work was never faulted, but at no time did I feel it really fulfilling. There were no sad farewells when my temporary exile ended and I was sent back to Belfast. My concern was that my colleagues in particular would think I had not made the grade.

The object of the exercise, I was to learn later, was nothing more than to afford me some office experience as a prelude to ventures into pastures new. I was destined to broaden my horizons with a transfer to Dublin.

One of my last stories before leaving Belfast again caught me on the hop as it blossomed into an unlikely personal romance against a bizarre background.

I first met the girl, who was to become a steady date, as she stood outside the General Post Office in Royal Avenue with her hands outstretched and dripping with blood. An excited crowd had gathered as an ambulance drove off with an elderly clergyman, who had been slashed across the face with a razor by a maniac. The assailant apparently held a grudge against men of the cloth.

The Reverend Alfred Harbinson of Ligoniel Methodist Church slumped to the pavement along with his wife, who had fainted. Women were screaming and amidst the hue and cry, a young nurse calmly elbowed a passage through the crowd to render first aid. She was 19-year-old Loyola O'Boyle from Castlefin in County Donegal, a student nurse at Belfast's Musgrave Park Hospital. She was in need of some care herself, as she stood alone and unaided in her bloodstained coat. After offering my handkerchief, I invited her to the *Daily Mail* office, just around the corner to wash her hands.

After the ablutions, Loyola settled down with a cup of tea and related what happened, not fully appreciating that her words, along with her photograph, would appear on the next day's front page.

By staunching the blood from a wound extending from the 65-

year-old minister's left ear down the side of his face, Loyola might well have saved his life and was hailed a heroine.

I don't think she was aware I was a reporter or that the man, for whom she meekly posed for a picture as she sat in our office, was a press photographer. She was in a state of shock, which probably accounted for her consent to see me again on a date.

We continued to meet for frequent walks on Cave Hill, overlooking the city. After my transfer to Dublin, we maintained contact in a romantic sort of way. Initially I spent weekends at home, travelling to Belfast by the Enterprise Express on Friday evenings and returning to Dublin on Monday mornings. The train passed Musgrave Park Hospital and Loyola and I used to wave to each other as she stood conspicuously on the balcony of one of the hospital wards and I leaned out of a carriage window on the Enterprise.

Alas, when my journeys became less frequent and Loyola no longer appeared on the balcony, it was the end of the line for our brief encounter. Of such stuff are films sometimes made.

PART TWO

eleven

MY DEBUT IN DUBLIN WAS FRAUGHT with consternation bordering on despair when I learned that the *Daily Mail* had no office there. The only briefing I had received was that Jack Murdoch was to be my new boss and I was to contact him at Leinster House in Kildare Street. Jack was the *Mail's* chief correspondent in the Republic and I was being assigned as his deputy.

As a complete stranger to the city, oblivious of its goings-on, it pains me to confess that I actually assumed in my woeful ignorance and innocence that Leinster House was Jack's Dublin abode. After all, it sounded like a posh family address to me and nobody told me otherwise. Now I know, of course, that Leinster House is the seat of the two houses of *an tOireachtas* or national parliament, comprising Dáil Eireann, which is the lower house or House of Representatives, who are known as deputies; and Seanad Eireann, which is the upper house or Senate. The building was originally the mid-eighteenth century residence of James Fitzgerald, the Earl of Kildare, who later became the Duke of Leinster.

However, for quite a number of years it was to become my own personal residence, or so it appeared. As time went on, it was even suggested that I had the safest seat in the Dáil. Governments would come and go, but I remained the constant, non-paying guest at

Leinster House. No one ever showed me the door, nor told me I had outstayed my welcome. In fact no one, not even the Captain of the Guard, Michael Loftus, ever asked me what the hell I was doing there or why I was spending so much time under its roof. What nice people.

Occasionally, other journalists who had every right to be there at all times — like Paddy Quinn, political correspondent of the *Irish Independent*, or Dick Dowling of the *Irish Times* and later RTÉ — would drop in during off-peak times and bump into me, wandering about the corridors of power.

I would invariably be asked in a jocular sort of way, 'You still here?' or 'Have you no home to go to?'

Jack Murdoch did not have to haunt Leinster House as I did. With the absence of an office in Dublin he worked from his home in Mount Merrion, part of which was converted for this purpose.

No such arrangement had been made for me, so what was I to do? Naturally it was the first question I asked on my arrival from Belfast. Jack suggested that all I really needed was a phone and this should be no obstacle as there was one in every pub in town. Much as I liked pubs, using them as a base was out of the question and working from my digs seemed just as impractical for a variety of reasons.

'Why not use Leinster House as an office?' Jack suggested. After all, a press room and a phone were there for the exclusive use of the *Daily Mail* when the Dáil was in session. Jack was absolutely sure no one would object to me using this phone, even when the Dáil was not sitting. What was more, I could also have my meals there since accredited reporters were welcome in the members' dining room. I was to go much further than that.

Short of sleeping under its roof, Leinster House became my full-time office and my part-time home for years to come. I could even use the Dáil bar as my 'local' and entertain friends there. All in all, it was a case of come and go as I pleased. My only regret was that the building was closed on Sundays, so I had to make the best of my leisure time outside its welcome environs.

It didn't matter if the Dáil was in session or in recess. I was always there. Thus, I got to know many Dáil deputies (*Teachtaí Dála*, or

TDs as they are more commonly referred to), and even some Cabinet ministers, on a personal, first name basis.

In hindsight, I'm amazed no one ever challenged my ubiquitous presence there during the greater part of the 1950s. I took the set-up so much for granted that I never questioned its professional rectitude.

My meals were state-subsidised. I had lunch practically every day in the Dáil restaurant, also an evening meal most days and breakfast occasionally. I enjoyed full office facilities including free heating and lighting, which must have saved my company thousands of pounds during my six or seven years as a lodger in the national parliament.

It never really occurred to me that all of this was at the expense of the Irish taxpayer. Yet I was using the Dáil for reporting almost anything, except Dáil business, for my paper. Everyone was so friendly, civilised, accommodating and unquestioning.

The *Daily Mail* had not the slightest interest in the day-to-day activities of the legislative assembly. We never reported on any of the debates as such. Apart from big occasions like Budget Day it was only when a member was ejected from the chamber for stepping out of line, or when there was a 'typically Irish' debate, that the newspaper showed any interest in what went on there.

When I think of it now I become quite shame-faced but at the time I thought nothing about using our exclusive phone line to chase up extraneous stories on a daily basis all over the country. These were not only for the *Daily Mail* but also for our sister paper, the *Sunday Dispatch*. Incredibly the phone bill was the only account our company was required to pay.

The telephone itself was in a private lock-up kiosk in a corridor off the Press Room. This phone box was specially fitted with shelves to hold files and a portable typewriter. In essence it was a private, compact and secure mini office.

All my correspondence, comprising personal mail as well as news and feature contributions from freelance 'stringers' all over Ireland, was delivered to me care of the Press Room and duly franked with the distinct oval *Oireachtas* stamp. Even my monthly salary cheque was sent to me care of Leinster House.

The reliance I placed on having access to the building was strikingly illustrated on my first St Patrick's Day in Dublin when I was covering the festivities for the paper. I arrived to find the entrance lodge closed and the giant gates locked, which was not surprising with it being a national holiday. Security was nothing like as strict as it is today. The resident Irish army guard and garda service employed a device known as a 'double-locking' of the gates — the only overt protection against intruders.

I was amazed to learn that all the pubs in the country were closed by law on this day above all days. This was designed to curb over-indulgence, which had apparently been a feature of past St Patrick's Days. There were ways, however, around the law. A person could get a drink at the St Patrick's Day Dog Show at Ballsbridge, courtesy of a special concession, or avail of a unique *bona fide* travellers' concession.

In the line of duty, I chose the 'one for the road' option. This entailed purchasing a rail ticket in Amiens Street station to travel to Donabate, some seven or eight miles from the city. The ticket established the holder as a rightful traveller for whom the provision of food, drink and shelter was an imperative under some ancient Innkeepers and Travellers Act. It did not, however, mean that a person had to physically travel all the way to Donabate for a jar. With ticket in hand, one had only to travel a few yards across the station to the bar — provided, that is, one could make it. There was scarcely any elbowroom as both the ticket office and bar were besieged by a sweltering, stampede-threatening throng.

'Jaysus, the whole country seems to be going to Donabate today,' gasped one tippler, whom I later quoted in a piece I wrote about this practice. 'I don't know where CIE (the state transport management company) is going to get enough trains.'

Of necessity, drinking glasses were not provided and bottles were distributed overhead to the masses in seemingly unending human conveyor belts, much like bucket chain gangs tackling a fire.

The heading for my article in the next day's edition read: 'Dublin's Dry St Patrick's Day — well almost!' However, to transmit the story in the first place proved to be just as difficult as getting a drink.

With Leinster House closed, I was aimlessly watching the St Patrick's Day parade from Stephen's Green and wondering where I could get a phone. I then spotted a garda friend outside the Shelbourne Hotel. He was one of the regular Dáil duty officers, whom I knew only as Ned. He was stout and red faced with a walrus-type moustache, a man after my own heart who liked a pint.

As it was an unseasonably sunny St Patrick's Day, Ned, in his heavy uniform, was licking his parched lips. He had tried to get a drink in Boswell's Hotel opposite the Dáil, and in the Shelbourne itself, but there was nothing doing. I told him I could get him a drink if he could get me into Leinster House to use the phone. I knew he had keys, not only for access to the building, but also for the museum adjoining it. Ned readily opened the museum gate on the Kildare Street side, which, unlike the Leinster House entrance, was not double-locked.

He led me through the echoing, eerie museum to a rear door, which opened onto a side entrance of the Dáil canteen. I followed Ned through the vast kitchen, noting with some surprise how old-fashioned the large copper utensils and rusty-looking cast iron ovens appeared, and how incongruous were the lines of washing hung out to dry: ladies' stockings, underwear and an assortment of garments.

The great dining room was unusually bleak and empty as we passed through, and it was then I began to have misgivings about my scheme. I had not told Ned that it was a bottle of poteen I had in store for him and just hoped he would take it in the spirit in which it was meant. A deputy from Galway had given me a bottle of the illicit drink at Christmas and I had left it untouched, afraid even to sample it because of its reputation for explosive potency. As I lifted it now from its shelf in the phone box, where it had lain for some three months, I was not at all sure how this guardian of the law would take it.

He looked at me suspiciously, held the bottle up to the light, uncorked it, sniffed it and then relented. He took a good swig and, smacking his lips, declared it a drop of good stuff. When I mentioned it had come from Galway he stunned me by declaring,

'Ah yes, that would be Paddy King's handiwork. King by name, king by nature, king of the poteen makers.' Then off he went, saying he needed a sup of water, and that was the last I saw of him that day.

The exquisite irony of all this was not lost on me. Here I was, a lone figure and an outsider at that, at the very heart of the nation's legislature, bribing a custodian of the law with a bottle of illegal spirits. And to make matters worse, it was all taking place on the feast day of the country's patron saint when the government decreed that all trading in intoxicating liquor was punishable by fine or imprisonment. As far as I was concerned, the end justified the means. I was simply obliged to carry on my business, courtesy of Dáil Eireann.

After phoning my story through to Manchester, I made my way out the way I came in. I knew Ned was still around somewhere because all the doors he had originally opened for me were still, thankfully, unlocked. Ned had, however, locked the tall Kildare Street entrance gate behind us and I had to climb over it to get out, at the risk of breaking either a leg or my neck. I still marvel that not one of the passers-by challenged me, though they must surely have wondered what I was up to.

Time was slow in passing when the Dáil was not sitting. I sometimes found myself the only outsider in the building when walking the empty corridors alone. At such times, Dáil members on visits from all over the country would occasionally drop into Leinster House and I'd often join those I knew for a drink or a night out on the town.

I knew the Labour Party members best of all, not least because they were the most constant visitors. Party leader Brendan Corish once told me over a meal that the *Daily Mail* was paying me more than the state was paying him as a Cabinet minister.

Seán Dunne, the Member for Dublin County, was a particularly close friend. I often accompanied him on his constituency rounds, which were a valuable source in my quest for stories. At the end of his meetings, Seán would introduce me and invite members of the audience to act as my news hounds. In this way, I got many offbeat news tidbits.

Seán and I also socialised quite a lot and were aptly known about

Leinster House as 'Mutt and Jeff', the tall and short cartoon characters in a Dublin newspaper. Seán was six foot three in height and I was five foot eight. I can claim credit now for giving Seán his election slogan: 'If Dunne can't do it, it can't be done!' I also introduced him to his future wife. It came about this way.

We were having a Saturday night drink in McDaid's pub off Grafton Street. Seán remarked that the woman sitting alone at the end of the bar was Cora Ryan, a member of the millionaire Monument Creamery family and a sister of film star Kathleen Ryan. She was obviously waiting for someone, as she kept her eye on the door. Towards closing time, no one had shown up and Seán suggested I should ask her to join us. I thought it a bit of a cheek, but being under the influence I consented, first introducing myself and expressing the hope I was not intruding.

I bought her a drink and asked her if she would care to meet Seán Dunne TD, who was eyeing me suspiciously as I continued to chat the lady up. The formal introductions being at last effected, we adjourned by taxi to the Silver Tassie near Bray to drink the *bona fide* hours away.

The encounter was to lead to one of the country's top society weddings of the year. The reception, in a grand marquee in the grounds of Bray's Royal Hotel, was attended by half the Cabinet in the coalition government. The National Union of Farm Workers, of which Seán was an erstwhile leader, was also well represented. Top hat and tails rubbed shoulders with rustics in their Sunday best.

My own standing in society was enhanced in a moment of levity. On arrival, the guests were formally announced by a flunkey in a scarlet uniform, gold epaulettes and white gloves. Both bride and groom were prompting this gentleman. As I arrived with my fiancée, Enda McAlister, we were announced in a loud voice, at Seán's insistence, as 'Colonel and Mrs Reynolds'. It must have left guests wondering how one so young could have attained such a rank, and left me with a title I was hard put to live down for quite a while.

Another moment of levity in which I aimlessly indulged offered a flashback to my boyhood in a haze of reverie.

I was alone in the Press Room one Saturday morning when the Dáil was in recess. The Taoiseach, or Prime Minister, Eamon de Valera was ambling along the corridor outside, arm in arm with a Fianna Fáil TD, Bob Briscoe. Bob was later to become Dublin's first Jewish Lord Mayor. Both men were audibly chatting about horse racing, of all things.

For a fleeting moment, I was back in east Belfast as a snot-nosed youngster playing in the street. To my Protestant pals, the Pope was a holy terror and de Valera an out-and-out baddie. They used to sing with gusto a pathetic, puerile doggerel about the Supreme Pontiff that went:

I heard the Pope was drunk last night
Fol-dol-dee-dee-and-the-daddy-o
On whiskey, gin and beer and stout
Fol-dol-dee-dee-and-the-daddy-o ...

For our part, we would only counter when we were brave enough and not outnumbered with chants of:

Up the Pope! Up the Pope!

As for the melodious derision of de Valera, the wee Protestant girls skipping in the street would intone:

De Valera had a canary
Up the leg of his drawers,
The canary came down
And sat on the ground
And whistled the Protestant Boys ...

To this, our lame, but loud, response was usually:

Up Dev! Up Dev!

Now, this very morning, I was in the presence of the great man himself and immediately sensed I had come a long way. I suppose, at that moment, something atavistic stirred deep within me and I could not resist it. Or perhaps it was for old time's sake.

As the Taoiseach walked off with Bob Briscoe, I gave vent to a loud cry behind his back: 'Up Dev! Up Dev!' and ducked out of sight, only to squirm slightly at the thought of my childish outburst.

The words echoed along the corridors of power and, somehow, I felt strangely fulfilled. Only I can understand the feeling I experienced, of having achieved something, however vague and indefinable. It was as if I had avenged a childhood injustice or squared some kind of circle.

I'm afraid I startled Dev. He swung around at the sound of my voice and seemed to stumble with arms outstretched and groping in the manner of a man with failing eyesight. He was, in fact, almost blind but was assured by Deputy Briscoe, whom I distinctly heard saying, 'It's alright chief, someone loves you.'

twelve

OF THE MANY FASCINATING CHARACTERS I encountered in Dublin, one of the most remarkable was Ignatius Patrick Quinn, alias the suspected 'Stratford Strangler'.

We first met on the morning of 22 May 1954. Born in Dublin and a brother of the top American-based singing star, Carmel Quinn, he was a 34-year-old nurse in Stratford-on-Avon General Hospital in England. He had travelled overnight on the Liverpool boat to Dublin and wanted to meet Seamus Brady of the *Daily Express*, whom he was told could be contacted through the Press Room.

The *Daily Express* in London, our paper's arch rival, had signed him up for an exclusive and were anxious to keep in touch with him when he said he was going to Dublin. I told him, quite truthfully, that Seamus seldom came into Leinster House on a Saturday. Now that he had fallen into my lap, I was not going to let him go.

Slightly hungover, he accepted my invitation to have a jar in Fleming's Pub, otherwise known as 'The Little Dáil', on Molesworth Street. It was just after opening time and I pretended that I badly needed a drink.

Over a few large John Powers whiskeys, he explained why the *Express* was so keen to tie him up for an exclusive. As he spoke, I could already visualise the front page headlines in my own newspaper.

He apologised for not being able to buy his round, but I meant it when I said it was my pleasure as I bought him drink after drink. We had quite a session and I invited him back to the 'office', where I talked him into switching allegiance to our paper, the *Sunday Dispatch*, with the promise of a few bob. Our editor, Aubrey Viggers, pledged a substantial fee of £100 to Quinn to allow me to ghost his 'tell-all' story. It was an offer Quinn couldn't refuse, especially when you consider that, in those days, one pound sterling was worth 240 pennies and a bottle of stout cost seven pennies. Thirty-four bottles for a quid!

Basically, Quinn's story was that he was arrested and questioned about the death of a 45-year-old midwife, Olive Bennett, in Stratford-on-Avon. She'd been strangled and dumped in the River Avon. An attempt had been made to sink the body with a headstone from the local cemetery. Interviewed by Superintendent John Capstick from Scotland Yard, Quinn denied he was the man seen 'pumping sherry' into the murder victim in the smoke room of the Red Horse pub before she disappeared, and he had an alibi to prove it.

The full exclusive story, with a large photograph under his own byline, was splashed across the front page of the next day's *Dispatch*. The eight column headline proclaimed: 'I Fled From Gossip', with the sub-title: 'Pointing Fingers And Malicious Tongues In Murder Town'. The story began with the words: 'In the eyes of the law I was only a petty thief. But in the eyes of many people in Stratford-on-Avon — indeed many people throughout the entire country — I was a murderer ... '

The account outlined his court appearance on a holding charge. He had been accused of the theft of a dressing gown, which he wore on overnight stays in the hospital where he worked. By taking it home on one occasion, he was charged technically with stealing it. Quinn regarded this simply as a stalling device by the police murder squad and, when the charge was eventually dropped, he immediately decamped to Dublin.

'Let's get it straight,' he wrote. 'I did not murder Miss Olive Bennett.' He was never charged with the killing, but he was, nevertheless, the centre of widespread public attention, speculation and controversy. After the story appeared Quinn, who was better known as Naish — short for Ignatius — was recognised wherever he went.

The *Sunday Dispatch* had a relatively big circulation and Naish kept in almost daily contact with me, frequently calling at Leinster House. In this way, he met quite a number of deputies and senators and became a familiar figure in the Dáil precincts. He was also quite popular, gifted as he was with a fine singing voice. As my guest in the Leinster House bar, he took part in a good few sing-songs, which were a feature of some late night sittings in the Dáil.

Out of work and with time on his hands, he was in the habit of tagging along with me for company when I went out on assignments, and local reporters came to regard him as a visiting journalist. On one occasion, he muscled in on a big story I was covering at Dublin Airport. It was the arrival of Limerick-born bishop Thomas Quinlan after his release from a Red China prison. He had served long-suffering years, enduring barbaric treatment and torture, almost to the point of death, because of his religion. The bishop became a human rights *cause célèbre*, with near martyr status.

Leaders of Church and State were at the airport to accord him a hero's welcome home. The press, which included a huge international corps, were confined to the VIP lounge, where a news conference was to be held. I warned Naish to behave himself, as he had a habit of butting in when he got a bit carried away.

As the aircraft taxied to a halt and the VIPs moved across the runway to greet the ailing bishop, I could hardly believe my eyes when I saw Naish joining them. Dressed in flannels and a smart, black blazer with a coat of arms on his breast pocket, he cut such a dashing figure that no one challenged him after he darted from the media pack to do his own thing.

As we viewed the proceedings through the observation window, one reporter asked in astonishment, 'What the hell is that Stratford bloke up to?'

Naish, the former murder suspect, was shaking hands with every

VIP in sight, including Cabinet ministers, bishops and archbishops. He even embraced the frail Bishop Quinlan himself, and had one arm around his shoulder while ushering him towards us in the VIP terminal for the news conference. I grudgingly marvelled at the audacity of the man, given his notoriety.

The photograph of him mingling with the distinguished welcoming party appeared on the front page of the Dublin papers, though his name was omitted from the captions, presumably because no one knew who he was.

After the news conference, where Naish sat at the end of the top table as if he was a privileged person, the party of eminent clerics was ushered to a fleet of sleek limousines to convey them to Maynooth College for an overnight stay. Nothing surprised me anymore about Naish and the last I saw of him that day was helping Bishop Quinlan into the leading limousine, and then getting in beside him.

I think those present were so overcome with the emotional nature of the occasion that Naish was somehow taken for granted to be a public relations officer or a bodyguard.

He caught up with me in Leinster House the following day to blandly announce, as if it was nothing really, that he had attended the lavish banquet in Bishop Quinlan's honour at Maynooth College the previous evening. Afterwards, he was allotted a special guest room at the college in which to spend the night.

I asked him why he had gone so far and all he could say, with a shrug of his shoulders, was 'Why not?'

Naish was also the centre of attention on a separate evening when he sprang another surprise in the back snug of Fleming's bar. This was a very democratic pub. Here there was absolutely no class distinction. They were an eclectic lot — Dáil deputies, senators, Cabinet ministers, well known writers, artists, actors, professional business people, together with proletarian Dubliners and women 'shawlies', all socialising as one.

Naish accompanied my girlfriend Enda and myself on this occasion when the other company present included: Dr Jim Ryan,

Minister for Finance; Senator Michael Ahern, son-in-law of Eamon de Valera; Frank Thornton, the War of Independence veteran and insurance company director; three Labour deputies — Seán Dunne, Maureen O'Carroll and Mickey Pat Murphy — as well as a few local regulars.

Naish was in great singing form and had been entertaining us with a parody of the song 'I Like To Go A-Wandering'. He substituted 'knapsack on my back' with 'Capstick on my back', in reference to the police superintendent he claimed had hounded him in England. This prompted someone to inquire about Naish's Stratford business. What had he really been up to?

Naish then embarked on an extraordinary and intriguing mime that left the entire snug spellbound. They had read, or were well aware by now, of his story in the *Sunday Dispatch*. Taking Enda to help demonstrate his mute show and indicating that he was playing the role of the Strangler, he took her by the throat, pretending to throttle her. He lifted her high and mimicked dropping her and throwing something on top of her.

It was a mock re-enactment, I presumed, of a real-life drama, which amazingly earned applause from all round the snug. But it left Enda embarrassed and complaining that her night out had been spoiled, having to play the role of a murder victim in front of a pub audience. Slim, petite and pretty, she had feared Naish, who was slightly under the influence, was going to drop her as he raised her prone figure above his head.

My future wife was also a regular visitor to Leinster House. We'd first met as a consequence of one of those small and innocuous quirks of fate, which have the potential to completely change the course and destiny of one's life. It was hatched in the form of a cracked egg — and it came about in this way.

Before moving in, as it were, to Leinster House, I had found temporary digs in the Phibsboro area of north Dublin. Enda's younger brother Malachy was employed by the landlord as a van driver for the family's wholesale egg business.

Guests and family shared the same breakfast table and I

happened to notice, with growing consistency, that the fried egg on Malachy's plate was different from mine in that his yolk was always broken while mine was always sunny side up and intact. Eventually, I discovered this was not by his choice, but by the landlady's design.

Malachy, with the benefit of inside information, revealed that his egg came from a batch of sub standard 'seconds', which were cracked and consequently less fresh. It was the paying guests alone who qualified for grade one eggs.

In no uncertain terms — well yes, I was a bit timorous about it — I made it known to the landlady that I was not prepared to share a table with anyone unless everyone was treated as equals. After all, there was a veritable mountain of eggs packed in the store at the back of the house. To be so niggardly in doling the eggs out at meal times was a breakfast too far for me.

The landlady was aghast when I told her I was packing my bags, but I plucked up the courage to tell her why. I was furious, but I'm afraid it wasn't as noble a gesture as it might sound. Malachy was leaving anyway and I was fed up with the digs.

'Why not come and stay with us?' he asked and I took him up on the offer, especially when I heard that his family had moved into a luxury Georgian house on Mespil Road in the upmarket Ballsbridge area of the city. Thus, I came to meet Malachy's sister Enda, whose father, it transpired, owned pubs in Monaghan and Cavan. And now that we've been married fifty years and have four lovely daughters, I say we owe it all to a fried egg. As for Enda, she just thinks I'm cracked up!

But returning now to Naish Quinn, I can recall an incident that occurred one Sunday when we hired a rowing boat at Howth to visit Ireland's Eye island. The saga began as we prepared to return in the late evening. The tide had gone out and our boat was stuck fast, some twenty yards from the water's edge. The heavy, wooden craft was firmly embedded in the wet sand and seemed to weigh a ton. Sweating profusely, we regretted having had so much to drink. We could only move the boat, inch after torturous inch, until we got it afloat.

A crowd had gathered on the distant pier at Howth as we tried valiantly to row against the treacherous, strong-running currents. Every time we neared the harbour bar, we found it impassable. As soon as we stopped rowing through sheer exhaustion, we began to drift back to the open sea.

A distress flare from somewhere ashore was fired high into the early night sky and a siren started to wail. The shoreline was receding rapidly from our view when we discovered we were not the only ones in distress. Another rowing boat appeared out of the gloom and someone with a foreign accent began hailing us for help.

To my great surprise, the boat was manned by a colleague from the Press Room, Monsieur Battefont, the correspondent for a French news agency. His wife was with him and both he and she were greatly alarmed. They had been on a similar expedition to Ireland's Eye, which left the woman in tears and her husband gesticulating in panic.

The local lifeboat duly arrived just as we had almost given up hope of rescue before dark.

After docking at Howth, an altercation took place between Naish and the man who'd hired us our boat. Naish threatened to throw him into the sea after he demanded a surcharge of five shillings for the boat, which was five hours overdue.

The last bus to Dublin, a double decker, was waiting at the end of the pier, but it moved off before we could reach it. It was lucky for us because, as we stood watching it drive away, something entirely untoward happened. The bus suddenly veered across the road and crashed through the sea wall with a shattering sound of grinding metal and splintered glass, leaving it firmly wedged and poised, see-saw fashion, above the water. Women's screams could be heard across the bay as the front of the bus protruded over a six feet drop.

True to his calling as a nurse, Naish dashed to the rescue. By the time I caught up with him, he had alerted a publican who lived almost opposite the crash, and secured a free bottle of brandy to administer to any of the passengers who needed it.

No one was seriously injured and only those suffering from shock required hospital treatment. All declined the proffered brandy, so Naish and I drank the bottle between us. Relief transport was sent from Dublin and we availed of it, posing as casualties, to save the price of a taxi into town. A photograph of the stricken bus appeared with a graphic story on the front page of the following day's *Irish Times*.

thirteen

THE PRESS ROOM AT LEINSTER HOUSE was the nerve centre for practically all my activities. It was, for example, at one stage an accommodation address for a notorious prisoner in an Irish jail, who kept in touch with me to maintain a long-running story in both the *Daily Mail* and *Sunday Dispatch*.

The central figure was a 29-year-old classics teacher at a school in Reading, England. His name was Ian Noel Harran, and he sparked a countryside manhunt when he escaped from Broadmoor Criminal Asylum for the Insane on 9 May 1951. He had been sent there in March 1946 as a convicted child molester. His escape with Ken Williams, a self-styled 'John the Baptist', caused a sensation and led to an extensive hue and cry.

Harran was branded a potential danger to children. He was so violent at his trial that it took seven policemen to drag him from the dock to the cells as he protested his innocence.

Williams was caught sixteen days after the breakout, but Harran worked his passage on a trawler to Ireland and was at large for nearly four months, back-packing his way between Dublin, Waterford, Cork and Galway. Arrested by gardaí in Limerick, who were unaware of his real identity, he had been using the alias John Drycer.

It was while he was being held at Limerick prison awaiting trial on house breaking and forgery charges that the authorities began to suspect he might be someone else. His fingerprints were sent to Scotland Yard, and practically every English newspaper, hungry for news of Britain's most wanted man, embarked on a frenzy of speculation stories.

I was sent to Limerick to write what we call in the trade a 'colour' piece. This meant unearthing any tittle-tattle, including such gems as what the prisoner had for breakfast, if only to prove that our paper was on the spot and also on the ball.

I called at the local garda station in William Street where the officer in charge was clearly fed up with all the phone calls from British reporters. In response to my desperate attempts to soft-soap him, he gave me a bit of straight advice: 'Why don't you go and ask the bastard himself who he really is? You know where to find him.' I took him at his word since I could think of nothing else. So it was that I found myself feeling a bit of an eejit, knocking on the door of Limerick prison and adopting what is known as the 'old soldier's act' for the benefit of the warder.

'Excuse me sir, but could I see John Drycer please, or whoever he is? I'm sure the poor man has had no visitors, him being a stranger in a strange land. Would you ever ask him if he'd like to see me?' I pleaded.

The warder told me to hold on and after an agonising absence returned to ask if I was a friend of the prisoner. Trying to be clever, I replied that I didn't have an enemy in the world. He then took my name and asked me to write down my address. Seeking to give the impression I was from England to enhance my chances of getting into the jail, I wrote down 'Northcliffe House, Deansgate, Manchester', which seemed, I hoped, to have the ring of my authentic family home. It was, of course, the address of the *Daily Mail* and *Sunday Dispatch* head office. I was banking on this English prisoner associating Northcliffe with the name of the well-known newspaper publisher and, by the same token, sensing my mission. It worked a charm.

In a small, arch-shaped cell painted all in white I found the prisoner sitting at a table with a warder at one end, and he pretending to be a long lost friend of mine.

'Delighted to see you, Patrick. It's so nice that you could come,' he said warmly, standing up to shake hands as if he had known me all his life. 'And how is everyone at home in Northcliffe House?'

First and foremost, I wanted him to confirm his real identity. A shrewd operator, he anticipated right away my unspoken question.

'I don't have to tell you, Patrick, I'm not John Drycer, of course. I'm your old friend Ian Noel Harran, in case you've forgotten,' he said with a disarming laugh. I could already see the front page headlines in the next day's *Dispatch* exclusive.

Harran went on to relate in great detail how he had escaped from Broadmoor with 'John the Baptist'. It was the first factual and authentic account of their story to be made public. He had filed a key in the prison workshop to fit his cell door. Before going to bed, he unlocked the door from the outside, then closed himself in by wedging a piece of metal to keep it shut and apparently locked. When the coast was clear, all he had to do was push open the door. A makeshift ladder then enabled him and his cellmate to scale the prison wall to freedom.

Clearly aware of what was necessary for me to pad out my story, he shrewdly revealed where he had been and what he had done while on the run in Ireland. There was such a wealth of detail to commit to memory that I felt I had to get something down on paper, particularly relevant dates, which he had mentioned. The warder politely told me, as I produced my notebook, that no writing was permitted during visits.

Having obtained all I needed for my story, I asked Harran to keep in touch with me, care of Leinster House. I realised then that I had blown my cover, but it didn't matter. I'd got my story.

After the half hour long interview, I had to wait for an escort out. In the meantime, the warder had obviously alerted the Governor. He stopped me as I was about to leave and said he now knew I was a reporter and accused me of breaching prison-visiting rules by false pretences. He also stressed that any communication conveyed by prisoners to the outside was subject to prison censorship, so I must not write anything about it. That didn't stop me phoning my story from Cruise's Hotel in Limerick to the *Dispatch* in Manchester.

As I left the telephone box, jubilant over my big scoop, a garda detective was waiting for me. He said he was investigating a series of hotel thefts in Limerick and wanted to question me as a matter of routine. I knew, of course, this was a bluff.

In William Street garda station, with an eye to possible legal repercussions, I made a statement about my movements since arriving in Limerick and what I had been up to. Cautioned not to leave the city without garda permission until further notice, I ignored the warning and was on the next train to Dublin. Before I left, I phoned Manchester to update the office and was told that the editor required a full memo immediately.

Back in Dublin, the editor dropped a bombshell. He informed me that the newspaper's legal department had 'killed' my story for reasons painfully obscure to me and against which I had no right of appeal. I was completely gutted and not even the subsequent bonus I received for my 'good work' could in any way assuage my bitter disappointment. I suspect the editor was taking no chances by crossing swords with the Irish authorities' sensitivities.

The *Sunday Dispatch*, in common with other English newspapers, enjoyed a relatively large circulation in the Republic, which they dared not jeopardise. Imported newspapers were subject to strict government censorship parameters and, running the risk of being banned, were always on their guard against offending officialdom, especially concerning such issues as internal and cross-border politics, books, films, pornography, divorce, contraception and other such affairs of Church and State.

The *Dispatch* had been banned on a previous occasion for a limited period with almost disastrous financial results because of an article that questioned Irish neutrality during the war. I have no doubt that it was this obsession with not putting a foot wrong and taking no chances that led to my Harran scoop being spiked.

Harran was eventually sentenced to a year's imprisonment in

Maryborough Prison, Portlaoise for house breaking and cheque forgery offences committed while he was on the run and, true to his word, he kept writing to me at Leinster House.

Just before his time was up, he tipped me off about his release date, hoping to provide me with another exclusive. Other English newspapers were very interested in the story and how it evolved. Harran's hour of freedom, however, lasted just a few seconds. As he stepped out of prison he spotted me and waved, but was prevented from approaching me by a detective sergeant, who emerged from the shadows.

A bewildered Harran was promptly bundled into a squad car, which had quickly drawn up, and he was whisked off to Portlaoise garda station, pursued by our photographer, Charlie Fennell, and myself in our press car. On being refused permission to speak to him, I went to the back of the station where I could hear Harran loudly calling my name. I shouted back, letting him know I could hear him.

'Listen, Patrick,' he replied in his posh English accent. 'The bleeders are sending me back to Broadmoor. There's no justice. The doctors here have certified me sane. The doctors over there say I'm nuts. Give me a good write-up, Patrick.'

Shortly afterwards, I spotted Harran sitting between two plainclothes officers in the back seat of a squad car as it was pulling out of the garda station. When it slowed down to turn into the street, Harran suddenly leaned over and nimbly let down the car window, beckoning me towards him. He grasped my hand to say farewell, but would not let go. The driver obligingly did not accelerate and the escort made no attempt to intervene. I had to run down the road for about fifty yards or so to keep up with the car, while Harran revealed he was being driven back to Dun Laoghaire to await a Scotland Yard escort to England. He only released his hold on me when the car started to increase speed. A large photograph of him, leaning out of the car window with me alongside appeared in the *Daily Mail* next day with my front page byline story.

In my report, I availed of the opportunity of quoting Harran, not only on what he'd said in the squad car, but also what he had told me during my censored visit to Limerick jail. The *Sunday Dispatch*'s loss became the *Daily Mail*'s gain. I felt I had fully recovered lost ground and was vindicated.

When Harran eventually appeared in court in England, prior to his commitment to Broadmoor, he refused to say anything until he had consulted his 'Irish advisor, Patrick Reynolds'. The *Daily Mail* was initially in favour of flying me over to meet Harron to see if there was any more mileage left in the story. However, for some vague legal reason, they finally dropped the idea and, thereafter, I ceased to hear from my prisoner friend.

The 'Galloping Major' was another high profile news personality to exploit Leinster House 'openness' over a long period. A self-styled gunrunner in the Middle East, he rejoiced in the name of Major Ralph Herbert Thomas Newman. He first made contact with me through the Dáil Press Room, having tried to sell his story to the *Daily Mail* in England before decamping to Ireland.

With twelve years' distinguished service in the British army with the Royal Artillery, and subsequently the Royal Army Ordinance Corps, he had fought at Dunkirk, in the Western Desert campaign and, finally, in Palestine. He'd twice been wounded there and acts of heroism earned him honourable mention in dispatches, and the nickname of the Galloping Major.

Sitting with me in the Dáil Press Room, he wrote his own account for the *Daily Mail* of his intriguing activities in Palestine before the British pulled out at the end of their mandate in the Middle East. It was dynamite in content and potentially libellous. At my insistence, he signed each page of what he wrote as indemnity against any legal comeback.

In his role as an Intelligence Officer, he'd eventually turned to gunrunning, but made it sound like his motives were purely altruistic. It was at the height of the Cold War and he sided with the Jews on the premise that the Russians would supply and arm the Arabs during the transition period in the wake of British withdrawal. Under orders to dump a large quantity of surplus arms in the Mediterranean, he decided instead to pass them on to the 'Haganah', the Jewish Underground Movement — but at a price. The sum was £50,000, and this was to 'cover risk and expense' and pay off fellow conspirators. The Haganah were short of £11,000 for which the Major was given a promissory note.

The clandestine consignment, worth much more on the black market, included a vast quantity of small arms, mortars and anti-tank weapons. These were American in origin and, under the terms of Lease-Lend wartime arrangements, they could not be resold by Britain and had to be dumped. The Major claimed that what he did was not morally wrong.

'My dear boy,' he stated, 'I merely flogged guns to the Jews to get one up on the Arabs, and it was in a good cause.'

But the army caught up with him. He was brought before a court martial and dishonourably discharged. Back in England, the 41-year-old Major could not find civilian employment and a warrant was issued for his arrest by Camberley police in Surrey for failure to settle a rates bill. He fled to Ireland, knowing that the warrant could only be executed for a criminal offence and not for a civil one, as in his case.

As the *Daily Mail* continued to give him write-ups in a long running story, I subsidised him for some time in food and drink. 'Broke?' he would say with embarrassing regularity. 'I'm right bang on the floor, old boy.'

Thus, he became a frequent visitor to Leinster House, freely using the Dáil Press Room, bar and dining room, and mixing *ad hoc* with deputies and senators, often being hailed as the Galloping Major, which he took in good spirit. In fact, he was such an effective raconteur and all-round entertainer that he became quite a popular figure. He used to say that he was perfectly enchanted by the general *bonhomie* of Leinster House.

On one occasion, which he thought was hilarious, he shared our table for lunch in the members' dining room. The company included Deputy James Everett, Minister of Posts and Telegraphs, of 'The Battle of Baltinglass' fame.

The 'Battle', over an allegedly rigged and 'political' appointment to a rural post office, was at its violent height and the Major took great facetious delight in referring to Mr Everett, who was at the centre of the controversy, as the Minister for Munitions. What especially tickled the Major's fancy at the lunch was the intervention of Deputy Seán Collins, a relative of the legendary Michael Collins, who came in for a meal and was invited to join us.

'Jaysus, I'd love to, but I can't sit down,' he said. Without batting an eyelid, he revealed he had nearly been castrated while having a sit-down in the Dáil toilet a few minutes earlier. He told us he was enjoying a relaxed perusal of the *Irish Independent*, oblivious to an inordinate build-up of noxious detergent gas, until he dropped his fag end between his legs into the bowl. There was a small explosion, which caused embarrassing scorch damage.

'The bang nearly blew my balls off,' he giggled, not in the least bit self-conscious. 'This is supposed to be the seat of power. I've a good mind to sue the bloody government.'

Despite his inability to sit at the table, Deputy Collins, who was a barrister, joined us nevertheless, remarking that it sure was a good stand up meal.

The Galloping Major continued to grace Leinster House with his presence, hoping to have his promissory note from the Haganah eventually honoured with the help of Jewish Deputy Bob Briscoe, who had links with Israel. But I never learned the outcome as the Major subsequently galloped quietly into obscurity.

Mention earlier of Cabinet Minister James Everett recalls our first meeting over lunch in my early days in the members' dining room, the setting for an embarrassing personal identity *faux pas* when I mistook him for the head gardener. Seating arrangements were on an *ad hoc* basis. There were no reservations as such and consequently I seldom knew, from day to day, who my table guests would be. Party political enmities were forgotten in a genial atmosphere, as lions sat down with lambs, no questions asked. So it was at our first encounter when neither of us knew the other. As he scanned the menu Everett turned to me, rather surprisingly, to criticise the rich fare.

'Roast rib of beef,' he said, 'one of the cheapest cuts of the beast — half a crown — you know that's not steak. You'd think, wouldn't you, in a place like this they could do better than that?'

I was under the impression that roast rib of beef was really a choice item, which made me rather question this good man's culinary inclinations. I wasn't to know then, of course, but the political inclinations of this same man were soon to become a national issue that would one day contribute to, if not in fact cause, the downfall of the government. But of that, more anon, as they say.

Meanwhile, I was somehow under the impression that here was a man, probably a true 'son of the soil', for he certainly had the hands of a member of the farming community, or perhaps a professional gardener. In the context of his remarking on the magnificence of the gardens of Leinster House, then in full bloom, and his passing knowledge of flora and fauna, my impression of someone with a distinct rural background was reinforced.

His fingernails also suggested some recent contact with mother earth, while the backs of his strong hands were matted with a robust growth of prominent black hair. All of which compounded my mental pen picture of a non-townie and left me wondering, not that it was of any consequence, from which part of the country he hailed. So I put it to him as tactfully as possible to establish his identity.

'Oh, I'm not a farmer or anything like that,' he said, 'though I once organised County Wicklow Agricultural Union. I'm the Minister for Posts and Telegraphs; and who might you be?'

Everett had been appointed to the Cabinet in 1948 in a coalition or inter-party Government that was to crash in June 1951. In 1950 he made what the outside world would have regarded as an innocuous parochial appointment. It turned out, in the eyes of many, to be a classic case of arrogant party political nepotism.

When a certain Michael Farrell was appointed by Everett as sub-postmaster of Baltinglass, on the border between counties Wicklow and Carlow, it was viewed as an attempt to arbitrarily oust one Miss Helen Cooke, of a rival opposition party. She had been running the shop for her invalid aunt, whose family had held the post for the previous eighty years. Helen was the darling of the local community and when the news broke of intervention from high places in their local affairs, the whole countryside seemed to erupt.

The locals formed a 'We Love Helen' fighting committee and laid siege to the post office to ensure that their heroine would not be supplanted. The bloodless 'Battle of Baltinglass' had begun and soon it became a frequent hot-tempered and fiercely contested subject of debate in the Dublin Parliament, both at Question Time and in Emergency Resolutions.

National newspapers took up the story and made it a *cause célèbre*, the popular theme being 'it's not what you know that counts, it's who you know'. Helen had assumed the role of David in the battle against Goliath. Baltinglass was now firmly on the map with far-flung sections of the international media descending on the sleepy village.

As part of the locals' battle plans to frustrate a possible government-backed takeover of their post office and the installation of an unwanted appointee by force, saboteurs cut down telegraph poles to make Baltinglass virtually incommunicado. In those days we journalists relied almost exclusively on the telephone to file copy, so coverage of the Battle of Baltinglass required much contingency planning. Locals also set up an early warning system consisting of makeshift sirens to counter any descent by the powers-that-be into the post office 'no-go' area.

Feelings had run so high for so long, and such was the countrywide support for the cause of the Battle of Baltinglass, that before the end of the year the government caved in to popular demand. James Everett himself bowed to the pressure of people power and reappointed Miss Cooke.

I often met the Minister in Leinster House during those arduous months and it was obvious the entire dramatic episode had taken its toll. Despite his outward appearance he was clearly a broken man. After barely three years in office, the coalition government was soon to fall with its defeat in the General Election of June 1951. In the eyes of most commentators of the day, this was in no small measure due to the backlash to the Baltinglass episode.

Down but not out, James Everett returned as Minister of Justice in the second coalition government of 1954-57 and was 'Father of the House' when he died in 1967.

fourteen

DESPITE THE *DAILY MAIL*'S VIRTUAL LACK of interest in the day to day proceedings of the Dáil, I maintained my presence in Leinster House, continuing to pursue news stories and other business, which had nothing whatever to do with central government.

On one occasion I had the effrontery, though indirectly, of being responsible for the suspension of all Dáil business, which led to a vote of no confidence in the Minister for Finance, Deputy Seán MacEntee. For my part, it was like biting the hand that fed you.

I had overheard Dick Dowling, the political correspondent for the *Irish Times*, giving forth on the upcoming Budget over a few drinks in the Dáil bar. He mentioned how remiss it was of the Minister for Finance, while posing for a pre-Budget photograph for his paper, to have the actual Budget itself and not a decoy on the table in front of him.

'I'm sure if the picture was blown up you could read some of the Budget's secrets,' Dowling said, almost as a jocular aside.

But what if that was actually the case, I thought to myself. I alerted my great friend, Deputy Seán Dunne, who became quite excited at the prospect, recalling that a Budget leak in Britain had once led to the resignation of the Chancellor of the Exchequer, Hugh Dalton.

The show window in the commercial office of the *Irish Times* in

D'Olier Street displayed prints for sale of pictures that appeared in the paper. And sure enough, there in the midst of them, was one of the Minister posing with his Budget opened in front of him. I bought it for half a crown.

Back in the Dáil, with the help of a magnifying glass, Seán Dunne was able to read the best part of a page from the financial document. It foreshadowed a rise in the price of bread, which was enough to constitute a leak as far as he was concerned. After consulting with the *Ceann Comhairle* or Speaker, he was granted leave to seek the immediate adjournment of Dáil business to enable an emergency debate 'on a matter of urgent, public importance'.

During the ensuing heated debate, members made a meal of it with the Opposition, led by Deputy Dunne, calling for the Minister for Finance's resignation. The upshot of the lengthy proceedings was that Deputy MacEntee narrowly survived a vote of no confidence, averting a government crisis. Although Dunne was deemed a loser in official records, it was hailed as a win in his publicity stakes.

I'm afraid to say that I was responsible on another occasion for the bringing of Dáil proceedings to a standstill, although it was not what I had planned or necessarily condoned.

On one of my frequent constituency tours alongside Seán Dunne, which usually combined sightseeing, pub crawling and extraneous newsgathering, I encountered a man in a Swords bar who, during the course of conversation, mentioned a matter which later threatened to provoke an international incident. He chanced to remark that he was a gardener employed by the Dutch Embassy in Dublin and I inquired what it was like to work for a diplomat.

Spluttering over his pint he remarked, 'He's a stingey oul bollocks. You won't believe this, but he refuses to stamp my health card because he thinks he's above the law and can get away with anything.'

Deputy Dunne promptly put down a question about the refusal of a Dutch Embassy official in Dublin to pay two shillings and fourpence a week in health insurance for his gardener on the grounds of diplomatic immunity. He had a field day and well he knew it. Dunne wanted to know from the Minister for Foreign Affairs, Mr Frank Aiken, to what extent diplomatic immunity was accorded to representatives of foreign countries and was he aware that, whatever it was, it was being abused by this Dutchman in Dublin?

Mr Aiken formally replied that diplomats were free from customs duty and internal taxation and enjoyed certain privileges, which were reciprocal. He would not go into details of special cases. A slanging match developed. Deputy Dunne was ruled out of order and told to sit down. Still on his feet, he crossed swords with the Speaker, Patrick Hogan, claiming that he had every right to defend a constituent whose very health was at the mercy of an indifferent alien parsimonious official using the cloak of privilege to dodge buying an insurance stamp for his poor gardener.

Amid heated exchanges from both sides of the House, which ended in uproar, the Deputy Prime Minister Seán Lemass proposed the suspension of Deputy Dunne for refusing to resume his seat. The expulsion motion was narrowly carried, but the Deputy refused to budge.

The Speaker called for the Captain of the Guard Michael Loftus who, with a tap on the shoulder, politely asked Dunne to leave.

'You'll have to carry me,' said big Seán, who weighed over twenty stone. The Speaker had no alternative but to adjourn proceedings.

The matter was resolved only when the session was resumed after a fifteen-minute break with Deputy Dunne an absentee. He had achieved what he set out to do with benign malice aforethought and gained for himself widespread publicity.

'Another fine mess you got me into,' he quipped gleefully as he joined me for a celebration drink in the Dáil bar.

When it came to canvassing for offbeat stories, big Seán was for me in the Republic what my Ma had been in Northern Ireland, although not quite as prolific. However, his many party meetings, which I attended all over the country and not just in his own constituency, were surprisingly fruitful. These meetings led to many quirky stories along the lines of the following:

The time when the ghost of Captain Moonlight, an Irish patriot-type on a phantom white steed, was observed riding high by independent witnesses in and around Bettystown.

The story of Little Jane Sherwin, the 69-year-old 'woman postman' of Whitestown Cross who, in her fifty-two years of work, reckoned she had made deliveries which took her the equivalent of five times around the world in terms of the miles she walked.

The case of Jolly Joe Butler the Dublin taxi driver who preferred indefinite imprisonment in Mountjoy Jail to paying a driving fine because of the principle involved.

The saga of Mary Anne Kelly from Rogerstown, a 70-year-old granny who lived in a house by the sea and had to climb a seven-feet-high wall to get in and out of her home when the tide came in.

It was Deputy Dunne's practice, before concluding a meeting, to invite members of his audience to come up with any suggestions that might make me a story. Sometimes I had to pinch myself at what I was hearing. But it convinced me of one thing: that wherever I went there was always a story lurking just under the surface, which required only a little scratching to unearth.

For example, at a meeting in Castledermot, County Kildare, where Seán was forming a new branch of the Labour Party, one obliging man put up his hand at the end of proceedings and said, 'What about the man who lives in a hole in the ground?'

He went on to paint an unlikely picture of a modern age caveman, John Fitzgerald, whose underground home was six feet long, six feet wide and six feet high, overgrown with blackberry brambles and wild roses. I was also led to believe there was carpet on the floor and pictures on the walls. The cave dweller, who heralded from Doon in County Limerick, had been living in his unusual abode apparently quite snugly for thirteen years. An ex-sergeant in the Munster Fusiliers, who had seen action in the First World War, he now earned a living making baskets from sally rods.

On the eve of the Second World War he got a job building air raid shelters and decided to build one of his own in a grass bank by the roadside, just in case Hitler ever bombed Castledermot. A smaller cave contained his larder, but when I heard he lit his fire with dried cow dung I decided to forget it.

One day a few months later, our photographer Charlie Fennell was pressing me to come up with a good picture story when I suddenly thought of our friend the caveman. It was blowing a blizzard at the time and the country was covered by the worst snowfall in years. How, I wondered, was John Fitzgerald faring in his hole in the ground?

Battling our way through the bad weather from Dublin to Castledermot in Charlie's battered old Volkswagen Beetle was a tortuous journey. The road out of town where old John lived was impassable and we got lost trying to make headway in snow that was waist deep. The entire countryside, under an immense, virgin white blanket presented a spectacular panoramic winter's scene with no sign of life anywhere. The air was crisp and freezing, the sky cloudless. Not a sound was to be heard.

At last, evidence of the caveman's survival suddenly materialised in the shape of a thin spiral of smoke in the distance, snaking slowly above the dazzling, snowy vastness and pin-pointing the object of our visit. It made a dramatic news picture spread in the *Daily Mail* the next day under the heading, 'John Fitzgerald Lives Here ... ' and Charlie subsequently picked up a national award for best topical news picture of the year.

Another far-fetched story I thought would never see the light of day actually evolved into a mini-series over some five years. Its launch in the *Sunday Dispatch* owed more to it having been instigated by that paper's editor than anything else. Whilst in a shop in Kilburn, London, he'd spotted an intriguing headline in a newspaper which catered for Irish exiles in search of news from home. The front page banner read simply, 'Brazen Bullock of Ballyclara'. Wanting to know more about it, he ordered a follow-up.

Ballyclara, I learned, was a small townland near Gort in County Galway and, while I had heard of brazen hussies, I had yet to meet a brass-necked bullock. But the powers-that-be had spoken and so I found myself haring across the breadth of Ireland on the trail of this wayward beast. On arrival I was directed to Bradley's bar, from where I was assured all reliable and exclusive information concerning the 'Brazen Bullock' emanated.

Through an alcoholic mist, I learned that old Pat Hynes was the original owner of the Brazen since its birth in 1951 when it had shown no initial signs of being a freak of nature. It developed, in fact, into a fine strapping young beast and, because it was in the wilds, no one had ever tamed it. Old Pat sold it on the hoof to local cattle dealer, Miko Kelly from Ardranan, for £60.

But when Miko arrived to collect it, try as he might, he could not catch it. Neither could anyone else. The Brazen took off and disappeared into 150 acres of wild and craggy countryside, greatly favoured by the audacious Galway Blazers. Every able man in the parish for miles around tried, time after time, to capture the fugitive.

Months passed and Miko demanded his money back. Old Pat reduced the selling price from £60 to £32. Miko then talked Jim Whelin, a supreme optimist from Rathcosgrave, into buying it at a bargain £25 as it was still at large. But you've guessed it: Jim couldn't catch the animal either, so *he* sold it still on the hoof to Mike O'Farrell from Cathercarna. Needless to say, Mike also failed to trap it.

Five times in all the Brazen changed hands over the years without anyone being able to catch it until, finally, a £5 price tag was put on its head. It was like throwing good money after bad as far as the locals were concerned. The offer was not taken up and the final sale of the Brazen went by default.

According to impeccable parish records there were no fewer than sixty attempts to capture the Brazen by all manner of means. On one occasion, a posse of at least one hundred local cowboys equipped with lassos, snares and nets — and many of them on horseback — was organised to try and trap the quarry in the stony expanse of his wild domain. But the Brazen was too good for them.

The legend grew to almost Loch Ness Monster-style proportions. The Brazen was perhaps best characterised by a Jack Gibben, who said he was allowing for no hyperbole when he insisted:

‘It stood sixteen hands high, had the shaggy coat of a lion, the fiery eyes and dilated nostrils of a dragon, the lightning speed of a deer, the cunning of a fox, the ferocity of the jungle, the jumping ability of a Grand National winner and an unearthly roar.’

One night in Bradley’s bar, I ventured to ask if it also had the horns of a dilemma. ‘Begob and it has,’ I was assured. ‘And they’re five and a half feet long.’

Not to be outdone, someone actually invoked the Bible, quoting from the Book of Job to substantiate the beast’s prowess: ‘The glory of his nostril is terrible. He mocketh at fear and is not affrighted. He swalloweth the ground with the fierceness of his rage.’

Many were the devices used to try and conquer the Brazen, including lamping it by night, springing underground traps and luring it with cattle decoys. Even Ireland’s ex-heavyweight boxing champion, Martin Thornton, came out of retirement to tackle the creature.

Martin owned a pub thirty miles away in Spiddal, County Galway, but his battle plan misfired completely with the Brazen showing more ring craft. After a two-hour chase, in which half the countryside took part, the Brazen was at last corralled in a stonewalled field. Almost exhausted and run to a standstill, as Martin thought, the Brazen furiously pawed the ground in snorting defiance.

‘I closed in and tried to grab it by the nostrils,’ Martin recounted for the benefit of *Sunday Dispatch* readers. ‘But it wrenched itself free and tossed me. Then it jumped the wall like a stag and was away in a flash.’

Such was the Brazen’s fame, thanks to the sizeable circulation of the *Dispatch*, that it was celebrated at carnivals, fêtes and fancy dress parades all over Ireland.

In the five years that I covered the story, with frequent but fleeting and glorious visits to Ballyclara to write progress reports, I must confess that I never actually saw the Brazen.

I did take part in several sorties into its domain, labouring under the handicap of impaired vision, attributed to the hospitality lavished so freely upon me by the generous patrons of Bradley’s bar.

Photographs of the Brazen were as illusive as any of the Loch Ness Monster and when a local photographer submitted his attempt at a picture, it was rejected by our art editor. He said it was so out of focus that it looked like a prehistoric monster grazing in the dim distance 'on top of a tree'.

The Brazen was born free, ran free and stayed free. It provided me with many unlikely follow-up stories over the years, especially during the 'silly seasons' when our paper was crying out for copy.

My fervent prayer is that the Brazen's noble spirit continues to roam the great plains of Galway. For, of course, its ghost has been spotted by witnesses whose veracity is beyond question.

fifteen

SINCE I SPENT THE GREATER PART OF my working life in Leinster House, a lot of my drinking was done in the Dáil bar. In fact, it was there that I had my first ever jar. Bridget McKeown, or Miss Mac as she was more popularly known, and with whom I was in good standing as a non-drinker, happened to remark one day that I was looking a little peaky. Her remedy was a Mackeson's Milk Stout.

Blissfully unaware that my first drink was to prove a defining moment in my life, this seminal draught was an exhilarating experience. 'Eureka!' I remember thinking. 'This is the answer, the great panacea for all my ills.' The instant euphoria it induced marked the start of a slowly evolving drinking career, destined to culminate in full-blown alcoholism.

For the first five or six years I drank with relative impunity, savouring every mouthful. A hangover was not something to be endured in those early days but actually enjoyed. By this I mean I used to pretend I was in need of the early morning drink just as an excuse to join the genuine sufferers in the quest for a hair of the dog.

Off-licences as we know them today were non-existent, so there were many early bird drinkers to be found, habitually lounging outside pubs waiting for the doors to open. Needless to say that this was not social drinking, and drinking in constant denial was to be my fate in years to come.

Meanwhile, I found Dublin in the pre-drugs era of 'the Swinging Fifties' to be a veritable tippler's paradise. Booze was the passion of my life, devoid as it was then of the demon of dependency, although I was drinking virtually every day.

My favourite bar was Fleming's, the 'Little Dáil' in Molesworth Street near Leinster House, where the craic was always great.

Near my digs in Mespil Road were pubs frequented by quite a few of the contemporary literati, most notably Brendan Behan, Strabane-born wit Brian Nolan, alias Flann O'Brien, alias Myles na Gopaleen, and pipe-smoking Frank Donovan who was a script writer for famed comedian Jimmy O'Dea. Ireland's 'Poet Laureate' Patrick Kavanagh had a ubiquitous presence in the Mespil Road-Baggot Street-Royal Canal area and while not a pub regular he enjoyed a flutter in any one of the local betting shops.

Brendan and Paddy were sworn enemies for whatever reason and I often witnessed altercations between them in public. They used to cross and re-cross the road whenever they met so as not to pass on the same side, and all the time shouting abuse at each other.

On sunny days, Paddy could be seen stretching out on the grass verge of the Canal, presumably in the depths of poetic composition. At intervals, he would suddenly jerk up to a sitting position, as if struck by a flash of inspiration, and snatch a few blades of grass to chew reflectively as he reclined again in contemplative repose.

On one occasion I saw Brendan on the bridge idly looking down with contempt on the recumbent Paddy. As Paddy bounced up for his periodic chew, Brendan bellowed, 'That's right, ye chancer ye. Live horse and eat grass. It's about all yer good for. Poet, my arse.'

Roused from his reverie, Paddy, tearing at his hair, gave chase to the fleeing Brendan, shouting, 'Ye ignoramus ye, Behan. Yer a drunken disgrace to the English speaking world.'

Passers-by seemed to accept it as par for the course and went about their business as if it was nothing untoward.

Conscious of the big brigade of the 'I knew Brendan Behan'

claimants in Dublin, and the many apocryphal stories about him, I hesitate to join the legion. Be that as it may, we often met in one of his favourite watering holes, Devine's, on the corner of Mespil Road and Baggot Street.

Brendan was writing a weekly column for the *Irish Press* and took some interest in my reporting activities, often providing me with news tip-offs. His sole income at the time was the six guineas he was paid for the column and in this context I think he was envious of my greater earning ability. He had not always the means to buy his round and complained of not being paid expenses, as I was, for his newspaper articles.

My expenses for entertaining people like Brendan were liberal and meant most of my drinking didn't cost me a penny. A psychiatrist was to tell me in later life that if all my drink was for nothing it would still be too dear for the likes of me.

When Brendan learned that my salary was a hefty £1,000 a year, he said the game was not straight. Why should you get three times as much as me, he moaned, underlining the difference between hack and genius. As his financial fortunes began to pick up and he was in need of getting from one place to another without engaging a round of taxis, I introduced him to a part-time chauffeur for the car he could now afford to hire — my future brother-in-law Malachy McAlister.

Malachy was also a drinking pal of mine, which meant that my contact with Brendan was more frequent than it might have been otherwise. My modest claim to fame, if you could call it that, was my role in inducing him to change the title of one of his epics.

We were drinking in Searson's pub in Baggot Street when Brendan was in the throes of composing *The Quare Fellow*, ably assisted by copious quantities of cider. With us were my future wife Enda and Brendan's wife Beatrice, who had arrived on a bicycle. For no better reason I suppose than to make conversation, I asked Brendan what he was going to call his latest work of art. '*The Rope*,' he grunted. 'Something wrong with that?'

I hadn't even suggested there was anything wrong, but now that he mentioned it I thought it was a rather unoriginal title; trite, hackneyed and more befitting a cowboy novel. He seemed peeved, so I told him, 'All I'm saying is that *The Rope*'s a quare title.'

I should explain perhaps, if only in the cause of etymology, that where I came from in Belfast the word 'quare' was a corruption of 'queer', meaning odd, curious, not apposite. 'Queer' had not yet been defined universally as the slang reference to being homosexual.

I don't know whether Brendan was having me on and had no notion in the first place of calling it *The Rope*, but he conceded: 'All right then, you win. I'll call it *The Quare Fellow*. Will that please you?'

It did indeed please me — and it has pleased me ever since, every time I think of it.

Speaking of titles, Brendan branded me 'the British object', a nickname that was to stick with me. It had its genesis in one of his columns in the *Irish Press*.

He loved visiting Belfast and fraternising — God be with the days! — with members of the Orange brethren, especially in pubs on the loyalist Shankill Road and Sandy Row.

The culture which consigned men to parade in black bowler hats, sombre lounge suits, starched collars, Orange sashes and white gloves, carrying ceremonial swords and beating Lambeg drums, while occasionally cursing the Pope, held a fascination for Brendan.

On one such fact-finding visit, he met a local man in the Boyne Tavern near the railway station, who proclaimed in the course of conversation, 'I'm a British subject — and proud of it.'

To Brendan's ear, not attuned to the local idiom, the man had declared he was a 'British object', leaving Brendan to ponder what the hell he was talking about. It formed the centrepiece of Brendan's column the next day, under the heading: 'I meet a British object.' And so it came to pass that, just because I came from Belfast, Brendan thereafter always referred to me as 'the British object'.

Enda was also saddled with a 'Behanism', suggestive to uninitiated innocent ears that she was something of a jezebel living in sin. The two had bumped into each other in Haddington Road when Enda was on her way to St Mary's Church one Saturday evening. Brendan was all set for a confab, but Enda excused herself saying she was going to Confession and was in a hurry.

The next time they met was in Grafton Street when Brendan hailed her in a loud voice from across the street, 'Have you been to Confession yet?' This was to be his style of greeting every time they met thereafter, with no concession to her blushes.

Brendan's contemporary, the much more erudite author, columnist and humorist-cum-top civil servant, Myles na Gopaleen, wrote a weekly column in the *Sunday Dispatch* for which he was paid a handsome twelve guineas. His copy had to arrive in our Manchester office by the Friday afternoon deadline to facilitate setting for the Irish edition. Not being the soul of punctuality, he sometimes failed to weigh in with his column in time and it fell to me to collect it at his daytime desk job in Dublin's Customs House to expedite its transmission.

I would arrive with little time to spare, only to find he had completely forgotten about it or had simply not bothered to put pen to paper. But such was his talent that he could rattle it off the top of his head, prefacing his effort with the remark, 'Now, let's see what I'll write today.'

Once, when he confessed his mind was blank and he hadn't a clue for a topic, he picked up an Irish dictionary on his desk, idly thumbed through it, selected a single Gaelic word, and contrived to base the entire column on it. I marvelled at his instant creativity and thought it a privilege to watch a literary genius at work.

For whatever reason, but probably indifference more than anything else, his weekly column in the *Dispatch* was not quite up to the standard of his daily 'Cruishkeen Lawn' column for the *Irish Times*, which had an avid countrywide following. Our paper toyed with the idea of dropping Myles' contribution on the grounds that it was not up to scratch. 'This is supposed to be funny and witty, but I don't see anything funny and witty about it,' the editor once complained to me on the phone. My response was that an Englishman could hardly be expected to see the funny side of it, but it was, in fact, absolutely hilarious and would go down a bomb with our Irish readers. It was my modest contribution to helping a genius consolidate his work.

Myles and I often met in the Pearl or Palace bars, which were the two Dublin drinking dens favoured by the literati, though the Scotch House and Mulligan's were close runners-up. His tipple was almost exclusively John Powers Gold Label whiskey, which he ordered by the double, always dubbing it a 'ball of malt'.

He coined the phrase 'a pint of plain is your only man', meaning that this lowest gravity 'plain' Guinness porter was the only true nectar of the gods for the ordinary people of Ireland. In all the time I knew him, however, I never saw him drink a pint of plain. Perhaps that's because he was no ordinary character.

Myles was knocking back quite a few balls of malt when he joined Enda and I in Smith's pub in Haddington Road one Saturday lunchtime. He was drowning his sorrows after the indignity of being locked up for the night in a cell at the Bridewell. He said it was the first time he had been arrested for simple drunkenness, having fallen flat on his face after leaving a local downtown pub, which shall remain anonymous since he accused them of selling bad drink.

His grudge was not so much against the publican who tried to 'poison' him, but against his jailer in the Bridewell. 'The swine wouldn't get me a cure,' he bristled at the thought of it.

He hadn't asked for much. All he'd wanted was the station sergeant to leave his post at six o'clock in the morning, cross the street to the Markets where the pubs were already open and return to the station, of which he was in sole charge, with a 'Baby Powers' for a badly hungover Myles. What could be more reasonable and obliging? But no, Myles would have us believe the gutless, misbegotten, son-of-a-bitch of a sergeant would not get up off his fat arse to save a man dying of thirst in jail.

There was a sting in the tail of Myles' diatribe. Before leaving us in Smith's, he ordered a take-away naggan of Powers, which he had great difficulty trying to fit it into his hip pocket. Placing the square, squat bottle on the bar counter — the better to grope more effectively in his pocket — Myles could not believe his eyes when he extracted another 'Baby Powers'.

He exploded, 'To think I was climbing the bloody walls of the cell for a cure half the night and all the time I had one in my back pocket.'

For a couple of hours he regaled us with anecdotes, particularly redolent of his role as a practical joker. Andy Clarkin was the butt of one of them. A big coal importer and respected citizen, Andy had offices, distinguished by a landmark street clock, in Dublin's city centre. Myles didn't like Andy's politics and I can't say what other grudges, if any, he had against him. But he kept sniping at him in his *Irish Times* column, which infuriated Andy no end.

Apropos and anent nothing in particular, Myles would randomly and regularly interject in his column a seemingly innocuous remark such as 'Andy Clarkin's clock was seven minutes fast at noon yesterday' or 'Andy Clarkin's clock was two minutes slow at half past eight last night'.

So it went on and on without any explanation or qualification until Andy could stick it no longer. He sought an interim injunction in the High Court to restrain Myles from pestering him in print, but Myles won the case for freedom of speech. It must have been like adding insult to injury for poor Andy.

Myles also made no secret of the fact that there was no love lost between him and the gardaí and, indeed, he was prepared to go to some extraordinary lengths to play games with them. Making a covert call to the local garda station from the Pearl Bar, he once reported seeing a drunk man trying to start his car outside the pub. It was Myles himself whom the guards found sitting in the car, well under the weather with the keys in the ignition.

In court, summarily prosecuted, Myles opted to defend himself and in cross-examination asked the garda witness if he understood the charge. The answer, of course, was yes.

The defendant admitted he might have had one over the eight, but denied being in charge of the car. Was the garda satisfied that the said car, under such-and-such section and so-and-so sub-section of the Act under which the charge was laid, was a 'mechanically propelled vehicle'? Would the garda swear to this? Well, of course he would. It was a car, wasn't it?

Did the witness look under the bonnet to confirm that the vehicle was indeed 'mechanically propelled'? Well, not really, not as such. It was suggested to the witness that if he had taken the trouble to look, he would have seen that there was no engine in the car.

And there wasn't, because Myles had earlier in the day taken the car to his local garage and had the engine removed for repair work. He then arranged to have the vehicle towed to the Pearl Bar. Not surprisingly, the case was dismissed on technical grounds and Myles left the court with a flea in his ear from the District Judge. But he thought the time, trouble and expense well worth it to get one over on the gardaí.

Unlike Myles, practical jokes were not my forte but on one occasion regulars in Fleming's Little Dáil suspected I was playing some sort of game. With commendable flourish, calculated to raise many eyebrows, I arrived with a string of 'ladies of the night' in tow.

I was covering a murder trial at Dublin's Central Criminal Court, involving a merchant seaman from Scotland who was accused of killing a young prostitute in Gardiner Street. Prostitutes packed the public gallery, and the grisly murder aroused widespread interest.

It was not unusual for reporters to collect photographs, wherever possible, to complement their stories. In this case, not even the Dublin newspapers had any pictures of the dead girl and the *Daily Mail* pictures editor was pressing me to find one.

During a lunchtime break, I asked one of the prostitutes if she had a photograph of the deceased or knew anyone who had. It turned out that, in the week before the murder, the victim had had her picture taken in a studio in North Earl Street. My prostitute contact agreed to come along with me and identify the photograph of her dead friend.

I bought a copy for half a crown, which left me broke. It was one of those days. My embarrassment was compounded by the fact that I had no money to airmail the picture to our Manchester office. Like many reporters back then, I didn't have a bank account. My salary was paid weekly and in negotiable money orders, which were cashed in the General Post Office or in a pub where I was well known.

In desperation and in a moment of sublime irony, I asked the prostitute if she had any money I could borrow for a short time, intimating that I could cash my salary cheque later in Fleming's and repay her. Being the very soul of generosity, she produced the two pounds and fifteen shillings for the Aer Lingus airmail fee at their office, which was then located off O'Connell Street. At the end of the day's court hearing, my benefactor asked if I'd mind if she brought some of her working colleagues along to the pub as she was sure they could all do with a drink.

The prostitutes had arrived in court with their pimp in a ramshackle van. Into the back of this conveyance, seven prostitutes somehow contrived to make room by sitting cramped together. I sat in the front beside the pimp, an elderly man with long wispy grey hair, a mottled face and large bulbous nose. A taciturn sort of chap, he drove us to Fleming's in grand style.

As the prostitutes filed out of the van and followed me into the front snug of the pub, old Mr Fleming nearly had a fit. He danced a short jig, screwed up his eyes as though they were deceiving him and rubbed his nose hard, not knowing what to make of it all. He drew me aside to inquire if I was aware these were all street women. I knew Mr Fleming to be a religious man and when I explained that the women were doing me a good turn in the line of duty he cashed my money order and I bought the first round. Fair play to the girls and the pimp, they were all willing to pay their way.

Our long session was the height of conviviality and at various stages we were joined by some of the regulars, including Deputy Dunne, his wife Cora and Senator Michael Ahern. They afforded my lady friends all the courtesies propriety demands. Generally speaking, the manners of some of the upper crust patrons in the same pub were not so impeccable.

I recall one early morning session of an *ad hoc* motley assembly, including a sprinkling of deputies, senators, journalists, the two distinguished oil painters Seán O'Sullivan and Harry Kernoff, and a certain titled 'Lady'. The celebrated O'Sullivan only hit the bottle occasionally, while Kernoff, known as 'lonely pint' because of his propensity never to be in any hurry to buy a round, was more regularly to be found in the Pearl Bar.

When the Holy Hour closing time arrived, the entire party was in full swing and someone suggested drinks could be had in the Kildare Street Club, where we could be signed in by a couple of our Dáil acquaintances. As I remember it, we were all half cut, but got into the club which was very posh indeed, with sumptuous carpets, rich period furniture and oak-panelled walls adorned with ancient portraits. It had that 'strictly private and members only' ethos written all over it.

'Her Ladyship' was particularly voluble and the only female in the company. Loudly proclaiming that she was bursting for a pee and could only find the Gents, her attention was discreetly directed by a knowing club member to a special panel in the lounge wall. Operated by the press of a button, the panel swung open to reveal a secret recess containing a large, cumbersome-looking chamber pot with colourful floral designs.

Ducking out of sight behind a comfortable armchair, our lady companion had her pee and audibly broke wind. It evoked neither a blush nor a murmur between us as we continued to drink, pretending we had seen or heard nothing while 'Her Ladyship' stood up and modestly adjusted her dress.

At the other end of the scale, a visit to an 'olde worlde' pub in the heart of Dublin's Coombe district provided a striking contrast for myself, Deputy Dunne and Brendan Behan. The pub was notorious for a tipple known as a 'pint and a needler'. The pint was plain porter, the poor relation of Guinness, and the needler was a shot of cheap wine, or 'Johnny-Jump-Up', calculated to inject more life into the porter.

While we were there, a typical Dublin 'shawlie' of the time was determined to make the most of the few coppers she had, and to savour and prolong to the full every drop of the drink she ordered with a dramatic flourish.

'Oh, man of the public house,' she intoned as if addressing the chairman of the Board of Directors. 'Oh, dispenser of the great nectar of the gods. With yer long arm and yer strong arm would ye ever be after pulling me a half pint of plain porter?'

Brendan explained that she was only parodying the comedian Jimmy O'Dea's Biddy Mulligan character. He then started a row with the publican, who had set him up his 'pint and a needler'. Behind the publican's back, Brendan emptied the 'needler' into the pint and insisted he was only going to pay for one drink. The publican contended that Brendan had either drunk the 'needler' or had poured it into his pint. Brendan denied drinking the wine and insisted that he was being short-changed. He further declared that if he was able to pour the 'needler' into the porter, as the publican had suggested, then there'd been less than a full pint in the glass, otherwise it would have overflowed. The hot and heavy argument went on and on until the publican gave Brendan his money back and unceremoniously ordered the three of us out, barring us from his pub for life.

By this time, I was drinking more than was good for me but would not admit it. If I wasn't in the Dáil bar, Fleming's Little Dáil or the Pearl and the Palace bars downtown, I was to be found in one of my several locals, be it Devine's, Searson's, O'Brien's or Walker's in the Baggot Street-Leeson Street area. As if that wasn't enough, I frequently availed of after-hour sessions out of town at such privileged hostelries as the Silver Tassie, the International or the Step Aside that often continued far into the night.

The writing was on the wall, but I refused to see it.

sixteen

PROBABLY THE FIRST POTENT SIGN OF my alcoholism was the onset of blackouts. On the morning after the night before, I would have to concede that I couldn't remember the last hours before tumbling into bed. How did I get home? Who had I been with? What had I talked about? Did I get into any trouble? The answer was usually a shrug of the shoulders and an acknowledgement, widely accepted, that there had to be a price to pay for over-indulgence. The test of a great night's drinking was the ability or inability to recall how it had ended.

My ephemeral amnesia, which I took so lightly and almost for granted, was to be explained to me in days to come as the precursor, if not already the result, of some brain damage.

The 'drink and be merry, for tomorrow we die' syndrome was dramatically brought home to me by one binge in particular, which was to change the course of my career in a drastic and traumatic way. It was to prove, in short, the death knell of my promising future with Associated Newspapers Limited.

In a devil-may-care spirit, I agreed to join big Seán Dunne and one of his lieutenants, leading trade unionist Dick McCann, on an expedition to assist a Labour Party recruitment drive in the West Cork constituency of Deputy Mickey Pat Murphy. It was the mother of all binges as far as I was concerned, not least because I felt we must have stopped at every pub between Dublin and Cork. The journey took three days with big Seán driving, amazingly without mishap.

A veritable feast of a supper in Mickey Pat's magnificent rustic home near Roaring Water Bay began at midnight and lasted until dawn. It marked the end of an intense, liquor-laced, three-day enrolment tour for new Labour Party members, which included all arts and parts of glorious West Cork. I had no stomach for the lavish supper. On the menu were richly garnished steaks of fresh salmon, which Mickey Pat was proud to boast had been caught that very day in a river at the bottom of his garden, and a brace of pheasant. Each guest also had a full bottle of Paddy whiskey set before him, which the host insisted was only a mandatory offering, there also being available a bewildering array of choice wines and liqueurs.

As dawn broke, we declined the offer of bed and breakfast, insisting that we had to reach Cork city for the start of the journey back to Dublin without further delay. The ever-hospitable Mickey Pat said there was no way we could reach Cork without his assistance, road signs being unreliable or non-existent. As he slowly led the way in his car I marvelled, in spite of my insobriety, at the sheer breathtaking beauty of the countryside as it unfolded, mile after mile. I marvelled even more that big Seán and Mickey Pat were able to drive at all and felt grateful that there was no traffic about.

But hark! Was I hallucinating or was our guide really pulling into this wayside pub at six o'clock in the morning? It was no mirage. 'One for the road, men,' said the laconic Mickey Pat.

In response to a knocking at the front door, loud enough to waken the dead, a window shot up in an attic bedroom.

'Is it yerself, Mickey Pat?' inquired the host, appearing later at the front door, looking for all the world like a character out of Dickens. Unfazed, with a broad cherubic smile and a ruddy face beaming all *bonhomie*, he wore a long, loose-fitting, pink-and-white striped nightshirt down to his ankles and a large tasselled hat.

'Your pleasure, gentlemen, and it's on me,' he greeted us, as if knocking him up at that unearthly hour was par for the course.

Big Seán had been drinking Hennessy brandy and asked for one with soda. 'No five star and no soda,' said our host, 'but I've a drop of the real stuff.'

From under the counter he produced a large, dark green bottle sealed by a stone stopper fitted with a spring, redolent of an ancient past. There was a cut-out brown paper label on the bottle with no attempt to disguise the scissors marks. Written in ink on the label was the legend, 'Finest Portuguese Brandy'. It was probably part of a haul smuggled in by local fishermen.

Our host poured out a large bumper for each of us without saying 'when' and not bothering to inquire if we would prefer something else. Even at this inauspicious moment, I was not averse to a pick-me-up.

Over my finest Portuguese, I basked in the enchanting atmosphere of the quaint little pub until I found myself dozing off. It was only when I woke up hours later that I discovered both big Seán and Dick McCann had also passed out and were still fast asleep. Meanwhile, Mickey Pat had baled out.

The sun was setting when we finally reached Cork and after a night in a Patrick Street hotel, with more dissolute drinking, we headed back to Dublin, which was a repeat performance of the three-day journey down. We stopped to meet deputy and senator acquaintances in practically every constituency on the way and, of course, we never declined the liquid expression of their hospitality, especially those who happened to be pub owners.

Shattering news awaited me in Dublin. My colleague, Jack Murdoch, informed me that the *Daily Mail* editor in Manchester had taken a serious view of my gross dereliction of duty by going AWOL and to expect the worst. A cryptic letter, brutal in its frankness, informed me the next day that, for reasons of which it was presumed I was well aware, my services with Associated Newspapers Limited were forthwith no longer required.

There was no word of complaint about my actual work, but no eulogies either, after some fifteen years' service. My going as a senior reporter was as unexpected as my arriving as an office boy and every bit as laconic in its announcement. Just as I had received, out of the blue all those years ago, a simple one-paragraph letter marking my appointment without the formality of an interview, I now received an equally curt one-paragraph letter ending it without the formality of a warning.

That was the law of the journalistic jungle in those days before the era dawned when specified verbal and written warnings were required as a prerequisite to dismissal. With no right of appeal and not much heart to launch one anyway, I meekly accepted my fate and tore up the letter.

I tried to put a brave face on it, but inside I was hurting badly. It was a devastating blow to my ego, leaving an aching knot in my stomach, betraying a great sense of loss, guilt and remorse.

One of the worst days of my life, as I came down to earth with a bang, was the day I said goodbye to Leinster House. Remembering how I had been teased about holding the safest seat in the Dáil, now that I had come to relinquish it after some seven years, the wrench was almost unbearable. Emotion choked me as I cleared out my things for the last time. Big Seán Dunne and Deputy Maureen O'Carroll accompanied me on my final, sad tour of the building.

In the bar, a tearful Miss Mac, who was not normally given to any form of ostentation, threw her arms round me and kissed me. The Captain of the Guard, Michael Loftus, a gentle giant, was also there to see me off. One of his duties was closing the Dáil bar after late night sessions and many a time he would gently scold me for being 'the last in the House'.

In the members' dining room where I had so many meals — more so there than anywhere else in Dublin — the manageress, who was known as Miss Mac the Second, actually said I would be missed. Beatrice McGurk, a waitress with dark, film star looks, whom I used to date, linked my arm and joined us on the tour.

On reflection, I should have been handed a bill if there was any justice for my long tenure in Leinster House as a non-paying guest, but the powers-that-be were just not like that.

Maureen O'Carroll, who had a great sense of humour and was

also a valued scout of mine in newsgathering over the years, thought it a good idea for me to pose for a photograph sitting in the hallowed chair of the Speaker of the House. Beatrice promptly sat on my knee while Maureen took our picture at the risk, perhaps, of a breach of parliamentary procedure or being held in contempt of the Dáil for such flippancy.

I continued to sit in the *Ceann Comhairle's* chair for some minutes, looking up at the press gallery. It was there that I'd spent so much idle time doing nothing but listening to endless debates down the years, ironically without needing to take notes since the *Daily Mail* couldn't have cared less what went on.

Maureen, by the way, used to say she owed me her seat in the Dáil because my slogan for her had won her the election. It was simply 'Housewives' Choice', which was the name of a new BBC radio programme that had not quite caught on in the Republic.

In the Press Room, the political correspondents were busy at their typewriters: Paddy Quinn and Dick Dowling, as well as Seán Cryan from the *Irish Press* and Jim Doyle of the *Cork Examiner*. As I took my leave, I had a sense of shame at coming to this sorry pass and felt like a soldier must on being dishonourably discharged after years of faithful and conscientious service.

Finally, with my portable typewriter and bundle of papers and files under my arm, I turned my back on Leinster House, marking the end of an extraordinary era in my life, crowded with memories I'll take to my grave. I had built up some great friendships among the Dáil's ushers and, soon after my departure, I threw a party for them in Fleming's, which helped to soften the blow.

I now began to shun the haunts of the news hawks, notably the Pearl and Palace bars, unable to ward off the dread of being treated as a has-been. On one occasion, a former close colleague I bumped into sniggered in his drunken state, 'How come ye blew it? Ye were only a chancer anyway, Paddy.'

My devastation at losing my seat was somewhat assuaged by the news that big changes were on the way concerning the facilities for the press in Leinster House. A separate dining room, open only during Dáil business hours was being provided, which would not have suited me at all. Changes were also mooted in the Lobby system for the political journalists, apparently to restrict privileges to genuine accredited correspondents, of which I was not one.

If this was merely the thin edge of the wedge there is no doubt I could not have survived much longer as a lodger in Leinster House. Perhaps I was over-consoling myself, but in these circumstances I believed I would have been forced to resign anyway, as trying to work without the use of an office was beyond me.

Financially I was fairly well off and could afford to rest on my tainted laurels for some time. The *Daily Mail* had a regular savings scheme, which I'd joined at its inception, and which constituted a handsome golden handshake. I was even able to continue modestly subsidising, by way of food and drink, two of my old pals from the past who had sustained me for so long with their newsworthy serial experiences. Naish Quinn, exonerated after being branded 'The Stratford Strangler', was still living in Dublin, but out of work. 'The Galloping Major', the self-confessed gunrunner in Israel, was making a modest living as a representative for a hardware store.

The dark cloud I was under began to show glimpses of a silver lining. Deputies Seán Dunne, Maureen O'Carroll, Mickey Pat Murphy, Brendan Corish and Senator Michael Ahern organised a petition to get my job back. Brendan Behan was well got with the *Irish Press* and assured me that he would put a word in for me.

The editor of the *Sunday Dispatch*, Aubrey Viggers, informed me that as far as he was concerned the door was still open to me on his paper. He immediately guaranteed me a lucrative Saturday shift every week as a basis to build a freelance career on. The paper had recently opened a circulation office in Middle Abbey Street next door to *Irish Independent* Newspapers and I was allowed to use it any time I needed to.

The chief reporter of the *Daily Mail* in Manchester, and personal friend, Harold Pendlebury, invited me over for a party, which was being given for a colleague who was leaving and he put me up in his home.

The *Daily Mail* news editor, Ronnie Jeans, who seemed to regret our parting of the ways and was highly embarrassed meeting me, asked me to contribute to the paper's daily social column, 'Who, Why, Where and When', and hinted there was a chance of me being reinstated before long.

Meanwhile, I continued to travel home to Belfast at weekends as if nothing had happened. Sorely hurt, pride prevented me from even mentioning to my family that I had lost my job, especially to my dear wee Ma. I think it would have broken her heart to learn that her 'big son', whom she'd helped in such an extraordinary way with her endless stream of neighbourhood news stories, was no longer employed by the *Daily Mail.* In fact both my parents died, God rest them, never knowing my secret, which was just as well.

Between jobs I visited Galway on a sentimental journey to Gort to renew acquaintances with old friends of the 'Brazen Bullock of Ballyclara' fame. They tried to tell me in Bradley's bar, with a view no doubt to more publicity, that the ghost of the Brazen was now roaming the plains of Connemara and I let on that I believed them. For old times sake, I rustled up a story for the *Sunday Dispatch*, which pleased them no end.

Life as a freelance was a complete turnaround, of course, and although I'd expected it would be more difficult to survive, I was not prepared for the consequences. It also brought home to me with grim reality just how much I had taken for granted in my role as a staff reporter.

Every morning I would leave my digs at Mespil Road with nowhere to go and with feelings of quiet desperation and isolation. All my working life I had enjoyed free access to a phone and never actually regarded it as a business line. Now, I had to pay for every single call. In all my years in the Dáil I never spent a penny on the telephone. The line between Dublin and Manchester was always open, and fixed-time incoming calls enabled me to transmit my copy without charge.

I found the use of my digs as a base from which to work to be highly impractical, and trying to operate from my local also proved to be a pub too far. Consequently, I didn't know where or who I was most of the time.

Transport was something else I had taken for granted. Until now I had availed of a taxi company to cover assignments and any pub-crawling contingencies. I had only to sign a docket and my office paid for it. As a result, I never really needed a car. Now, having to resort to travelling by bus was an innovative irritant.

In the generosity of their hearts, the *Daily Mail* had also met my hospitality bills for food, drink and tips incurred for the entertainment of clients in the line of duty. All in all, I was now destined to spend most of my time in the pub.

One morning on my aimless meandering, I met the Galloping Major who invited me to join him for a drink. This was something rare in my experience of the worthy, erstwhile gunrunner. But with nothing better in prospect, I went along with him.

We arrived at Pelican House, a blood transfusion centre in Leeson Street, where the Major explained that in return for a pint of blood the donor qualified for a snipe of Guinness, which was a third of a bottle. And if you were really nice to the nurse you could expect two or three more snipes, which made it less of a recuperative measure and more of a cure for the morning after the night before.

seventeen

JUST AS I WAS BEGINNING TO despair of ever making a go of freelancing, a lifeline was suddenly thrown to me by Paddy Scott, the Northern Ireland editor of the *Irish Press*. He phoned me at my digs to say he was taking up an appointment in Belfast as chief of staff in the North of the new nationwide Irish News Agency. The Agency was set up by the coalition government in Dublin, ostensibly to counter what was perceived to be a growing anti-Irish bias, or misinformation, in certain sections of the international media and, in short, to disseminate 'the Irish truth in the news'.

Paddy offered me the job as his deputy in Belfast and I readily accepted it. While greatly relieved at the prospect of a staff job again, I also had certain reservations. Not least of these was my preference for life in Dublin rather than Belfast. My adopted city had decidedly more attractions than my roots.

The Dublin people, I found, had a better concept of how to enjoy life. They were generally more relaxed, not taking life or themselves too seriously. Above all, they seemed blessed with a special brand of humour, particularly the ability to laugh at themselves. They also seemed to be more at peace with the world than their dour, insecure, separated brethren in the North. This was reflected in their art of conversation which, to my ear, made

Northerners sound almost illiterate. Even those at the bottom of the social ladder had an enviable command of the Queen's English, as expressed so often in the ethos of the Dublin pub.

Before packing my bags for Belfast, the 'Black City', which owes its name to lying in the shadow of the Black Mountain rather than its dark sectarian or industrial history, I advised Paddy Scott that I had some final business to attend to in Dublin.

My marriage to Enda in St Mary's Catholic Church, Haddington Road on 14 August 1956 was memorable for all the wrong reasons. (Enda, by the way, is a boy's name, but it was given to her in the expectation of her being born a boy. It didn't matter that she was born a girl because it stuck with her anyway.)

My sister Molly, who was living in Belfast, was engaged to a Protestant by the name of Tommy Ferguson, and mixed marriages in that era were not the flavour of the month. They wanted to keep it as quiet as possible. We decided on a double wedding in Dublin and a large advance party arrived from Belfast to make a long weekend of it. We all descended on Shelbourne Park for the big Saturday night final of the Irish Greyhound Derby. Tommy had a dog running in the race called 'Keep Moving', the pride of the North and second favourite. I knew nothing about greyhounds, but Tommy said his dog would win by three lengths.

When the betting opened, I backed Keep Moving at seven-to-two. The price dropped to three-to-one and, on the basis of it being unlikely to go up, I piled more of my wedding money on it to make sure I got the best odds. When the price fell back to five-to-two, I plunged again, convinced it would go no higher. Then the price started to rise and I couldn't resist it at three-to-one. Back went the odds to seven-to-two, so I made more hay while the sun shone.

In fact, the price went up and down like a yo-yo, so fast that I could hardly keep up with it. I don't know exactly how many bets I put on the dog, but my pockets were bulging with dockets. Everyone else in our party seemed to be plunging fearlessly and I reckoned we would either have a hell of a wedding or a nuptial wake.

Deputy Maureen O'Carroll's husband, who joined our company,

seemed knowledgeable about the sport and put the wind up me when he said that 'Prince of Bermuda', the pride of Eire, looked unbeatable at four-to-six. Apparently, all the Southerners thought the same.

When the traps went up, I couldn't bear to watch. I stood under the stands listening to the continuous roar of the crowd, convinced with stomach-churning fear that they were cheering on their favourite to victory.

Then silence. From somewhere, high up in the stands, a punter toppled over in the excitement and fell at my feet. I thought for a second he was dead, but he got up none the worse and, dusting himself down, looked the picture of misery.

'What won?' I gasped.

'That fecking Northern dog,' he answered. 'By three bloody lengths.'

Joy of joys, where was my blushing bride that I might kiss and hug and tell her we were rich? Rich enough, in fact, to pay for our wedding several times over.

The Lord Mayor of Dublin presented the cup filled with champagne at a grand reception, which left us reeling. What a curtain raiser to our wedding. The partying continued half the night and all day Sunday. I was banking on spending all day Monday recovering for the wedding on Tuesday.

But then it struck me. How could I make such a mistake? Monday the fourteenth was to be our wedding day, not the Tuesday. I knew the fifteenth was our original choice, but because 15 August was a Church holiday, it was ruled out. I was so mixed up I wasn't sure whether I had remembered to change the date on the invitation cards, which had already been printed and sent out to my guests. I had a sneaking feeling I might have made a mess of it, but it was too late to do anything about it now. Finally, I decided to let the hare sit, hoping the drink was not playing tricks on me.

In the end, all the guests turned up — but on different days! Most of them got it right, but those I had personally invited, including my Dáil friends, arrived a day late when it was all over.

For me, the wedding itself was not quite a day to remember. For starters, I wore the wrong suit. I had commissioned an old school pal of mine, Des Tanner, who was a master tailor, to fit me out. The cloth I chose could only be had in England. Such was the delay in the order that the material did not arrive on time. So Des, who was also one of my guests, arrived in Dublin on the Friday night before the nuptials without my wedding suit.

It meant me spending Saturday shopping around Dublin for a replacement. I settled for one off the peg in the Fifty Shillings Tailors, even though the sleeves and legs were too long. But Des said he would sort it out.

Now Des, like the rest of us, was in no fit state on Sunday night to tailor anything. Shuffling up the aisle the next morning I noticed a small thread hanging from one of the sleeve turn-ups. I gave it a tug. It was not a short thread. It was a long one and the sleeve end disintegrated the more I pulled at it, leaving me with what looked like one arm longer than the other.

The trousers had not been taken in at the waist as required and, in trying to hold them up, I kept tripping over them as the legs were too long.

I had such a hangover after Keep Moving's victory that I deemed it prudent to have a hair of the dog handy to keep my spirits up. As I stumbled more or less up the aisle, the John Powers Gold Label Baby whiskey, which I had in my pocket, was clanking against a bunch of keys and I imagined everyone in the church could hear it.

The Church laws against breaking fast or quenching thirst before Communion precluded me from availing of my hidden cure. By the time I reached the altar my equilibrium had gone to hell altogether, to say nothing of my manners. I blustered forward, breaking ranks to lead the way towards the altar instead of waiting for the other composed members of the wedding party.

There were two kneeling stools in front of the high altar, with it being a double wedding. Already in front and totally confused, I was the first to kneel down and in doing so made a holy show of myself. For some extraordinary reason, I knelt with one knee on the end of the first stool and my other knee on the end of the second, causing them both to coup over with a clatter, which must have alarmed everyone in the church. Someone sitting at the back later told me he thought we had started a fight.

As we finally knelt down, I realised that we were on an elevated level and in full view of the congregation. Afterwards I was to learn that I had neglected to remove the price tags from the soles of my new shoes, which were clearly visible from the front pews of the church. Anyone with half-decent eyesight could have read how much they cost and what size I wore. Guests also noticed that my blushing bride, in her beautiful trousseau, had occasion to nudge me frequently as I self-consciously twitched and tugged at my ill-fitting suit.

With my tongue stuck to the roof of my mouth due to my weekend's excesses, I cannot vouch for uttering a single word during the ceremony. At the risk of alarming my four lovely daughters, I cannot honestly remember pledging 'I do' or 'I will', or articulating any such phrases. I can only hope I have not been living in sin all these years!

My first task after the ceremony was to unstick my parched tongue. While everyone else was signing the register in the vestry, I knew there was no way I could append my signature as a married man without having recourse to my Baby Powers to stop the shaking. Not partial to neat whiskey, I needed some water. Eventually, I located a carafe and, not caring whether it was water from the tap or water blessed by the Holy Mother Church, I promptly mixed it with the whiskey and felt like a human being again.

I still see the wedding reception through a haze and if I made a speech I can't recall it. The commercial photographer we engaged failed to turn up, but a quick phone call brought my old *Daily Mail* friend, Charlie Fennell, to the rescue.

The limousines I'd booked for guests leaving the reception also failed to arrive and a phone call to the company in Baggot Street elicited the news that the drivers were on strike. In desperation, I contacted the public taxi rank at Stephen's Green and, at regular intervals, they responded with transport in various stages of dilapidation. Many street taxis in Dublin in those days were of an extreme vintage, being throwbacks to the postwar era. Some had broken door handles tied with string, or missing mudguards — not a pretty sight for wedding guests.

It was a salutary thought as my wife and I left for our honeymoon in Galway that the guests whom I had not been able to contact would be turning up for our wedding the following day. Drink can be such an awful curse.

PART THREE

eighteen

MY NEW JOB WITH THE IRISH NEWS Agency (INA) induced a certain sense of *déjà vu*. It was like starting all over again in similar circumstances and with the same sort of set-up. I had not applied for the post, had not been interviewed for it, and had never met or knew anyone in the INA. The managing editor, Brendan Mallin, and news editor, Matt Farrell, though prominent in Irish journalism, were strangers to me.

The Belfast office, opposite the *Irish News* building in Donegall Street, was every bit as small and dingy as the old *Daily Mail* premises in Rosemary Street, where I'd started as an office boy. It was two rickety flights up in an ancient edifice, with a funeral director's on one side and a pub on the other — a virtual death trap, it might be said, for a burgeoning alcoholic.

There were two rooms: one for editorial use and the other subdivided into a darkroom for developing photographs and an area for the teleprinter to transmit copy to Dublin. The badly worn linoleum, carelessly nailed down, exposed patches of bare floorboard. The thin plaster walls were distempered a fading yellow and the single, small front window was so begrimed with emissions from busy passing traffic that it was almost opaque, blacklisted by window cleaners for years.

There were but two tables in the editorial office. One was for the boss, Paddy Scott, which was devoid of a typewriter as he'd never learned to type and wrote all his copy in laborious longhand. The other was for me and placed on it was a cigarette ash-choked portable typewriter. As with the *Daily Mail* office, the heating was provided by a single element, dust-laden electric fire.

Dilapidation seemed to be the hallmark of all the newspaper branch offices I knew in that pre-Troubles era, and it was impossible to imagine that this was the home of a government news agency with headquarters in the Dáil.

The mere breadth of a wall separated me from Rogers' pub to the right of the office and O'Kane's Funeral Directors to the left. I had only to walk downstairs, take a sharp right at the bottom, one step forward and I was within an arm's length of a drink.

At this stage in my life, an early morning shot of whiskey to set me up for the day was an incessant imperative. The pattern varied to facilitate a cover-up. For example, I would give Rogers' a miss in favour of Ned Johnston's pub fifty yards along Union Street or the Brown Horse almost opposite to it in Kent Street. This small area became known to its habitués as the Bermuda Triangle because, having entered it, there was a danger of getting lost.

I can now appreciate the validity of the paradox, that alcoholism is a sickness that tells the sufferers they haven't got it. I regarded my early morning sallies into the Triangle as nothing more than one of the vicissitudes of social drinking and not for a moment as nascent alcoholism.

Reporting the Troubles began for me not in 1969, but in 1956, a year after I joined the INA. It was then that the IRA launched its border guerrilla warfare, which it designated 'The Campaign of Resistance to British Occupation'. It was to continue for six years, consisting mainly of shooting up and bombing police stations, and blowing up customs posts.

The first big story I was assigned to in this campaign was an all-out raid on the police barracks in Brookeborough, County Fermanagh. You could say that I covered the incident on the spot by proxy. It made New Year's night in 1957 memorable for a high-profile exclusive interview I obtained, quite by chance, while a gun battle between the IRA and the Royal Ulster Constabulary (RUC) was actually in progress.

Paddy Scott phoned me at home, saying he had been tipped off about heavy gunfire being heard in the Brookeborough area and I was told to get cracking. The only person I could associate with the picturesque village was the Prime Minister of Northern Ireland, Lord Brookeborough, who lived at nearby Colebrooke.

His son, Captain John Brooke, the Second Viscount, was visiting his father at the time and answered the phone in his residence. Even as we spoke, he said he could distinctly hear the shooting I was inquiring about. He went on to say he was able to discern vivid flashes of gunfire, flares and smoke from exploding mines and grenades. Against the distant din, he outlined a descriptive newsworthy picture, explaining that the barracks under attack was in the middle of the village Main Street in a large old stone-built house no different from the houses adjoining it.

Detailing the layout, he told me that Main Street was the only street in the village and legend had it that 'the further up you go, the mainer (meaner) it gets'.

In providing his running commentary, Captain Brooke called on his military experience to identify the weapons being used from the sounds they made. He could differentiate between the police Bren guns, the IRA Thompson sub-machine guns, the rifle fire on both sides, and was even able to relate to me how the sound of a grenade was dissimilar from that of a landmine explosion.

We were not to know it then but two prominent IRA men were killed in the raid. Seán South from Limerick was shot and wounded by gunfire from the upstairs window of the barracks. Fergal O'Hanlon was hit when the raiders' getaway truck came under police fire. Both bullet-ridden bodies were later found in the byre of a farmhouse at Baxter's Cross, some distance from Brookeborough. Republican sources claimed that South and O'Hanlon were unconscious when left by their fleeing comrades to await medical help at the farm. When the police in pursuit arrived at Baxter's Cross, there were reports of a long burst of automatic fire indicating, it was claimed, the delivery of the *coup de grâce*.

In the course of a subsequent tour of the border area to write a series of articles, one of which was an interview with Lord Brookeborough, I was invited to afternoon tea at Colebrooke. With me was Noel Conway from the *Irish Press*, who was working on a similar article for his newspaper.

The Prime Minister was not known to be the most co-operative of people when it came to the Irish media. Dressed in rough tweeds and cravat and smoking a cheroot, he was very much the image of a quintessential country squire. He had been Prime Minister since 1943, a post he was to hold for twenty years, and was a nephew of Field Marshall Brooke, Chief of the Imperial General Staff of the British army. Founder of the exclusively Protestant 'B' Specials, the back-up force of the RUC disbanded by the British Government in 1970 for its persistent excesses, Lord Brookeborough made no secret of his mistrust of Catholics, whom he regarded in general as being rebels at heart. He had once notoriously remarked in public that he would 'not have one of them about the place'.

After a rather innocuous interview, which was more of a congenial chat than anything else, he invited us to have tea on his sunlit patio, while hinting at the same time that he had a surprise in store.

Sipping his tea, he broke off a small piece of cake, keeping his eye fixed on an open window and issuing a low whistle. His face beamed as a bright-eyed, chirpy little robin flew into the conservatory and settled on the dining table. Noel whispered paradoxically that the bird was 'wild tame'. Finally, the robin flew over, landed on His Lordship's outstretched hand and started to peck at the crumbs.

'This little chap visits me every day and trusts me unconditionally,' Brookeborough said. 'Why wouldn't he?' The tacit suggestion was perhaps that if such a little thing could trust him then anyone could.

Another border incident was to provide a foretaste of what the

Troubles had in store. On 2 July 1958 police intercepted an IRA patrol on a railway line near Clontibret in County Fermanagh. In the ensuing gun battle, the leader of the ambushed IRA column, a 21-year-old unemployed labourer called Aloysius Hand was shot dead. He had in his possession a loaded Thompson sub-machine gun from which, according to the inquest evidence, two bursts had been discharged.

Next morning I interviewed his widowed mother in their border home. On the mantelpiece was displayed a clip of highly polished bullets and, above the fireplace, a copy of the 1916 Proclamation of the Irish Republic. An extremely frail little woman, bent almost in two and her body racked by arthritis, she clutched a Rosary in her twisted, claw-like fingers. Despite being in obvious pain, she insisted on making me a cup of tea though she was hardly able to lift the kettle or handle the cup.

Her son, she said, was a great lad who would do anything for anybody. She had last seen him the night before when he'd left the house telling her he was going to 'lamp rabbits'.

A handsome young man, she produced photographs of him playing a guitar. The pictures, which she allowed me to have for publication, appeared in newspapers all over the country and further afield. Aloysius Hand was soon hailed as 'the man who swapped his guitar for a machine gun'.

His mother stated simply: 'His vocation in life was to fight for Ireland. He died for it.' She was the only one left to mourn him. 'I'll manage somehow,' she said, shuffling to the door as she led me out. Crippled as she was from head to foot, she added piquantly, as if the pain which riddled her body was nothing: 'Thank God at least I still have my health.'

The IRA's border campaign ended in 1962 after six years with a sudden, dramatic announcement from the leadership explaining that, because of sheer lack of support, this latest chapter in the 'war for Irish freedom' had ended. All arms were being dumped and all volunteers stood down 'for another day'.

Another precursor of what lay ahead occurred in 1955 near

Kilkeel in the heart of the mountains of Mourne. History was to record it as 'The Battle of the Longstone Road'.

The incident centred on the right, claimed by Orangemen, 'to walk any road anywhere at any time' in pursuance of their civil and religious liberties. Over the period from 1952 to 1954, the government had banned, in the interest of public order, local Orange Order members from marching along the Longstone Road through an area that was exclusively nationalist.

In 1955, the Orangemen pledged to go ahead with the parade and to hell with the consequences. They were led indiscriminately by Brian Faulkner, a junior minister and Chief Whip in the Stormont Government, who was later to become Prime Minister and finally Chief Executive of the ill-fated power-sharing Executive of 1974.

Faulkner denied the march was simply a coat-trailing exercise, claiming the Orangemen meant no offence to the local Catholics. 'We will yield no longer, not an inch, not one iota of our freedom, to parade the Union Jack anywhere on the Queen's highway in Ulster,' he proclaimed. It was a sentiment to be echoed throughout Northern Ireland for years to come.

Two days before the parade, local Catholic militants used dynamite to underline their protest. Three large craters were blasted along the route, but the huge holes were filled in and the road repaired by flying columns of council workers drafted in from outlying areas. Overnight, six hundred fully armed police, including commando units and 'B' Specials, were drafted in. It was the first time I had seen police in full riot gear and, needless to say, it wouldn't be the last. The partisan police presence on the Longstone Road was there to protect Orangemen and to aid and abet an unlawful procession.

On the morning of 12 July, prior to the parade, I drove along the Longstone Road with Denis McGrath of the *Irish Independent*. For him too, it was an historic first in this type of news coverage. The police wore steel helmets and visors, bulletproof uniforms and jackboots — all alien accoutrements to us, which were likened in local newspaper reports to resembling Hitler's storm troopers' garb. It's strange to reflect now, but walkie-talkies, with which so many of these policemen were equipped, were not generally in vogue in those days and we had certainly never seen them before.

All along the route in practically every ditch and under every tree and hedge, the police squatted in readiness with their rifles and pistols. We saw boxes clearly marked 'CS Gas' and elaborate mobile radio communication stations along the road.

It is worth noting that the IRA was non-existent and there was no other overt paramilitary guerrilla activity at the time.

The local people were up in arms, though with nothing more threatening than basic farm implements, mainly sticks, cudgels, hayforks and spades. The defiant Orangemen planned to march along the road from the Annalong end to link up with other lodges from Kilkeel and Cranfield before proceeding to the 'Field', where the triumphalist speeches were delivered. Both sides of the Longstone Road are marked for miles around with drumlins or small hillocks. It was on the crest of these that the local protestors began to muster with their makeshift weapons.

From our vantage point Denis and I commanded a panoramic view of an unfolding spread of violent clashes between riot police and civilians, which were long drawn out and bloody. As the Orangemen progressed in safety along the route, it was clear that the locals had attracted a strong outside support overnight. Everywhere I looked, hordes of civilians were descending like ants across the fields towards the Orange procession only to be repelled, wave after wave, by the ruthless baton-wielding police guard.

Hopelessly outnumbered and outflanked, the protestors were no match for the Orange protectors. In pathetic defensive engagements, they fell like ninepins, bruised, bloodied and beaten as they fled in retreat all over the countryside.

The Battle of the Longstone Road and its aftermath went on for hours. It was incredible that no one was killed, but scores upon scores of people were injured. It was a terrifying first in my reporting experience of violent confrontation, but I had the satisfaction of knowing that my exclusive report for the INA scored high ratings in the media at home, in Britain and America. Yet the 'Battle' was a veritable picnic compared to the orgy of bloodletting of the Troubles that was brewing on the horizon.

My two-year tenure with the INA was, otherwise, a generally humdrum affair, relieved only by run-of-the-mill stories. The axe finally fell as swiftly and cruelly as it did when I got the chop from the *Daily Mail*.

The trouble was that the Irish media, for the most part, were reticent to avail of the Agency's services and there were not enough big news stories in Ireland at the time to generate consistent international or overseas interest. This all conspired to make the INA not the most viable of propositions.

Doomsday came out of the blue one afternoon in May 1957. While idly watching the teleprinter monitor in our Belfast office, I observed my fate being spelt out in the few words of a cryptic news flash: 'Finance Minister announced in Dáil 2.15pm closure Irish News Agency due heavy financial losses. Ends. More later.'

At that moment, as if on cue, Paddy Scott arrived back from lunch. Stunned by the no-warning blow, he seemed unable to accept it at first and kept checking the news flash as if, somehow, we had misread it and it was all a terrible mistake.

Unfortunately, it wasn't.

nineteen

WITH NORTHERN IRELAND VERY MUCH IN the backwater of media interest back in the late Fifties, the prospect of landing another job, or even freelancing, was decidedly unpromising. Paddy was destined for a career as a producer with Ulster Television while I was lucky to join the *Irish Press*, succeeding the renowned Eileen O'Brien who'd moved to the *Irish Times*.

I was the sole staff correspondent in Northern Ireland for the *Irish Press* and *Sunday Press*, but the post did not have proper news editor status even though I considered that it merited it. For several years thereafter, such was the dearth on the news front that life as a journalist took on a banal nine-to-five aspect. The *Irish Press* was not interested in the type of stories that had stimulated and inspired me during my days with the *Daily Mail*, and parochial events were not in my line.

The Reverend Ian Paisley, however, was beginning to attract media attention. In 1951 he had opened his first Free Presbyterian Church on Belfast's Ravenhill Road, but it was not until 1963 that he finally emerged as an important political animal. That was the year when, on the occasion of the death of Pope John XXIII, Paisley organised his first public march in Belfast to protest against the lowering of the Union Jack on the City Hall as a mark of respect on the Pontiff's passing.

Paisley took centre stage at once as a hate figure for many. Such was the depth of public outrage at his act of blatant bigotry that the Stormont Government invoked the Special Powers Act to ban his parade. It was the first loyalist march in history to be outlawed under the draconian act and Paisley defied it to bring shame to Belfast in the eyes of the world. He was fined a nominal £10 and, perversely ecstatic over all the publicity he had attracted, tried to exploit it by electing to go to prison rather than pay the fine. His stunt misfired, however, as the £10 was paid anonymously and Paisley promptly branded the donor a government agent.

I was soon to cross swords personally with 'the Big Man' himself. The editor of the *Sunday Press*, an ex-Irish army colonel by the name of Matt Feehan, planned to run an in-depth first interview with Paisley, which he wanted me to do and about which I was not keen. Truth to tell, I was badly hungover on that Saturday morning when Matt had called with my assignment, having imbibed over-wisely and for too long the previous night.

Accordingly, I tried to dissuade the editor and contended that Paisley's rantings and ravings, especially about His Holiness and members of 'the One True Church' would get the *Sunday Press* denounced from every Catholic pulpit in the country.

'Publish and be damned' was Matt Feehan's motto, long before it was patented by a Fleet Street editor. He wanted the interview on his desk by 3pm. It was then 10am — pub opening time. I nipped downstairs to Mick Rogers for a 'cure' and some Dutch courage to square up to the Big Man. I assured Vincent the barman, as was my wont, that I was dying, that the drink was killing me so I needed a large one and be quick about it.

I downed the Powers in one gulp and felt instantly so revived that I ordered another, and another, and another. By noon I was hardly able to stand, but made it back upstairs to the office. I wasn't able to see too well, so I knew my note taking was going to be a problem.

Into the bargain, my Dutton shorthand was suspect. As an office boy in the *Daily Mail* I had tried to learn it by a correspondence course, but I never really mastered it. On this occasion I was also not quite as articulate as the situation demanded when I phoned the Reverend Ian. He did not have the same reservations back then, as he was later to acquire, about speaking to Sunday newspapers. I inquired if that was 'Mr Paisley' speaking and he corrected me, saying he was the Reverend Doctor Ian Paisley, Moderator of the Free Presbyterian Church of Ulster. I asked how he was doing and he told me he was doing all right, but he did not think I sounded too good. I had been deliberately vague about my credentials in case he would turn me down, telling him only that I was a press reporter without saying I was from a Dublin paper. Apart from his uncompromising fundamentalist Sunday observance, he followed a strict unyielding hands-off policy towards anybody or anything from the Irish Republic. All things Irish were absolutely taboo.

He suggested that I was under the influence of the demon drink: 'I think, brother, you have been supping the devil's buttermilk.'

'Not at all, Doctor dear,' I replied, trying hard not to slur my words. 'I had a bit of a cold and there's a frog in my throat. But to get down to brass tacks, your Reverence, what's all this you're going on about the poor Pope and the Church of Rome and all that? ... Jesus, Doctor, you're an awful man to be saying things like that ... No, no ... Sorry ... I was not being blasphemous ... '

On and on I scribbled through an almost brain-dead alcoholic mist and by the time the interview was over I felt I needed a drink. A few more jars, I thought, and I would be able to read my notes better. As it was, I could make neither head nor tail of them and the deadline was approaching.

Back in the office and still befuddled, I was in a sweat trying to decipher my shorthand when there was a knock on the door. To my utter astonishment it was Paisley himself, with a Bible underarm and an associate in tow. All at once, I regretted having given him our office address.

'Just as I thought,' he said. 'You're drunk, young man.'

While he was inveighing against the evils of intoxicating liquor, I pleaded that it was as much as my job was worth to file my story as soon as possible. I begged his help pledging, God forgive me, that I would never touch another drop if only he would repeat the interview.

I led him to the teleprinter and pressed the start button, affecting to demonstrate how it worked. It seemed to intrigue him, for he wanted to know more about it. To make sure I was through to head office, I explained I had only to press the 'Who Are You?' button and back would come the reply 'IP/DN'. I dared not tell him that 'IP' meant *Irish Press* and that 'DN' stood for Dublin. I didn't want to put him off.

What amazed me was that he never once asked about the destination of the transmission. Perhaps he was not into gadgets and had never seen a teleprinter, and thought it was just some sort of glorified typewriter.

Anyway, despite my insobriety, I was so expert at automatic two finger typing that I could do it in my sleep. I started to key in the introduction: 'Rev Ian Paisley, Moderator of the Free Presbyterian Church, in an exclusive interview in Belfast said yesterday ... ' before inviting the Big Man to carry on.

With his hands clasped behind his back, and pacing up and down the office, he dictated the interview to me in measured words so that I could keep up with him. It was much the same as he had given on the phone: a fierce tirade opposing a planned visit by the Archbishop of Canterbury to Pope Paul. As he fulminated against the Supreme Pontiff, branding him the 'anti-Christ' and 'old red socks', I kept typing away like the hammers, grateful that I was able to transmit the interview straight from the horse's mouth. In language totally alien to the uninitiated, he described the Church as 'the scarlet lady' and 'the harlot of Rome', continuing his diatribe to the bitter end as I muttered involuntary expletives under my breath at the shocking things he was saying.

Like an iconoclast in full swing, he branded the central act of worship in the Catholic Church, the Mass, as 'an idolatrous fable and a dangerous deceit'. Finally, as I marked my copy 'ends', I stated cynically, 'That'll go down a treat with every Catholic in Ireland.' To which Paisley replied, 'That's good.'

As he departed I gave him my own blessing, while he abjured me to keep my word and never to touch another drop of 'the devil's buttermilk'. Whereupon, I immediately retired to Rogers' for what I considered a well-deserved *Te Deum* drink.

I honestly believe to this day that the Big Man did not really cop on that he had done his bit for one of de Valera's hated 'republican papers', edited as it was by a retired colonel who had fought in Ireland's War of Independence. Still, I was grateful to him for saving my bacon.

Though not an elected public representative then, Paisley was the dominant figure on the political stage and continued to hog the limelight. During the Westminster General Election campaign in 1964, he set the scene that led to the first serious street rioting in the run-up to the outbreak of the Troubles. It centred on the rather inconspicuous republican centre in Divis Street, adjoining the Catholic Falls Road in Belfast. This was nothing more than a street corner sweet shop, but Paisley was tipped off about a small Irish tricolour in the display window.

The green, white and orange flag was like a red rag to a bull for the fundamentalist Church leader. By decree of the Stormont Government, it was also unlawful to display it publicly anywhere in Northern Ireland. Passers-by in Divis Street would have had to stop and have a really close look in the dark recess of the Sinn Féin shop to spot the offending article. Certainly, I personally had difficulty in picking it out. Yet Paisley bullishly insisted on its removal and threatened to get rid of it even if it meant leading his hard-line Protestant supporters into the staunchly Catholic area at whatever the cost.

Of course it was a colossal bluff, but the police fell for it. They knew if Paisley turned up gung-ho in any part of the Falls he was in danger of being lynched, and Paisley knew it too. But he kept up his strident campaign and finally, while he stayed well out of the way, the RUC carried out his dirty work. In a sudden swoop, heavy police reinforcements saturated Divis Street, taking residents completely by surprise. Under sledgehammer blows, the locked and barred front door of the Sinn Féin centre splintered open and the outlawed flag was taken away.

However, local people promptly replaced it and, when police in full riot gear returned for a repeat performance, serious disorder erupted. As baton charges raged for several hours I was to witness, for the first time in my reporting career, blatant instances of indiscriminate police brutality. Women, young and old, were pummelled to the ground and kicked. I saw one high-ranking officer strike several screaming women with his ceremonial dress-parade truncheon.

Paisley was in his ascendancy the following year, 1965. The occasion was the historic, though tentative, summit at Stormont between the Taoiseach Seán Lemass and Northern Ireland's Prime Minister Terence O'Neill. Before anyone could assess the far-reaching implications of the event, Paisley was branding it the beginning of the end of Ulster's union with Great Britain.

As summits go, this one was somewhat bizarre. At Stormont House on 14 January, for the first time since the partition of Ireland, the leaders of the two governments were breaking constitutional ground by doing nothing much more than simply meeting overtly and shaking hands in public. You had to go back to May 1921 for a comparison: the meeting in Dublin between Sir James Craig, the Prime Minister-in-waiting of the new Northern Ireland state and Eamon de Valera, the head of the new republican government of Ireland.

The incredible difference about this Stormont summit was that it had been arranged under the cloak of utmost secrecy and on the strict understanding that there was to be no mention of politics. That was why, from a journalist's point of view, the whole set-up was so strange. While it was an unprecedented meeting, I still find it an unaccountable fact that I never heard a reporter ask a single question.

Press conferences, as we know them today, were not so much in vogue then. In fact, as I recall it, the only television crew present at this particular history-making event remained very much in the background.

We were initially advised by Ken Bloomfield, a top Stormont official, that the summit was concerned solely with economic co-operation in the areas of agriculture, tourism, transport, fisheries, drainage and such like. Thus, when the two Prime Ministers emerged from Stormont House for a short stroll in the weak winter sunshine it was for a news photo-call only.

I found myself walking side by side across the lawns with the two men of destiny, yet uttering not a word. Why was I struck so dumb on such an auspicious occasion? Was it the sense of history in the making, vague as it was? Was I overly conscious of the restraints placed upon us because the question of politics was officially taboo? Was I afraid that it would be a breach of some kind of protocol to open my mouth and intrude? It reminds me of the way journalists used to behave in the presence of royalty.

My only consolation was that I was not alone in my speechless bewilderment. Walking with me on that brief stroll, as newspaper photographs published the next day showed, were Jim Creagh of the *Belfast Telegraph* and Mervyn Pauley of the *News Letter*. Neither of them broke their silence, summit or no summit.

Of the accredited political correspondents of the day, the only one present that I can recall was Dick Dowling from the *Irish Times*. I don't know how many other reporters were there, but again I ask myself why we collectively were so devoid of even a semblance of investigative motivation.

There was a golden opportunity to intervene as the two leaders stopped to pose for pictures, shaking hands and smiling on their return to Stormont House, but we blew it.

All we got out of the pair was talk of the sudden nip in the air, and how the weather had been, and what we could expect it to be in the immediate future. In the event, we were reduced to writing about how historic it all was and how it augured for Ireland's political future.

An example of our 'waffling' was perhaps best illustrated by Alexander 'Sandy' Boath, the renowned *Daily Express* reporter in Belfast. After describing the perfect setting in which the talks were held, waxing lyrically about Stormont House's 'high-ceilinged dining room overlooking green lawns, fringed by trees', Sandy went on to refer to the 'wan winter sunshine that had followed a night of gales'. He had gone one better than myself in discovering what the two great men had for lunch. As they sat round the 'highly polished mahogany table, adorned with a wealth of tulips, chrysanthemums and daffodils', they had feasted on 'smoked salmon, fried fillet of chicken on a bed of rice, leeks with cheese sauce, creamed potatoes, trifle, coffee, cheese and biscuits. They also drank champagne, a rare burgundy with the main course and finished with a rich port.' Sandy concluded his colour piece, noting the lunch was a 'relaxed affair' with the whole party 'studiously avoiding politics', while adding as a footnote that 'the two Prime Ministers swapped ... fishing stories'. For me, it was the big one that got away.

The summit had, however, marked an overdue recognition in public by the two governments of the need for economic co-operation, if not unity. It was along these lines that I wrote my report for the *Irish Press*, embellishing it with a speculative background of the secrecy involved.

Feelers had gone out the previous Christmas from Belfast and Dublin, which culminated in the historic meeting. Neither Prime Minister had told their respective Cabinets of their covert plan until virtually the last moment in an effort to forestall any extremist reaction. Lemass might have subscribed to the idea of a Gaelic speaking united Ireland, but he also preached the gospel of economic union with Britain. O'Neill might have marched with his Orange sash on the Twelfth of July, but he was also a visionary in terms of his country's economic future.

Paisley, as might have been expected, saw it all in a different light. He launched a virulent anti-O'Neill campaign, proclaiming in his customary booming oratory that the threat of a united Ireland had been awakened by the 'treachery' of the Prime Minister. He also demanded that 'O'Neill must go'.

Paisley's 'gospel of fear' soon developed into a strident onslaught against Church ecumenism. On Monday 6 June 1966, he aroused the ire of Church and State leaders with an unseemly march to the General Assembly of the Presbyterian Church in Belfast's city centre to protest against its 'Romeward trend'. Outside the hall, banner-waving Paisleyites hurled vitriolic abuse at the Governor of Northern Ireland, Lord Erskine, and his wife, and other dignitaries who were attending the Assembly. In Parliament, Prime Minister O'Neill deplored what he called 'these alarming tendencies towards fascism'.

The Assembly protest was the sequel to another incident, which had taken place that very same day. Paisley had upped the ante by announcing his intention to lead his followers from his church on the Ravenhill Road to the Assembly Building via Cromac Square in the exclusively Catholic Markets area of Belfast. It was here that I sustained my first, albeit not serious, injury in the line of duty.

Billy Simpson of the *Belfast Telegraph* and I seemed to be the only reporters covering this particular march. Singing their favourite battle hymn, 'O God Our Help In Ages Past', the marchers gingerly approached Cromac Square, where eerily there was not a Catholic in sight. We didn't realise that an ambush had been planned and that Billy and I would end up in the middle of it.

Out of sight of the marchers, residents were lying in wait in and around the area with a stockpile of missiles. Suddenly the heavens opened with a fierce downpour of bricks, stones and bottles. Many of the marchers fell under the hail while others, with arms covering their heads, took to their heels towards the safety of the Albert Bridge.

With stones bouncing off us and thudding all around, Billy and I recklessly sought refuge in a telephone box. Every pane of glass in the kiosk was shattered as we took shelter, but we managed to escape in the end with only cuts and bruises.

twenty

THE WINDS OF CHANGE, WHICH HERALDED the civil rights era in America and Europe, were now beginning to stir in Northern Ireland.

Militant unionism fiercely opposed the new liberal expressions of Prime Minister O'Neill, as reflected in his meeting with Seán Lemass. Shortly after the Stormont summit the UVF, in a statement by spokesman 'Captain William Johnston', threatened war against the IRA and said it intended to kill their members 'without mercy'. Six days later an innocent Catholic, John Scullion, was gunned down on Belfast's Falls Road.

If the gun had been taken out of politics in late 1962 at the end of the IRA's six-year-long Fifties campaign, it was introduced again in 1966 by the UVF under the leadership of Augustus 'Gusty' Spence. He was to become a folk hero in the eyes of extreme loyalists, especially in the Shankill area of Belfast where he was born.

Before the year was out I had the opportunity to observe this man at close quarters and, if looks could kill, I reckoned this man was a killer. Nearly thirty years later, I was to hear Spence denounce violence and abjectly apologise for the terrible excesses of his terrorist organisation.

In the early hours of 26 June 1966 an innocent Catholic barman,

18-year-old Peter Ward, was shot dead by the UVF as he left a pub in Malvern Street in the heart of the Shankill. It was not uncommon in those halcyon days for Catholics to venture with impunity into the staunchly Protestant stronghold for quiet after hours drinking. In fact, a policeman friend assigned to the nearby Brown Square barracks had first acquainted me with the Malvern Street hostelry. We had a few sessions ourselves there not long before the grim benchmark murder of young Peter Ward.

Spence and another leading UVF member, Hugh Arnold 'Dandy' McClean, were arrested and charged with the Ward murder. In a statement given by McClean after his arrest, and subsequently read to the court during his and Spence's trial, the name of the Reverend Ian Paisley was introduced into the proceedings. McClean declared: 'I am sorry I ever heard tell of that man Paisley or decided to follow him.'

When this statement became public, Paisley denied any association with the accused, claiming that McClean 'has never been associated with me at all'. Through his *Protestant Telegraph* newspaper, Paisley further insisted that he himself 'has never advocated violence, has never been associated with the UVF and has always opposed the hell-soaked liquor traffic which constituted the background to this murder'.

During the trial I watched Spence closely, especially during the evidence of Liam Doyle, who'd been badly injured in the shooting which had claimed Ward's life. Doyle broke down and wept as he told the court that he'd been struck by a bullet and fell as he left the bar with Ward. Spence, he alleged, stood over him. 'He fired five or six shots into my body as I lay on the ground pleading, "Please don't",' said Doyle.

I can still recall what I regarded as arrogance on Spence's face as he listened to the testimony, sitting with his elbows extended on the rail of the dock, his chin resting upon it. Sporting an apparent smirk of contempt as the evidence unfolded, his body language as far as I was concerned suggested only one thing — guilt.

Spence pleaded 'not guilty' and declined to give evidence. He was convicted of the murder of Peter Ward and, along with McClean, was sentenced to twenty years in prison. He served seventeen of those years, while McClean died behind bars.

During his incarceration, Spence continued to maintain his innocence and on several occasions embarked on hunger strikes. Among militant loyalists he became something of an icon. His portrait adorned tea towels and T-shirts. Facsimile five-pound notes were printed on which the Queen's head was replaced by Spence's. 'His only crime was loyalty' became the slogan used by those who campaigned for his release.

Gradually it became apparent that he was undergoing a remarkable personality change. He became an avid reader of Irish history and communicated with the then Catholic Primate of all-Ireland, Cardinal Tomás Ó Fiaich, who regularly visited him in prison. He even chided the Cardinal on one occasion about his belching, pipe-smoking habit and advised him to cut down on it for his health's sake. Indeed, he once gifted the Cardinal with a supply of prison-issue tobacco stressing it was a special treat, but omitting to mention it had been spiked with illicit prison-made alcohol. The Cardinal informed Spence it was the best smoke he'd ever had.

Spence started to learn the Irish language and, in a surprise message supporting reconciliation and condemning violence, he at least sounded like a man of peace. He believed that loyalists had achieved their aim of self-determination in Ulster, but not all UVF prisoners welcomed his general stance. In March 1978 he resigned as the prison's UVF commander.

He was finally released in December 1983 when he was said to have been in poor health. He spoke then of how his future would be in community politics and, to this end, he would devote the rest of his life. He also consistently maintained he was not the one who had pulled the trigger in Peter Ward's murder.

If Spence was indeed the first man to introduce the gun into Northern Ireland's 'long war', he was also one of the first men to try and remove it. On the occasion of the loyalist ceasefire of 13 October 1994, he was chosen as the most appropriate man to announce it. The declaration was made in the name of the Combined Loyalist Military Command, the umbrella organisation of the UVF, the Ulster Defence Association (UDA), the Ulster Freedom Fighters (UFF) and the Red Hand Commandos (RHC).

David Ervine, spokesman for the UVF's political wing, the Progressive Unionist Party (PUP), described the selection of Spence to publicly declare the ceasefire as 'highly significant, securing for him an important niche in modern Irish history'.

Ervine continued that: 'Gusty Spence represents the alpha and the omega — the beginning and what we all hope is the end of violence.'

In expressing sorrow for the terrible misdeeds of the past, Spence faced the world's media to assert: 'In all sincerity, we offer to the loved ones of all innocent victims over the past twenty-five years abject and true remorse. No words of ours will compensate for the intolerable suffering they have undergone during the conflict.'

It was subsequently revealed by journalist and broadcaster Peter Taylor in his book *Loyalists* that Spence had since phoned Peter Ward's mother, Mary, to apologise for the murder of her son by the UVF. Mrs Ward is quoted as saying: 'Yes, I'll forgive you, on one condition — that you bring peace to this country because I don't want any mother to go through what I went through.'

But back to the protracted era of the civil rights street campaign, which constituted the most time-consuming, stressful and often one of the most frustrating ongoing assignments of my career. By its very nature it demanded unremitting on-the-spot coverage, frequently around the clock.

Although the bomb and the bullet reign of terror was to be infinitely more damaging, it was relatively easier to cover and more suited to the armchair reporter. Since the incidents were all in the past tense by the time the journalists showed up and basic details were readily available through police and army media information offices, the story was much more straightforward to piece together. However, reporters covering the civil rights marches had to become marchers themselves, running the same risks of attack as the demonstrators and not knowing what trouble was around the corner.

The first direct action of the civil rights campaign was staged in June 1968 at Caledon in County Tyrone when Austin Currie, the local nationalist Member of Parliament (MP), led a sit-in at a council house in the village. The protest began when the house was allocated to an unmarried 19-year-old Protestant girl rather than a homeless Catholic family of six who were deemed to be less deserving. For the first time, the blatant and widespread discrimination in Northern Ireland featured on the national news as a result of this protest, and it inspired the first localised civil rights march in Dungannon, which passed off largely unopposed.

The first major civil rights march in Derry on 5 October 1968, however, erupted in violence and provided me with my first and only real life experience of the 'hold the front page' legend.

Under the Public Order Act, the marchers were prohibited from entering Derry's inner-city walls, an area which was by tradition preserved as sacrosanct for the loyalist minority in that divided city. The drama began that dank, dark afternoon outside the railway station at the bottom of Duke Street in the Waterside. A crowd of about five hundred had sung their 'We Shall Overcome' anthem but, just before the march got underway, RUC County Inspector William Meharg stepped forward with a megaphone to deliver a chilling warning: 'Women and children clear the streets.'

It was nearing the deadline for the final city edition of our *Evening Press* in Dublin, so I alerted the news desk that it appeared that the first blood of the civil rights campaign was about to be shed. The ominous words of Officer Meharg still echo down the years.

'Any person who wishes to parade or hold a meeting is at liberty to do so, provided it is other than in the area specified in the Public Order Act,' he declared. 'It is the desire of the police to prevent trouble ... we want to give a warning especially to those who are not interested in their own safety and the safety of women and children.'

The gauntlet was down. Slowly the marchers moved up the hill towards the top of Duke Street, which was blocked by a solid phalanx of police in full riot gear. Parade leaders appealed to the marchers not to be provoked, to avoid violence at all costs.

Confident that all would be well, some of the leaders retired to a local tavern for a round of hot whiskies. They included Gerry Fitt MP, Frank Gogarty, Betty Sinclair and Paddy Kennedy MP. Since I had been drinking with them earlier, I rejoined them only to announce that the balloon was about to go up.

Gerry Fitt was one of the first to fall, with blood streaming from a head wound. It was my cue to contact our Dublin office, as the front page could hold no longer. This was a history-making event in so far as it marked the inaugural full-scale bloodletting suffered by the civil rights movement at the hands of the RUC, and probably did more than anything else to focus international media attention on Northern Ireland's plight.

Our evening paper must have been one of the first, if not *the* first, to hit the streets with the dramatic news that was to have such far-reaching consequences for the Stormont Government and the people of the North.

The *Evening Press* copy-takers had finished their normal Saturday shift when I phoned through with my copy from a telephone in a chemist's shop on Duke Street. Since the final City edition was being held back for me, the news editor Mick O'Kane typed my story himself in 'short takes' to build up the front page 'scoop'.

Oddly enough the shopkeeper, who had been eavesdropping, told me if he'd known I was going to use his phone to send such 'propaganda' he would not have allowed it. Derry, he added, was a peaceful, law-abiding city and I was giving it a bad image. I told him to take a look out of the window.

Duke Street that day was like a battlefield. Long before nightfall, more than one hundred people had been treated in Altnagelvin Hospital and the police had made twenty-three arrests. The fighting went on through the night and most of the next day, and the Altnagelvin casualty list rose to 171. Many of the injured preferred not to go to hospital, so it was not known exactly how many people suffered in the mayhem on Duke Street. But the total ran into hundreds.

That Saturday night and the following Sunday, the City Hotel was like a casualty clearance centre, where many people were given first aid. It was in the same hotel that Gerry Fitt, who had been released from hospital after treatment for his injuries, waved his bloodstained shirt aloft shouting, 'We shall overcome.'

Paddy Kennedy, a Republican Labour MP at Stormont, promptly predicted with uncanny foresight the unthinkable outcome which was to be fulfilled in a few years: 'This is the beginning of the end of Stormont and the Unionist monolith.'

Another hair-raising event in the history of the civil rights marches, and one which scared the pants off me, was staged in Armagh city a short time later on 3 November 1968. Overnight, hordes of Paisley supporters from all over Northern Ireland, led by the Big Man and his henchman Major Ronald Bunting, had invaded Armagh and claimed it as their own. Armed with a bewildering array of weapons, ranging from fiercesome wooden cudgels studded with six-inch nails to iron bars, axe-handles and pitchforks, they saturated the city centre in an effort to prevent a civil rights march taking place there.

Local people awoke to find that their city had been completely taken over by an army of thugs, its streets patrolled by menacing groups of paramilitaries. The night porter in the Beresford Arms Hotel, where I was staying, told me I would be safer staying in bed.

I had to be up and about to file a story for the *Evening Press*'s first Country edition, with a 10am deadline. Tension was electric leading up to noon, when the civil rights march through the town was due to start. The Paisleyites announced that the march would only be held over their dead bodies. Riot police reinforcements were dramatically drafted in from all over the country.

I teamed up with Billy Simpson from the *Belfast Telegraph*, both of us sharing a common cause of pressure by working for 'stop press' evening newspaper editions.

The civil rights marchers were massed on the main road outside the city, facing a potentially explosive situation, while police set up an armoured buffer zone.

During a parley at the barricade between a high-ranking RUC

officer and Paisley, Billy and I made our way through the throng to eavesdrop. As Paisley turned to address his followers about the crisis, he spotted me close to his platform.

'And what have we here?' he bellowed, by way of a pleasantry diversion. 'Why, we have a man from de Valera's paper.'

I froze as a roar went up from the crowd, which sounded to me rather like 'crucify him, crucify him'.

'The hands of this man's republican editor are like all republicans',' Paisley exploded, 'stained with the blood of our Protestant martyrs.'

Convinced that Paisley had taken leave of his senses, I found myself mouthing back to him, 'Good Christ, are you trying to get us lynched?' hoping the police officer in charge might take me into protective custody. Whether the officer heard me or not, Paisley then turned to Billy.

'This is getting better,' he continued. 'Here is a man from the *Belfast Telegraph*. His editor is another enemy; he won't even publish my Church notices or any of my advertisements.'

The air was filled with another unmerciful roar of maledictions and Billy, who was as shit-scared as me, suddenly threw up his arms and unaccountably declared, 'I have great faith in the Lord!'

He told me later that he didn't know what came over him to utter these words, saying he was probably trying subconsciously to invoke divine intervention. Be that as it may, it seemed to strike a chord with Paisley. The Big Man suddenly relented, perhaps sensing at last the danger we were in at the hands of his hyped-up supporters who were baying for blood.

'Listen now,' he urged. 'These men are only doing their jobs. It's their editors I'm against, not them, so I want you to give them free passage out of here. Come on, make way for them.'

The mob was in no mood to effect a Moses-style parting to facilitate our passage to safety. So it was with extreme difficulty that we made our agonisingly slow escape. We had to run the gauntlet of venomously tongued louts breathing down our necks and spitting out words of hate. Those on the fringes were especially hostile, too far back perhaps to have heard Paisley, and they assumed we were the enemy. A section of the mob gave chase as Billy and I took to our heels and dashed for the cover of the Beresford Arms. Billy ran up the stairs to seek refuge while I dived under the bar counter, our pursuers being finally repelled by police who had followed them.

The rally in Armagh was officially deemed an unlawful assembly and its two leaders, Paisley and Bunting, were arrested. The following year, Paisley served a prison sentence for his part in the whole affair. But that was not the last of my nerve-tingling encounters with the Paisley circus. A month after the Armagh episode, I had another alarming run-in with them in Larne, County Antrim on the occasion of the arrival of the old gunrunning schooner, the *Clydevalley*.

During the 1912 anti-Home Rule campaign, which had posed the threat of civil war, a Protestant force claiming loyalty to the Crown but ready to fight the legitimate forces of the Crown was established in Ulster. This was the original UVF, referred to sometimes as 'Carson's Army' after Lord Carson. Its logistics officer, Major Fredrick Crawford, was tasked to provide weapons for the underground army. In April 1918 he secured some 35,000 rifles and three million rounds of ammunition in Germany, which were loaded aboard the *Clydevalley*.

In a daring exploit, he smuggled the consignment under the noses of the Royal Navy and into Larne Harbour. Although not a gun was fired — the question of Home Rule was shelved by the bigger issue of the First World War — the gunrunning event continued to be celebrated by Ulster loyalists.

In the late 1960s, the old *Clydevalley* was traced to a breakers yard across the Atlantic. A plan was hatched to convert it into a floating loyalist museum and when it eventually arrived at Larne Harbour it was greeted by a large gathering of Paisley supporters. My Armagh experience ensured that I kept a prudent distance from the platform where the welcome committee was based. Paisley was having a field day and emotions were running high.

I was taking notes when a group of noisy louts surrounded me, berating me for not taking down all the Big Man was saying. They threatened to throw me into the harbour and, as I was standing dangerously close to the edge of the pier, I started to write furiously, pretending that I was recording every precious word.

I was told I looked like a 'Fenian bastard', and one of the thugs produced a wooden baton inscribed with 'UVF 1912', which he placed across the bridge of my nose inviting me, while calling me an 'effin' so-and-so', to read it. Meanwhile, I was being nudged ever closer to the brink until I was within a few inches of being edged over the side and into the deepwater dock. At that moment, the Larne-to-Stranraer passenger ferry, which was alongside the *Clydevalley*, was casting off and the thought crossed my mind that I might at least have a 'man overboard's' chance of being saved if someone spotted me drowning.

As the ferry came slowly abreast of the Paisley platform party, there suddenly emanated from the bridge a loud blast of the ship's horn, which completely drowned out the Big Man's voice. This drew an asinine remark from Paisley that the horn sounded like 'the Pope blowing his nose'.

Taking advantage of this God-sent diversion, which the crowd thought was hilarious, I made a break for it. Pursued by the thugs who had threatened to drown me, I made a record-breaking sprint to my car. In my flight I noticed *Irish Press* colleague, Cormac McConnell, nonchalantly advancing towards me. Normally based in Galway, Cormac had been sent North to help me cover the Larne assignment, but was late on arrival.

Unaware of what had befallen me, he had remained in the Laharna Hotel for a quiet drink. But the cigarette dropped from his mouth in astonishment when he saw me running for my life towards him. He turned and joined me on the last leg of my dash to safety. Even as we sped away in my car I still had to shake off a carload of pursuers, who only abandoned their chase when we reached Carrickfergus some miles away. It was from there I phoned through my story, which made the front page of next day's *Sunday Press*.

As previously indicated, coverage of street demonstrations and protest marches was the most arduous of all the assignments. In the late Sixties and early Seventies they began to proliferate alarmingly.

I was the only staff reporter for *Irish Press* Newspapers in Belfast, which meant working for three issues: the morning paper, the *Irish Press*, the daily *Evening Press* and the *Sunday Press*. Initially, Head Office helped out by sending reporters from Dublin on relief work. It was not a marking that these journalists generally welcomed.

I recall one reporter, who'd never been in the North before and asked me to meet him arriving in Belfast on the train from Dublin. He clearly had the wind up, inquiring about the Troubles and how we managed to cope.

Some distance from the station, a British army Saracen, a personnel carrier known as a 'Pig', pulled out in front of us and a petrol bomb was thrown at it. Nothing out of the ordinary really. As it exploded in flames, my colleague was terror-stricken and suddenly remembered he had misled an item of luggage at the railway station. I drove back and left him to pick it up. He must have boarded the return train to Dublin for I never saw him again. It was a classic case of 'instant hail and farewell'.

Not only was I expected to report on the day-to-day news stories, but I was also required to write in-depth news analysis and commentary pieces. As a result, the burden became almost unbearable. Correspondingly I was drinking more and more, trying to cope.

Tension was mounting all the time, especially with regard to the civil rights campaign. A pattern had developed whereby when legal notice of a parade was given to the police a defiant counter protest was announced. The counter protest, like the civil rights march, would be banned, leading to a simultaneous double dose of confrontational violence.

There was scarcely a city, town or village in Northern Ireland from which I had not reported on the occurrence of a riotous situation, and the personal toll began to mount. Eventually I could no longer cope with the danger of being battered, stoned and petrol-bombed without recourse to the bottle. Most of the ubiquitous on the spot reporters I knew also ended up turning to 'Dutch courage' simply to face the violence, which the street protests were throwing up day in and day out. It was all very well for local campaigners. They didn't have to participate in each and every protest parade, as we non-combatants were duty-bound to do.

One of the most tortuous of the civil rights marches was the ninety-mile trek from Belfast to Derry, which began on 1 January 1969. At various stages along the route we came under attack from well-organised loyalists who had been mobilised by that most ardent of Paisleyites, Ronald Bunting. It was a nightmare to cover, culminating in the infamous 'Battle of Burntollet', which I'm ashamed to admit completely escaped my notice.

I was driving at the head of the march, accompanied by Denis McGrath of the *Irish Independent*, according to a pre-arranged plan. The idea was that we would cover any trouble up front while colleagues looked after the rear. On the very last leg of the march as we neared Derry, we thought it would be plain sailing. Thus, we blissfully drove through Burntollet, which did not even feature on our map. There was neither a soul in sight nor the slightest sign of trouble.

What we didn't know was that a trap had been set in the form of an elaborate and meticulously planned loyalist ambush. It involved over three hundred die-hards including, as we were later to learn, some 160 men associated with the sectarian 'B' Special police force. The mob had at their disposal a huge stockpile of literally tons of stones from a local quarry.

As Denis and I enjoyed a drink in a pub on the outskirts of Derry to celebrate the end of the marathon march, a fleet of ambulances began heading in the direction from whence we had just come. At first, we speculated that it would take a plane crash or some such major disaster to account for so many ambulances. It was only when we tried to head back along the route, which was now congested with casualties, that the full scale of the bloodshed began to dawn on us.

In the end we had to rely on our colleagues who had stayed behind to report on the battle, which left most of the five hundred marchers injured and scattered in disarray across the countryside.

'Battle' was a misnomer, for it was mainly a one-sided onslaught on defenceless civilians. The shocking pictures from the site were flashed around the world, the loyalists claiming it a great victory, which would subsequently be celebrated in song and verse.

As veterans of the civil rights campaign, there is one question that Denis and I always dreaded being asked: 'Where were you during the Battle of Burntollet?'

twenty-one

THE ENDEMIC STREET VIOLENCE ENSURED THAT it was only a matter of time before the guns came out. We were caught on the hop, nevertheless, in October 1969, when there was serious rioting in the Protestant Shankill area of Belfast.

Constable Victor Arbuckle was the first member of the RUC to be shot dead in the 'Troubles'. Police had thrown a cordon across the Shankill Road at Townsend Street to prevent rioters mounting an attack on the Catholic Unity Flats at the bottom of the road.

Most of the reporters covering the event were concentrated at the Unity Flats complex in case of a break-through. A sudden outburst of shooting further up the Shankill Road caught us by surprise.

At first we suspected that armed republicans had intervened since we assumed that it was almost inconceivable that people who pledged loyalty to the Crown would open fire on Crown forces. But when the Crown forces had a duty to protect the residents of Unity Flats, be they republican or otherwise, someone on the Shankill decided that a price must be paid for that protection.

After the first volley of shots rang out, which had the effect of pinning down reporters at the flats, Colin Brady from the *Daily Telegraph* and I decided to try and get closer to the action, though certainly not out of any sense of bravado. We drove up the Antrim Road to cut across to the upper part of the Shankill, by way of Northumberland Street. The place was in uproar. There was complete pandemonium as police mounted wave after wave of baton charges to keep the rioters at bay. We saw a man with his back to us standing in the middle of the road near Agnes Street, firing a revolver. All around us, people were going berserk, looting shops, smashing windows, erecting barricades and lighting fires.

With deadlines approaching for our papers, it was time to contact our respective offices. However, a drunk was using the public phone box at the corner of Northumberland Street as a toilet. Smell or no smell, Colin was determined to contact his news desk. I had no stomach for using the phone and decided to get out as parked cars were being broken into and hijacked.

I escaped in my Cortina Estate, feeling very much in need of a drink. All the pubs were closed, so I headed for Gerry Fitt's house on the Antrim Road. The Republican Labour MP was always good for a jar, but there was no one at home when I called. Directly across the road from his home was the Elsinore Hotel, but it too appeared to be closed with all the blinds drawn. As I was about to move on, I noticed a slight parting of the front door curtains and someone peeping out. It was one of the joint owners, Brendan Farrelly, who let me in without demur. He had a bottle of brandy under his arm and told me he would be glad of my company, as the hotel was empty. All drinks were on the house.

Brendan also offered me free use of the phone in reception, which meant I had regular access to the Police Press Office to keep abreast of developments, while enjoying an armchair reporter's perspective. I was chuffed, since my copy was well ahead of what was going out on the Agency wires and radio reports. It was then that I learned about Constable Arbuckle's murder, an incident about which the reporters on the scene were oblivious.

Unaware that I was reporting away from the maddening front line, surrounded by the comforts of a hotel, with a cigar in one hand and a brandy in the other, the news editor in Dublin, Gerry Fox, was concerned for my safety. It turned out to be a defining moment in my career.

While I was on the phone to Gerry, an ice-making machine or something in the hotel's plumbing system went on the blink and started to emit loud and rapid cranking noises, sounding for all the world like intermittent bursts of semi-automatic gunfire. Gerry could hear it on the phone in Dublin and, with a note of alarm in his voice, asked what it was. Under the influence of the Hennessy 'Five Star' brandy and adopting the role of a hero, I replied with an air of off-handed bravery, 'Some bugger has opened up with a machine gun.'

Gilding the lily a bit, I told Gerry that I was trapped in a phone box, blandly announcing, 'The bullets are flying all round me here.'

To maximise the drama I held the phone near the sham machine gun noise for another burst, casually complaining, 'Good God, the bastard has opened up again.'

'Jaysus!' replied a seriously concerned Gerry. 'Get to hell out of there, man. Your life's worth more than your job.'

By this stage, Brendan had fallen asleep so I let myself out by the front door. But it was not long before I was back in again. To my horror, I heard real gunfire to my left in the New Lodge Road area and more real gunfire to my right at Carlisle Circus. So I stayed put in the safety of the hotel for the rest of the night.

The guns which came out that night, arguably the first to be fired in Northern Ireland's Troubles, were not to be silenced for another thirty years.

For my heroic Elsinore Hotel performance, deemed to be beyond the call of duty, I was awarded a £75 bonus in my next pay packet. Although no one in our office would officially concede that it was 'danger money' for fear of creating a precedent, our trade union leader in Dublin eventually got wind of it. He raised the matter at once with management. As a result, and at the insistence of the National Union of Journalists, every member of staff of *Irish Press* Newspapers — be they journalists, photographers or wire men — who came to the North on relief duty qualified for the same ill-begotten bonus. God forgive me, but it must have cost the company a fortune over the years.

There was scarcely a reporter or photographer on the entire pay roll of the three papers in Dublin who did not, at one time or another, engage in temporary relief work in the North.

The contingencies were such that staff reporters in the outer reaches, such as T P O'Mahony, who was based as far away as Cork, and Cormac McConnell in Galway, had occasionally to be drafted in. Thus, the bonus system or 'danger money' payment, which I so gratuitously instigated, soared over the years. It's my fervent hope that this sum total did not unduly contribute to the eventual financial collapse of the company in 1995.

My own financial viability was itself at risk as my drinking escalated. The well-worn bleat of being overworked and underpaid gradually became a perpetual moan. I was certainly not as well off as I had been with the *Daily Mail* and expense accounts, to cover hospitality drinks, were not overtly recognised by the *Irish Press*.

One day, my poor wife Enda casually remarked, with a knowing shake of the head, that it would take two salaries to keep up with my drinking and provide for my family, which now comprised four lovely young daughters. It was then the thought occurred to me: why not be a ghostwriter? I was certainly well placed to collect two salaries. Local freelance correspondents throughout Northern Ireland often submitted their contributions to me in Belfast for transmission to Dublin for one or all of our three newspapers.

Journalists like Mick Cannon, a former *Press* Belfast correspondent before joining RTÉ as their man in the North, and Cecil Deeney, a former contributor before joining the *Belfast Telegraph* and later the BBC, were welcome to continue to write for our three publications. Why not join the party? Why not indeed? And so it was that I became the man who never was under a new alias.

It was either a measure of my gift of originality, or a commentary on my insobriety at the time, that I could conceive no more original a name for the new me than the prosaic, quintessentially Irish 'Paddy Murphy'.

The problem of collecting and cashing my alter ego's payment cheques was soon resolved. I instructed Head Office that all monies earned by our new correspondent, Paddy Murphy, were to be sent to number 15 Albert Drive in Belfast — my old address where some family members were still living. Of course I also advised my family of my newly acquired pseudonym and, just to make sure everything went to plan, I suggested they tell the postman they'd taken in a lodger called Paddy Murphy. I could not have been more meticulous about covering my tracks.

To allay any suspicion that I might be a thief who had stolen someone else's cheques, I told Sam Casey, the owner of the Brown Horse pub that for professional reasons I had changed my name. All future cheques made out to Paddy Murphy, I informed him, could be safely cashed on my behalf. He accepted my assurance that it would in no way render him liable to any fraudulent charge of conspiracy.

I might have been misleading the company, but not for a moment did I consider that I was doing anything dishonest. Income tax was deducted at source by the *Press* group, which must have left the Revenue commissioners wondering why anyone who was not on their registrar, and therefore somebody who did not officially exist, should be paying tax.

Granted, I was freely availing of office facilities to promote Paddy Murphy, but I still considered my deception to be fair and reasonable given that it was of mutual benefit to both parties.

All the sterling work I did in Murphy's name was accomplished, I would like to think, in my spare time, even though there were arguably occasions when Paddy Murphy was every bit as active as yours truly, Paddy Reynolds.

The *Sunday Press*, forever on the lookout for offbeat stories and features, was by far Murphy's most lucrative source of plunder. The news editor, Gerry Fox, soon acquired a sneaking regard for Murphy's constancy and expertise. He would phone requesting that I do this and that for the paper. When I complained that I was too busy with the other two papers, he would invariably say, 'Get Paddy

Murphy to do it!' And naturally, the always obliging and grateful Murphy could be relied upon to come up with the goods.

Although payments to Murphy were relatively small by modern standards, I found them rich pickings indeed in contemporary values, particularly in settling my ever-growing drinks bill. Month after month, year in and year out, my ghost writing continued unabated.

'You better watch out, or you'll be caught,' my good wife used to caution. 'Long runs the fox, you know ... '

Sure enough, one day I received a phone call from Dublin, summoning me on urgent business to Head Office. I suspected right away that my cover was blown and Enda didn't help with her response, 'I told you so.'

My initial apprehension was compounded when I inquired why my presence was required and was told: 'It's about that man, Murphy.'

I dared not pursue the matter, but pondered over it with dread as I drank all the way to Dublin in the bar of the Enterprise Express.

Fearing the worst, and somewhat befuddled, I entered the lion's den in the O'Connell Street Head Office. The line-up of the execution party in the Board Room as I recall it included: Mr J C Dempsey, managing director; Mr William Redmond, editorial manager; Colonel Matt Feehan, editor of the *Sunday Press*; and Oscar Trainor, personnel manager.

If they were about to administer the chop, then they were certainly going about it in a civilised manner. Mr Redmond at once called on his secretary Ms Ferguson to bring in the elevenses and, ominously, while she was at it to bring in Mr Murphy's file as well.

I found the opening gamut somewhat reassuring. In fact, I now began to think this might not be a sacking matter after all and instead suspected that maybe 'Mr Murphy' had landed us in a libel action or something of that nature.

We sipped our teas and coffees, served in china cups on a large silver platter, and nibbled our rich assortment of chocolate biscuits while I reflected that this was surely not a prelude to giving me the hammer. To my great relief, Mr Redmond opened on a work-friendly note. He remarked that news was beginning to hot up in the North and, with the Troubles getting worse, the company had decided to increase staffing levels in Belfast. Flicking through Paddy Murphy's comprehensive file, which Mr Dempsey had handed to him after his own perusal, Mr Redmond asked how I rated this Mr Murphy, whom he noted seemed to be earning nearly as much money as me.

I reckoned Paddy Murphy was as good as you would find anywhere, and said so. Mr Redmond concurred with a nod of approval and then floored me completely. *Irish Press* Newspapers were prepared to give him a staff job as my number one assistant!

The company was sure Murphy would find this proposition more attractive and secure than freelancing. I said I could not agree more, not really knowing what I was saying.

'He's already proved himself, so we don't need to interview him,' added Mr Redmond. 'Just send him down as soon as possible to sign the contract.'

In the bar on the return journey home, weighing up the pros and cons of this intriguing new development, I speculated on the feasibility of me continuing to play a dual role.

How was I to get around the tricky question of signing Murphy's contract unless I did it myself in disguise, or found an obliging proxy? And what would happen about annual holidays, when one of us would be expected to cover for the other? I could never again have any time off. And what if Murphy and I were ever required to appear somewhere together at the same time? How could I be in two different places at once, carrying out two different assignments when Paddy Reynolds and Paddy Murphy were one and the same?

No, I told my wife. It would never work and she said I was mad to even think about it. I resolved to settle the predicament during a post-Dublin drinking spree to celebrate my survival.

In my cups, and in a moment of mischief, I phoned Mr Redmond at Head Office. Choking with emotion as best I could and in a broken voice reeking, if only he could have smelt it, of a prodigious quantity of John Powers Gold Label whiskey, I told him to compose himself and prepare for some bad news. Although he had never met Mr Murphy — and that was a shame, I said, because no nicer man would you meet anywhere — it was my painful duty to inform him that Paddy Murphy had dropped dead of a heart attack that very day.

He had been cut down in his prime, God rest him, on the eve of fulfilling his cherished ambition of becoming a staff reporter with the *Irish Press*. In my maudlin state I shed tears as Mr Redmond, with a catch in his voice, suggested sending a wreath on behalf of the company. Since it was coming off a broad board, I made no effort to dissuade him. I advised that the flowers to be sent to Murphy's address on Albert Drive, but he told me to attend to this myself and charge the wreath to my expenses' account. When I sobered up, however, I had neither the heart nor the gall to exploit Paddy Murphy even in death.

Mr Redmond was toying with the idea of sending a company representative from Dublin to attend the funeral, and even considered attending himself. I hastened to assure him that I would do the honours. Thus, Paddy Murphy, the man who never was, was laid to rest at a mythical funeral service at which I was the sole mourner as well as the very corpse itself.

As if that wasn't enough, I even had the cheek to suggest that if I wasn't around when anyone needed to contact me in the course of the next few days, I was sure he would understand. That way, with the bosses in Dublin off my back, I was able to continue on my drinking spree.

'If you'd been sober you'd never have gone so far and made such an idiotic mess of things,' my wife remonstrated when I told her of Paddy Murphy's demise. 'Why didn't you just say in the first place that he turned down the job and left it at that? This drink will be the death of you.'

Of course, I couldn't afford to suffer the loss of Paddy Murphy's earnings. So, hey presto! The very next day I was reborn, this time under the new pen name of Joe Lamont.

The king is dead. Long live the king.

twenty-two

OUR EDITORIAL STAFF IN BELFAST WAS eventually increased to three, if we counted Joe Lamont, the new resurrection man. We were joined by Colin Brady, an extremely bright young journalist who found himself suddenly on the street when the *Northern Whig*, a leading morning newspaper in Belfast, was wound up almost without warning.

Apart from being an accomplished writer, Colin was also a gifted artist. With his tremendous sense of humour, he could well have made a name for himself as a newspaper cartoonist. In fact, he had quite a few of his efforts published and I mention this only because his *pièce de résistance*, as he used to call it, was exhibited in the Belfast office of the *Irish Press*. Such was its excellence that expert opinion pronounced it worthy of a place in the Tate gallery, except that this would have meant dismantling the wall it adorned.

It was a portrait in crayon of our esteemed managing editor, Mr William Redmond, which Colin dedicated to him in gratitude for having employed him as an *Irish Press* reporter. After its completion, it became a living thing as the result of an extraordinary, some might say miraculous, set of circumstances. People came from far and near to marvel at it. Indeed, it was celebrated in the world of local journalism in much the same way as some people revere moving or weeping religious statues.

It takes some explaining this, but one must first understand that the winkle picker shoes Colin wore, then at the height of fashion, had an indispensable role in the inception of this remarkable work of art. He was demonstrating to me how he had scored the winning goal for his team in a vital five-a-side indoor football match the previous evening when he kicked a hole in the wall that separated the editorial area from the teleprinter room with his right winkle picker.

The wall was wafer thin, made of cheap plasterboard. The hole he made, three feet above the floor, was a gaping one about the size of a lemon. It even looked like a lemon in silhouette. With artistic dexterity and a black crayon, Colin fashioned the hole into a replica of our managing editor's mouth, wide open as in the act of hearty laughter. Then he added a deft likeness of the nose and twinkling eyes under Denis Healey-like black, bushy eyebrows to complete the impeccable physiognomy of the jovial-faced Mr Redmond. It shone by its own light as a mute work of art but its transformation, or indeed transmutation, into a real living thing takes a little more explanation.

A frequent visitor to our office was Ernie Camlin, widely known as 'Ulster's Singing Frogman'. He used to sing underwater for some obscure reason, and make recordings while diving in the seas around the Irish coast on treasure hunts among sunken wrecks. Apart from providing us with novel stories of his underwater exploits and adventures, he also generously supplied us, by way of reward perhaps, with regular supplies of fruit, vegetables, flowers and plants from the big nursery his family ran in Newtownards. One day he arrived with a box of small tomatoes, which he recommended would make nice chutney. Colin and I found a better use for them in our idle moments. We played a game of seeing how many tomatoes we could throw into Mr Redmond's mouth, and whoever got the most into the cavity was the winner.

The heat of the office, the debris in the cavity, of whatever composition, and the seeds of the competitive tomatoes eventually combined after several weeks of germination to stimulate nature.

Tiny tomato plants started to sprout out of Mr Redmond's mouth. Delicate and spindly as they first appeared, Colin fed them Guinness in small doses and Guinness seemed to be very good for them indeed. The leaves took on a brighter hue of green. The slender little branches got stronger by the day, even showing tentative signs of reproductive tendencies. Lo and behold, tiny yellow flowers began to blossom and Colin suggested that perhaps a little manure would bring them on a treat. All being well, we could look forward to a healthy crop of 'toms' in the not-too-distant future. I don't know what kind of fertiliser Colin had in mind, or from whence it would come, so we left it at that.

Journalists who frequented the Brown Horse, Ned Johnston's and McGlade's bars were known, after a hard day's session, to vote for a diversionary visit to the nearby *Irish Press* office just to see for themselves what could emanate from an editor's mouth. It was good for a laugh.

Mr Redmond himself, on one of his infrequent visits to the Belfast office, was intrigued to find the embryo tomatoes growing there before he realised that he had played a part in the scheme of things. He was so taken with his own portrait, which he conceded was a good likeness, that he thought it a pity he could not take the masterpiece home to Dublin.

I offered to cut it out of the wall so that he could frame it, provided he would pay for the damage. But environmental concern for the welfare of the growing tomatoes ruled that out. So he took a photograph instead.

Meanwhile, my drinking was certainly no joke and was beginning to take a serious turn. Colin, within a matter of months, left to join the *Belfast Telegraph* and later went on to become Ireland correspondent for the *Daily Telegraph*. This meant I was back to square one as the only staff reporter in Belfast for *Irish Press* Newspapers, expected to cover three papers, each of whose editors was continually demanding copy in times of ever rising civil unrest as if their paper came first in order of priority.

I had now reached the stage when I felt I needed a drink to start work and a drink to help keep me at it. I also felt I needed a drink to help me sleep and eat. In fact, I felt I needed a drink to function, to survive — to do anything.

Still, I was living in total denial that it was a problem. Hiding drink under the bed or out in the garage was not a symptom of serious trouble, but rather a simple matter of expediency. I had not become so much a fall-down drunk as a topper-upper. No sooner had the drink died in me than I revived it at once with another, ensuring that alcohol was never really out of my system.

I was shedding weight like snow off a ditch. It dropped alarmingly, by nearly three stone to nine stone. My hangdog expression became ever more pronounced, but I never suspected I was as haggard looking as one sardonic remark I overheard suggested.

As I approached the bar counter in my local pub, the owner's son turned to his father and, in an audible aside, exclaimed, 'Here's creeping Jesus back.'

Now I might not have known the precise meaning of this epithet, but there was no doubting its contemptuous and derogatory tone. I felt totally humiliated.

To be characterised as such a base, snivelling creature did not do justice to my sartorial elegance, or so I felt. My good wife Enda always saw to it, whatever my degree of insobriety, that my executive suit was well pressed, even if I had slept in it; that my shirt was immaculate, my tie unstained and my shoes well polished. Fortunately, that morning there was only one other customer in the bar to witness the insult.

This customer was, by the way, a 'regular' during illicit out of hours drinking sessions in the pub and he fascinated me. I knew him only as the 'quiet man' since he never engaged in conversation, even of the aimless pleasantry variety for which pubs are renowned. Not even in ordering a drink did he utter a word. He had only to nod his head and the barman knew what to set him up — brandy after brandy, and large ones at that.

A typical 'lonely pint' customer, he showed no interest in the morning papers and with his characteristic staring eyes he would survey himself for hours in the mirror behind the bar. Then he would shuffle off, briefcase in hand, to go about his business, leaving me to wonder about who he was.

On the morning of my insult, I departed the bar shortly after the mystery drinker had left, as Enda had made an appointment for me to have a medical check-up. I had not seen a doctor for years and didn't even know what panel I was on, if I was on one at all. As the receptionist ushered me into the surgery I felt like doing a runner. Behind the desk was none other than the 'quiet man' himself, he of the staring eyes.

'And what's wrong with you?' he asked and, though I'd known him by sight for a long while, this was the first time I had ever heard him speak.

So taken aback was I that my only response was pathetic. 'I'm bad with my nerves, doctor,' I told him.

'You are an' my bollocks,' he grunted in his gruff voice. 'You're an alcoholic.'

Well, stone the crows: I was absolutely stunned. Whatever the precise meaning of the word 'alcoholic', and I don't think I had ever heard the word before as it was not in fashionable use then, I sensed what it ominously implied and it struck me like a death sentence. Life would not be worth living if what was once my best friend was now deemed to be my worst enemy. How would I be able to cope when I felt I needed a drink, even to buy a pair of shoelaces? I had come to depend on alcohol so much that I might as well be dead if I had to stop drinking.

Perhaps the doctor's diagnosis was wrong. After all, his examination, if you could call it that, was not even cursory. He hadn't taken my pulse, sounded my heart; he'd not even told me to drop my trousers.

'You have to go into hospital,' he concluded with another grunt.

Nonsense, I thought. Hospitals were for sick people. I only drank too much.

Striking a note of blunt finality he added, 'You're a physical wreck and for all I know, you're off your head.'

There was no way, I protested, that I was going into hospital. The stigma and humiliation were just too much. How would poor Enda and our lovely daughters feel? What would the neighbours say? I could even lose my job.

'If that's all you're worried about, I'll park you where no one will be any the wiser,' said the doctor, making it clear he would not be dissuaded.

He wrote me out a hospital admission note, which he then handed to me in a sealed envelope. The address was in Dublin.

'Is this some sort of nut house, doctor?' I asked fearfully.

'You could say that,' he replied.

In a last desperate throw of the dice, hoping he would have second thoughts, I asked, 'Do you really think, doctor, that this place will do me any good?'

'I hope so. I'm bloody well just out of it myself,' he replied with complete equanimity.

Grudgingly accepting the inevitable, it says something about my state of mind that, on leaving the surgery, a cheering thought occurred to me. I would be able to drink in the bar of the Enterprise Express all the way to Dublin. I did just that and still felt the need for a 'last drink' before the demon was exorcised. My ever patient and loyal wife, who came along to make sure I did not get cold feet, raised no objection when I dropped into the pub nearest to the hospital. Fearing it might well be my last drink in an age of miracles, I ordered a double.

My new home looked more like a hotel than a hospital and one of the inebriate arrivals at the admission desk, who was identified as a leading Dublin bookie, was so drunk he really thought he was setting off in search of the sun. He told the receptionist he wanted an early morning call, breakfast in bed and a taxi to the airport. Letting everyone know what a comedian he was, he loudly and laughingly proclaimed he was going on his 'alcoholidays'.

I was not amused when I was put to bed without my usual nightcap. I was given a handful of tablets instead. Patients were drugged for three or four days' oblivion to counter withdrawal symptoms, especially of a hallucinatory nature to which I had laterally become prone.

My first thought on waking was the need for a drink and this seemed par for the course, for other patients within my hearing range were requesting similar succour with pleas of 'No, not orange juice, nurse. I need a real drink' and 'I need a cure, for Christ's sake.'

We were encouraged to drink as much liquid as possible, but none of the hard stuff, of course, to combat dehydration.

Patients were divided into groups and mine consisted of a Dutch sea captain, a retired British colonial judge and a leading psychiatrist. The thought naturally occurred to me that if there was a medical answer to my problem, then why had the doctor who'd hospitalised me not found it for himself? By the same token, why was the top psychiatrist in the bed next to me not able to cure himself when he was supposed to be capable of curing others with the same complaint?

As the so-called 'recovery programme' progressed, I developed a close friendship on a patient-to-patient basis with the psychiatrist, who was surprisingly self-effacing. He confided that he was in overall charge of psychiatrists in a provincial circuit of hospitals and was on six months' probation to straighten himself out or 'get the boot', as he put it.

Recreational facilities at the hospital were of a very high standard and included a swimming pool, indoor gym, golf course, running track and sports pitches. Patients in our group availed of these facilities, not so much to make use of the amenities as to escape for a while from our rigid treatment regime. This provided my psychiatrist friend with the opportunity he seemed to relish, to mingle with patients undergoing different psychiatric treatment and with whom he chatted freely on a sort of busman's holiday basis. After conversing with some of these people he would remark, not I felt in any way to impress me, but as a matter of course, that so-and-so was schizophrenic, this one a psychosomatic, that one a psychoneurotic, and so on.

In a fit of irritation, I asked him that if he knew so bloody much, then how the hell was he not able to cure himself, or me for that matter. He floored me by explaining there was no cure as such for alcoholism, although the disease could be arrested on a daily basis if the sufferer went about it the right way. The only surefire answer was total abstinence and to effect this was imperative.

I challenged him about alcoholism being a disease, suggesting that despite its potentially lethal nature it was more a bad habit than anything else. Be that as it may, he went on to say that the World Health Organisation regarded it as a disease and that should be good enough for me. Then he explained his personal dilemma.

There was only so much the medical people could do in terms of the physical and mental or emotional aspect of the illness. But there was another dimension with which he personally had not yet come to terms. This was of a spiritual nature and, of course, he was neither priest nor minister. In his view, alcoholics were in need of some form of moral psychology or psychic change because of what he called their 'soul sickness'.

Addiction made them powerless, so they had to find a power they did not possess if ever they were to recover. Intrinsically self-destructive, alcoholism condemned its victims to an addiction so overwhelming that willpower was practically useless to overcome it. In short, alcoholics inclined to despair of life itself because of an inability to cope with what it threw up, and compulsive drinking was a recipe to self-destruct. It was a form of slow suicide, born out of despair, bereft of any faith or trust in anything or anyone outside of themselves. And because it was morally wrong to self-destruct, there had to be a spiritual remedy. My psychiatrist friend confided he had not yet found it.

The Dutch sea captain in our group was not much given to such analysis. His philosophy was that if alcoholism was a fact of life, then the sooner he accepted it and stopped fighting it, the sooner he expected to be released from his addiction. He also recognised his need of a personality change, since up to now he knew really nothing about the art of living a normal life and turned to drink to cope with any problem. His whole attitude and outlook on life was flawed, he conceded, as was his reaction to people, places and things with the capacity to destroy him if he let them. Indeed, he told me that he had grown up so ignorant of the facts of life that when his wife had their first baby, he was surprised to learn that it had not come into the world by way of her belly button.

As a self-confessed alcoholic, he recognised the need to have a complete overhaul of his persona. 'Change I must, or the old me will drink again,' he said.

The joker in our pack was formerly a circuit judge in the British Colonial Service. He was no longer convinced, he said, that drowning in a vat of beer was a great way to die.

Irish-born and clearly a man of great humanity, he said he detested the elitism of the colonial system in India, so much so that he'd made a point, during his entire service on the Bench there, of never sending a native to jail.

He also claimed he never once sat on the Bench without hiding a bottle between his legs. Such was his notoriety that when he was required to preside in the Court of Appeal, the two other judges used to make sure he sat in the middle because of his tendency to doze off and keel over.

It was during my incarceration in Dublin that I first heard alcoholism described as something that was 'cunning, baffling and powerful'. The aptness of this aphorism was brought home to me by the case history of one of my fellow patients.

He was the elderly father of a Belfast doctor, and his son was concerned about the old man's heavy drinking. Hospital treatment was deemed an imperative. But the father would have none of it. He invoked family honour as an insurmountable obstacle. What would people think of a doctor who committed his dear old dad to a mental institution to be treated, above all things, as a common drunk? Think of the shame of it, the indelible stigma.

The father, however, was finally inveigled into it on the promise he would travel to Dublin, not by ambulance with sirens blaring, but by sedate and anonymous taxi. More compelling was the assurance that the driver was under strict instructions to stop for the father to have as much drink as he liked, anytime anywhere along the way, so long as he got to the hospital.

Four days after the patient had emerged from round the clock sedation the son received a bemusing phone call from Dublin. The recently revived patient kept insisting that he was a humble taxi driver, not the father of some Belfast doctor. An accurate description was urgently required, and the doctor's worst fears were confirmed. His father had pulled a fast one — 'cunning, baffling and powerful'!

It transpired that the wily old man had managed, more or less, to stay off the booze until the last leg of the journey. In a pub near the hospital which, in jovial mood, he dubbed 'The Last Stop Saloon', he plied the taxi driver with so much drink the poor man passed out, while he himself only pretended to be indulging drink for drink. With the help of some customers, the sleeping beauty was carried to the taxi, which was then driven to the hospital by the erstwhile passenger, wearing the taxi man's cap.

It was not unusual in those days for patients under the influence to be admitted to hospital so the taxi man, still in the land of nod, was duly put to bed after being 'signed in' by the crafty pretender, who then set out unshackled on a countrywide drinking spree. He was later to explain it was all 'a bit of devilment' to get his own back on his son. But the scheme backfired when the son eventually caught up with him and had him returned to treatment under the Mental Health Act.

Against medical advice, I myself left the hospital after two weeks, not having done full justice to their rehab programme. The treatment course was expensive and beyond my means, and my good brother Willie had generously footed the bill. I made this my excuse for cutting the programme short.

To tell the truth, I acknowledged I that had a drink problem, but could not accept that I was an alcoholic.

twenty-three

PREDICTABLY, I WAS SOON BACK DRINKING again, causing inevitable hurt and heartache to those I loved. Alcoholism has rightly been described as a family disease and, while realising that it is not a matter for levity, I cannot help mentioning that even our pet dog Nipper was a victim.

In the dead of night when the old craving was on me and the sleep was gone, I would steal downstairs with the comforting thought of at least some company. Nipper, a lively little mongrel terrier, liked nothing better than to join me for a jar. He loved Guinness, which he supped with relish from a saucer as I conversed with him in hushed tones.

Sometimes I got rid of my empty bottles by pitching them into the overgrown back garden, which was so neglected it could have served for a safari. Provided Nipper had not too much to drink himself, he would dash out and retrieve the empties, which was a bit of a nuisance. Sometimes he would return with a bottle I hadn't thrown at all. It made me wonder about my neighbours. More often than not, however, he was generally too tipsy to retrieve, although the instinct was there.

Christmas was a busy time for him, scouring the neighbourhood for empty festive bottles, which he used to drag home by the neck from dustbins, thinking he was doing me a favour. I once inadvertently put Enda to the expense of taking him to the vet, as she attributed his inebriation to rickets.

While out walking with Nipper one morning to relieve our collective hangovers, I met a good friend, Brendan Murphy, who inquired about the little dog's welfare before asking me about mine. Not to put too fine a point on it, I told Brendan that I thought the dog was a bit of an alcoholic.

'There's no such thing,' Brendan rejoined. 'Either you are or you're not. It's like saying a woman's a bit pregnant.' But Nipper had a drink problem and I could prove it.

Brendan, who went on to assume the post of picture editor with the *Irish News*, had then only recently taken up professional photography. I suggested that Nipper would make a good guinea pig, not only to prove a point, but also to provide Brendan with a bit of picture-taking practice.

We were in the Grove Park near my north Belfast home and, from one of the drinking dens in the bushes, I selected a dozen or so empty beer cans. I slipped in a decoy and ordered Nipper to retrieve. And a dozen or so times he returned with a beer can in his mouth. However, he could not be persuaded under any circumstance to fetch the decoy. It was a lemonade tin.

Brendan, by the way, is the only man I know with roots in the republican Falls area of Belfast to boast that he followed in the footsteps of the former Unionist Prime Minister of Northern Ireland, Captain Terence O'Neill, which was literally true. Brendan was working then as our photographer and we were carrying out an interview and photo opportunity with Captain O'Neill at his home near Ahoghill in County Antrim. The Captain suggested posing in his beloved arboretum but, since it was raining heavily and the ground was sodden, Brendan was not over enthusiastic. However, Captain O'Neill insisted and tempted him with a pair of his Wellington boots, inviting him to try them on. They fitted like a glove and so it was that Brendan could state that he did indeed follow in the Prime Minister's footsteps.

There were times during my addictive drinking when my out-of-character behaviour suggested nothing less than a subconscious death wish. On one occasion, I conceivably risked life and limb in the throes of my reckless meanderings. I had been drinking, not too wisely, and staggering aimlessly from one company to another all day in the Somerton Inn, a pub near my home and my favourite watering hole.

At closing time, feeling restless, irritable and discontented, the need for 'one for the road' was paramount on my list of priorities. A married couple in the pub, whom I knew only by sight and who were otherwise complete strangers, announced they were going to a club to continue drinking. They wanted company to share the taxi fare.

I had never once spoken to them, although I knew the husband's name. His wife was inseparable from her pampered white poodle. She seemed to be either carrying it everywhere in her arms or had it on a leash, implacably defying all 'No Pets' signs. I regarded them as typical, middle-aged, bowling green types and assumed it was to the Salisbury Bowling Club that we were taxi-bound. It was only when we entered the fiercely loyalist Westland housing estate in north Belfast that I realised this was dangerous territory for any lone Catholic.

The craving for drink quickly overcame initial misgivings as we entered the brightly lit, bustling, boisterous drinking den. This was the Westland UDA Club, and no mistaking.

Ulster's loyalty to the British throne was proudly proclaimed in banner and bunting, augmented by myriad tokens of Protestant paramilitary allegiance.

As my married couple friends innocently, though rashly, insisted on giving away my religion by openly calling me Paddy, I began to get the wind up. Any Paddy in those days and in those circumstances was at risk of being deemed a legitimate target. It was high time I indulged in some well placed name-dropping to save my skin. Even though journalists were generally regarded as being vaguely neutral by both loyalist and republican paramilitaries, I decided discretion was the better part of valour.

As a reporter I was in contact, as occasion demanded, with staff at the Newtownards Road headquarters of the UDA in east Belfast, which was at that time a non-proscribed organisation despite its overt militancy. So I began asking all and sundry around me if Sam Duddy was one of the regulars. Sam, an erstwhile poet, was actually a media relations officer with the UDA and someone with whom I spoke on a regular basis by phone.

In my anxiety to cover my back, I even hinted that I was a buddy of Andy Tyrie, the UDA's Supreme Commander. In fact, I was merely on speaking terms with Andy and was certainly not as intimate as I made out.

My confidence began to rise in ratio to the impact I felt I was making. Although I was a Paddy, my name-dropping hinted that I had influence in the upper echelons of the UDA.

As the night progressed I blacked out and was left with only a vague recollection of what happened.

The next morning, not knowing how I'd got home, and recalling with stomach churning snatches of fear my feeble efforts to join in drunken loyalist singsongs while letting on I knew the words, I began to panic. Whose company had I joined in the club and what had I been slobbering about? Words could kill so easily in those days. Worst of all, where did I get the money I'd found in my pocket when I'd awakened? I froze in terror when it dawned on me what might have happened.

The previous day in the Somerton Inn, I'd tried to cash a cheque only to discover I had no cheques left. All that remained was the stub used to order a new chequebook. Surely to God, in my drunken state I hadn't used the stub to write out a cheque in the UDA club? It was one thing for a Paddy to get into such a joint in the first place, but it was infinitely much worse for a Paddy to get money on the strength of a dodgy pseudo-cheque.

My fear was confirmed when I found the stub missing from my empty chequebook. I shuddered to think of the awful consequences for pulling a fast one in such a club. The penalty could well be a kneecapping or a bullet through the head. There was only one way to find out: I had to return at once and make amends. But where exactly was this club? I had only seen it in the dark the night before and I knew it was located somewhere on a patch of waste ground in the Westland housing estate.

Retracing my steps, I returned to the Somerton Inn, but was unable to find the couple who'd introduced me to the drinking den. I finally decided to hire a taxi in the Westland area expecting, quite rightly as it turned out, that the driver would know the whereabouts of the club.

To gain admission as a non-member, I told the doorman I had a slate to clear and, after frisking me, he pointed to the barman. Much to my astonishment the man behind the counter actually greeted me saying, 'You're all right. You don't have to explain. We knew you'd be back.'

From a drinking glass above the till, he extracted the self-same stub from my chequebook and handed it to me. I could scarcely believe my eyes.

Scribbled in large, spidery, handwriting I had scrawled across the stub: 'Pay UDA £20 only'. I'd also had the audacity, or drunken foresight perhaps, to invoke the name of the UDA's Supreme Commander by writing, as guarantor on the bottom of the stub, a footnote: 'See Andy Tyrie for OK'. As I redeemed the IOU stub, which I promptly tore up in sheer relief, the barman invited me to 'have one on the UDA'. I downed the whiskey in one gulp and, for a brief moment, thought about taking the pledge.

But this was not the only madcap episode in my drinking experience I can recall to illustrate the 'fatal attraction' aspect of alcoholism.

At the height of the sectarian murders in north Belfast I found myself, early one morning, craving for a 'cure' at any cost in the loyalist Tiger Bay area. I had wandered from my Antrim Road environs, where all the usual haunts I knew near my house were closed.

Outside a pub in North Queen Street, which was said to be favoured by the UVF, a group of men, clearly hungover, were waiting impatiently for the bar to open some three hours before shutters normally went up at 10am. As a relative stranger in the district, I had to be on my guard. An outsider in such an area ran the risk of being regarded a loose canon, a spy or an easy target.

All such considerations, however, were secondary to the overwhelming need for a drink. In my covert role, I sought to ward off any suspicions by giving the impression I knew exactly what was afoot. I shared in the collective impatience of the drinkers-in-waiting, openly cursing the pub owner for his lack of punctuality. After all, it had now gone seven o'clock and there was still no sign of the proprietor, who must have overslept. How dare he keep us in agony.

Perhaps in my anxiety to be one of the boys I overdid the whingeing bit. One of them cynically remarked that by the look of me I didn't need a drink — I deserved one. That was the ultimate sanction.

Two of the men said they could wait no longer and were going to 'The Club'. To my consternation, they put me on the spot by inviting me to join them. More than anything, I now feared entering into a dialogue that could so easily give the game away. But I had to go with the flow and pretend I knew the set-up. I dry-retched as we walked along North Queen Street, which helped to check verbal exchanges.

I was still dry-boking from stomach nerves more than anything else as we turned into Albion Street, which has long since been redeveloped. Halfway up a dirty, litter-strewn alley behind a small, dingy two-up and two-down terrace house we reached a back door, left invitingly wide open. The tiny backyard was stacked with empty beer barrels and wooden crates. Entrance to the drinking den was through a dark, dank and damp, smelly scullery. At the foot of the house's narrow staircase, a drunk was slumped snoring. We simply stepped over his recumbent body to gain access to the upstairs 'bar', for the want of a better word.

The dividing wall between two small bedrooms had been knocked down to make more space. A large Union Flag, a huge blown-up photograph of Glasgow Rangers football team, a portrait of the Queen and a banner, which proclaimed 'For God and Ulster, UVF' adorned the walls.

Through the heavy haze of tobacco smoke I noted, despite my

lack of focus, that there were different patterns of faded wallpaper in the two halves of the room. But that wasn't the first thing I noticed on entry. Above the door was a sign that read: 'Would all patrons kindly check in their guns at the counter before going to the bar.'

Even if the sign was meant to be frivolous, it managed to be chillingly sinister. The place resembled the set of a Hollywood western and, as I surveyed the patrons of this loyalist shebeen, I could tell that the sign might not actually be a joke. Sinister men squatted on wooden benches lining each wall. They were dressed in black leather jackets, wearing black gloves and dark glasses. There was no doubt in my mind that they were in the business of killing Catholics. And here I was, an innocent Catholic if only they knew it, right in their midst.

As the two loyalists I had joined approached the bar counter, which was simply a wooden shelf across one corner of the room, I dreaded to think there might be someone there from the Antrim Road area who might recognise and finger me. Sure enough, after I ordered a 'bottle and a half 'un' — a beer and a shot of whiskey — which seemed to be the flavour of the day, I spotted a man I knew on a casual basis. He was sitting only a few feet away and I froze. As he caught my eye, he sent me a mute signal. Pressing his forefinger to his sealed lips he gave me a slow reassuring wink, indicating that he would not let the cat out of the bag.

This man was a distant neighbour and, only a week earlier, we'd had a few drinks together in the Labour Party Club in Waring Street. On that occasion he was 'strapped', as he put it, for money and put the bite on me for three pounds. It was the best few quid I had ever parted with. And now I felt I'd been paid back, with interest.

With a broken pane of glass the only visible source of air conditioning and a steady influx of shebeen patrons building up, the atmosphere became unbearably stifling. Apart from being decidedly in the wrong place at the wrong time and having secured the initial dubious 'cure', I was ready to beat a retreat. I failed, however, to shake off my two drinking pals, who must have thought I had a few bob and was an easy touch. They insisted on enlarging our drinking circle with a visit to the Naval Club in North Queen Street. This, as it turned out, was like jumping out of the frying pan and into the fire.

The clientele in this drinking den were also loyalist. After several lusty renditions of popular Protestant ballads, hand-to-hand fighting suddenly erupted for no apparent reason. Within minutes, baton-swinging police descended upon us, and everyone fled.

Befuddled as we already were, the demand was for more and more drink. With all the pubs closed on that bleak Sunday afternoon, and at a loss as to where to go, I announced that I knew the very place, even if it was in a republican area. It was the Felons Club on the New Lodge Road. I blandly assured my loyalist friends that I was in the know and could vouch for their safe passage.

Our mutual craving for drink overcame all patriotic and partisan leanings, although my two friends might well have been taking their lives in their hands as I had done in Albion Street. They were as mad as I was.

I have no recollection of how or when the night ended. The last thing I remember was my loyalist companions trying to read the 1916 Proclamation of the Irish Republic, which took pride of place on the wall near the front door of the Felons Club.

twenty-four

EARLY IN THE TROUBLES, I HAD a passing flirtation with radio and television, which was not at all to my liking.

My health was in decline, aggravated by a suspected stomach ulcer, when I applied for the post of news assistant with the BBC in Belfast. I regarded my chances as slim, since I was up against several newspaper colleagues with better qualifications.

From the start, my approach was of a cavalier fashion. I had been to a party the night before the interview and, with a bad hangover, was of a mind to call the whole thing off.

My wife, however, had different ideas and insisted that I showered and shaved and was sartorially correct for the big occasion. I tried to look the part, carrying an expensive briefcase. But it contained nothing more than a half bottle of vodka.

In the taxi on the way to the BBC I was fidgeting, fearful my cover as a secret drinker would be blown by the gurgling of the vodka, swirling in the bottle inside the briefcase.

Whatever the taxi driver was thinking, I ordered him to stop at a public toilet at Smithfield in the city centre. It was stomach churning, stinking and most unbefitting as the last port of call for anyone aspiring to join the establishment BBC.

As I sat in the toilet quaffing the vodka, I speculated on what the interview panel would think if they saw me now. Scanning the graffiti on the back of the door, I found one particularly intriguing item, if only for its remarkable logic: 'Eat shit. A million flies can't be wrong.' The thought of it unaccountably kept resurfacing during the interview, a pointer to just how well focused I was on this important occasion. Despite this inane distraction, I breezed through the interview, which was relaxed and informal.

One of the interviewers, by the way, seemed to be a man after my own heart. They say it takes one to know one, and this one, I suspect, could have done with a drink himself.

He had a touch of the shakes, fiddling with papers he pretended to consult, and a giveaway nervous twitch about his dry lips. Thus, I felt I had a kindred spirit to bank on.

After the interview, I was ushered into a room for a written test which was really a dawdle. I was provided with a timer and a typewriter, and was politely requested by a secretary not to leave the room before the expiry of the test. I had hoped to nip out to the Elbow Rooms pub, not far from Broadcasting House, for a quick one as the vodka had died in me. It was all the more frustrating because I had completed the test in fifteen minutes, half the allocated time.

It was then that I spotted a cocktail cabinet in a corner of the room, which was obviously for use by some of the BBC bigwigs. As a guest of the world's most famous public broadcaster I could see no reason for not helping myself. Unfortunately, the cabinet was locked and for the life of me I couldn't discover how to open it. In desperation, I shook it until the bottles rattled and I swear that if I had found a jemmy I would have used it.

Later, in the Elbow Rooms, I joined the other candidates and not one of them reckoned they had any chance of getting the job. For reasons beyond my comprehension and against all the odds, I landed the post.

On the eve of taking up the new job, I collapsed with acute stomach pains and was rushed to hospital. A perforated ulcer was suspected, but the operation was aborted when gallstones were diagnosed to be the trouble, and this required further surgery. During a lengthy recuperation, brandy and milk were the recommended restorative, which only served to add fuel to the flames of my alcoholic progression.

By newspaper standards, my job at the BBC was relative child's play. For the first time in my career I was desk-bound and consigned mainly to early morning shifts. My job was compiling and editing news bulletins for BBC radio, which in those days were of a brief duration, lasting only minutes. They consisted of severely compressed items, more in the nature of extended headlines, with the bones being only barely fleshed out. It was in sharp contrast in both quality and quantity to what I had been used to. This was the era just prior to the outbreak of the full-scale Troubles and consequently I had a lot of time on my hands. I was often bored and, although I was being more highly paid, I was by no means any happier.

Undoubtedly, I preferred the rough and tumble of the newspaper world and the loveable hacks and characters I encountered in its denizens. Not that the BBC types were intrinsically different. Most were newspaper graduates themselves, but quite a few struck me as being superciliously ambitious with a newly-acquired affectation and aloofness — a tendency to take themselves and their jobs too seriously. These were the would-be prima donna types, overly prone to adopt phoney accents.

In the midst of this egotistical ethos, I felt not so much out of my depth as out of place. I missed my old drinking pals in the print media, who enjoyed a freedom now denied me.

Drinking patterns had changed drastically and because of the BBC security set-up I couldn't nip out for a jar at any old time. And besides, pubs were closing early in the evening with the onset of the conflict on the streets.

Unlicensed drinking dens and shebeens began to flourish and I often had recourse to them when a jar was not otherwise freely available. A select few BBC colleagues regularly joined me. Like myself, they all had a drink problem but were unwillingly to admit to it.

Top of the list of the dives we were wont to frequent was the

Baker's Club in east Belfast, which had a variable 5am or 6am opening time. It was licensed ostensibly for night workers who provided the city with its daily bread. To me, it was an open house with anybody and everybody welcome. Members could legally entertain visitors and, more often than not, a sizeable cross section of the population could be found there imbibing and revelling in pre-dawn singsong sessions.

Other last resort watering holes to which we had occasional recourse included open-all-hours shebeens rejoicing in such exotic names as The Sweetie Bottle, The Cracked Cup, Doctor Hooks and The Swingin' Diddy, more politely known as The Spanish Rooms.

My ephemeral BBC experience lasted just under a year, by which time I knew my heart was no longer in it. The entire ethos was incompatible with the old lifestyle I preferred.

The parting of the ways was by mutual consent and compounded by the promise that the door remained open for my return to the *Irish Press* group.

Ill health dogged me while I awaited further surgery. A gallstone had lodged in a duct after the earlier operation for the removal of my gall bladder. For weeks I had bouts of excruciating pain, which delayed my return to print journalism.

Meanwhile, pending an opening in the *Irish Press*, I embarked on a spell of freelancing, which produced some surprising ramifications.

Despite my poor health, I rapidly built up a lucrative contract with the American United Press International (UPI) organisation through their Dublin office. The highlight of this venture was the attainment of a personal record for the number of outlets that simultaneously published one of my articles about the Troubles. UPI's Head of Bureau took time off during a visit to Jerusalem to send me a cable-graph, marking the achievement of a record one day 'score' in hundreds of publications throughout the world.

RTÉ had not yet built up a permanent staff on the scale currently employed in Belfast and was open to freelance contributions. I was also paid a retainer.

Other occasional outlets for my freelance activities were as diverse as *Business and Finance* in Dublin, *Lloyds List* in London, the *Cork Examiner* newspapers, the English *Spectator*, Associated Newspapers (including my old alma mater the *Daily Mail*), the *Sunday Empire News*, the *Sunday Chronicle* and the *Catholic Herald*.

The uncertainty of these markets, the constant insecurity and the substantial overheads involved, ruled out freelancing on a permanent basis. But a bonus arrived when the *Sunday Empire News* ceased publication. I qualified for a golden handshake, despite the fact that I'd only been their freelance correspondent for a few months.

The opportunity to rejoin the *Irish Press* was not long in presenting itself and I was soon back with my old employer. Two former high profile colleagues during my *Daily Mail* days were later to join me in the *Press* group: Seamus Brady of the *Daily Express* became political editor while Jack Murdoch, my former colleague in Dublin, was appointed as crime reporter and literary critic.

Jack and I had shared many experiences in the past, but he was personally involved in a real-life drama, so bizarre as to be almost incredible, while working on a story for the *Evening Press*.

As a brilliant investigative journalist, he was covering the brutal 'body on the beach' murder of a Dublin prostitute, which was a big long-running story at the time. The suspect arrested for the murder turned out to be Jack's own son, Adrian.

A lieutenant in the British army and son of a bishop's daughter, Adrian, who was on leave in Dublin, was alleged by the police to have confessed to the crime during a drinking spree. Jack was a vital witness at the trial, which he would normally have covered himself in his capacity as a crime reporter. He gave defence evidence to the effect that, at times during the course of conversation, he had discussed the murder with his son, and his investigations for the newspaper were often conducted by phone in their home within earshot of Adrian.

In short, Adrian had access to all the details of the murder he had allegedly confessed to, either by hearing his father discuss the case on the phone or from reading his father's reports of the murder in the papers. Jack's son had actually been on sick leave while receiving attention for a nervous breakdown, which left him in such a confused mental state, it was argued, that he had imagined that he'd committed the gruesome deed himself. The jury accepted this, the alleged confession was rejected and Adrian Murdoch was found 'not guilty' and discharged to undergo psychiatric treatment.

I continued my demanding work in Belfast, but it was soon evident I could not carry on single-handed for the *Irish Press* group as the Troubles intensified and became more widespread. As a stopgap, an aspiring young journalist from the *Irish News*, Paddy Topping, joined me as a full-time freelance. He declined a staff job.

Paddy shared my partiality for a drop of the hard stuff and, freely mixing business with Bacchanalian pursuits, we earned a newspaper reputation locally as 'The Terrible Twins'. We certainly got into some scrapes together, but in truth, this did not really inhibit us professionally, or so I would like to think.

One escapade I associate with Paddy involved an innocent brush with the security forces when he triggered off a major security alert.

Paddy lived in Ballymena, about thirty miles from Belfast, and travelled daily to the city by rail or bus. Returning home on the train one night, he nodded off, missed his stop in Ballymena and woke up in Derry. After an overnight stay in a hotel there, he fell asleep again on the train back to Ballymena, passed by the town a second time and woke up in Belfast.

Travelling home again the next night, this time by bus, Paddy fell asleep after stretching out on a back seat in the upper deck. Presumably the conductor didn't spot him as the bus drove into the depot in Ballymena to be locked up for the night.

It was pitch dark when Paddy awoke and he couldn't see a thing. Terror-stricken, he thought he had gone blind when he checked his eyelids and found them open. Oblivious to the fact that he was on a bus, he stumbled down the stairs shouting for help. Paddy was also unaware that the bus had driven over a 'bear pit', used for repairs, and he fell into it. He clawed in vain at the pit walls, heavily smeared with black sludge, yelling louder than ever until he stumbled onto stairs leading out of the pit.

It was still pitch dark when a stentorian voice boomed over a loud hailer, 'You are surrounded. Come out with your hands up.'

At the top of his voice Paddy shouted back, 'I'm not breaking in. I'm bloody well trying to break out.'

A door was gingerly opened and out stepped Paddy into the light of dawn, covered from head to foot in black, oily grime and besieged by armed police and British army soldiers.

Not daring to go home in his bedraggled state, nor venturing to travel to work by bus or train, he hitch-hiked a lift to Belfast. He called at a petrol station near our office to clean up and I got him a change of clothes.

With an alarming escalation in the violence of the Troubles, the *Irish Press* bosses were forced at last to make big changes in staffing arrangements. New offices were opened in Royal Avenue in the heart of the city centre, and a new post of Northern editor was initiated. I had no quarrel with the redoubtable Vincent Browne being appointed. In fact, I welcomed it. I had to concede that there was good reason for my being overlooked for promotion. Not only had I broken service with the *Irish Press* group, but I was also drinking too heavily to take on added responsibility. For Vincent it was his big breakthrough into journalism. He later went on to greater things in Dublin as *Sunday Tribune* editor and RTÉ presenter.

Vincent was not the type of person to suffer fools gladly. I reckon he made an exception in my case and, although there were times when he sent his secretary to shadow me and monitor my drinking propensities on assignments, he was sympathetic, or at least not unsympathetic, to drink addiction victims.

A permanent reporting staff was set up in Belfast and a new employee by the name of Kieran McGill was given the Derry brief, assuring adequate coverage in the Northwest. This was to take a tremendous burden of responsibility off my shoulders.

Another addition to the staff numbers was Ciaran McKeown, who was appointed as political commentator. Later to gain prominence because of his involvement with the Peace People, I will always be grateful to Ciaran for the generous help he gave in helping me to combat my alcoholism. Not only did he encourage me to take remedial steps, but he devised and actively put into effect a recovery programme, based on his own appraisal of the situation.

In this he was supported by his good wife, Marianne, to such an extent that they opened their home to me. I was undergoing a particularly bad patch at the time and, unsparingly, they converted their front living room, installing a bed to accommodate me in my 'drying out'. Their help and support aided me in overcoming my withdrawal symptoms.

Michael Keane, who was to succeed Vincent Browne as Northern editor, and our immediate boss in Dublin, Michael O'Kane, were equally understanding and supportive, something I will always remember with deep gratitude. Despite their best efforts and finding my own willpower unavailing, I tried to regulate my drinking, which by now was totally compulsive. I would still not accept it was out of control.

Among other things, I started experimenting with my 'poison', switching from brandy to beer, or vodka to Guinness, blindly repeating the same thing and, each time, expecting a different result.

My perception of the alcoholic was the stereotyped drunk — unshaven, unkempt, in rags, smelling of the gutter and with a bottle of 'plonk' sticking out of his pocket. I certainly did not fit that bill. I simply drank too much.

'I'm not one of those people,' I rationalised with a psychiatrist. 'After all, I'm a journalist holding down a good job.'

'All right then,' he replied cynically. 'Come back to us again when you're not holding down a good job and when you're not a bloody journalist.'

My dilemma was the age-old paradox of being unable to live with drink and unable to live without it. The unbearable pain of such conflict finally drove me to take the first step on the road to recovery. I sought help. Left to my own devices, I finally had to admit that I would either die or go mad.

Such was my physical condition that my doctor of old, 'the quiet man', he of the staring eyes, suggested I take up where I left off those several years earlier in the Dublin hospital.

I was now seeing hideous crawly things that weren't there and hearing weird music that didn't exist. This time, the doctor recommended a local psychiatric hospital. But no, it was asking too much. Whatever else I might have been, I was certainly not insane. Nevertheless, he insisted that it was the only place in Belfast which treated people in my condition. Knowing his own track record as an alcoholic, I ventured to inquire if he personally had sampled this hospital as a patient. He made no bones about it.

'I had no choice,' he admitted. 'It sobered me up in the end and I'm no nut case.'

I looked at him and noticed that he was certainly a different man, clearly at peace with himself and with the familiar stare gone from his eyes. To my certain knowledge, the good doctor thereafter stayed sober for thirteen years until his retirement. Alas, it was then that he brought out the bottle again and it killed him within a matter of months.

The severe hospital regime condemned me to be kept and treated as a prisoner. My clothes were held under lock and key. In common with other patients, I was issued with Belsen-style pyjamas. In my domain, there were bars on every window and locks on every door. For the first few days I was drugged so that I couldn't think straight. I was not permitted to shave with an open razor and even safety blades were doled out under supervision. I was also forbidden to retain such items in my toilet bag.

'Now we don't want you to slit your throat, do we?' an orderly explained when I naïvely questioned the taboos.

For no other reason, I suppose, than accommodation purposes, we alcoholics were hospitalised with patients suffering from other mental illnesses. This could be disconcerting at times and occasionally objectionable. Nevertheless, I couldn't fault the psychiatric treatment which, as I understood it, was designed to promote and encourage personality changes and a new way of contented living without the use of booze.

It was based on the simple truism that, in the absence of change, the 'old me' would drink again. First and foremost, it was explained to me that I had to fully concede to my innermost self and accept that I was an alcoholic. It was no use not merely acknowledging that I had a drink problem. Once the admission came that I was an alcoholic, that was half the battle. It required a willingness to face reality as a prelude to a massive dose of self-honesty. At the risk of sounding didactic, I was to discover in the final analysis that acceptance was the key to my drinking problem and, indeed, the key to contented sobriety.

'Grow up and cut the bullshit,' I was urged. Turning to the bottle to cope with living problems was the hallmark of immaturity.

Eventually, my obsession for alcohol and the terrible craving that went with it was finally removed.

For years, even though I didn't recognise it, I was powerless to control my drinking. Therefore, if there was to be any hope of recovery, I had to find some power beyond myself. This I discovered by the simple expediency of cultivating the company of people in pursuit of the same goal. In my case though, and don't ask me to prove it, I suspect I needed a touch of 'divine intervention' to get there.

twenty-five

AFTER TWO YEARS' SOBRIETY, I WAS given a hard-earned vote of onfidence by being promoted to Northern editor of the *Irish Press*.

During a difficult period prior to this, I'd been impelled to conceal a dark secret. I considered it prudent to eschew publicity on a traumatic experience which, conceivably, could have seriously affected my family's security as well as my own.

At a time when words could kill and suspicion was often equated with guilt, I was arrested as a suspected terrorist. To the best of my knowledge I was the only news journalist up to that point to have been subjected to such an ordeal.

This all happened during a period of unusually high tension and an intense IRA bombing campaign. The security forces embarked on a major drive to round up suspects in a bid to apprehend those responsible. It was not quite on the scale of the activity surrounding the introduction of internment on 9 August 1971, but proved to be every bit as ineffectual. The internment operation by police and troops, when more than three hundred republicans were scooped in dawn raids, was seriously flawed. As history would confirm, many innocent people were arrested on the basis of false or misleading intelligence reports. To accuse was to proclaim guilt in those days of arrest without trial and, in a way, so it was in my case.

My home was in a middle class mixed Protestant and Catholic area. One night, as I was about to go to bed, a sudden commotion erupted in the normally quiet cul-de-sac outside. A rumbling of heavy traffic, chugging and grinding, was accompanied by a cacophony of loud door slamming, excited shouting and feet stamping.

The street was chock-a-block with army Saracens. As I looked out of the window, a powerful searchlight mounted on one of the vehicles was making a swoop of the houses. It stopped and focused on mine. Soldiers of the Parachute Regiment were running helter-skelter up and down the street, scurrying around and squatting amongst flowerbeds and bushes, to take up positions in neighbours' gardens.

In response to a loud knock, I opened my front door to an army officer, who was standing stiffly to attention, a baton under his left arm and a clipboard in his right hand. In the glare of the spotlight trained on me, I saw a soldier lying behind a rose bush in our garden with his rifle pointing at me.

After establishing my identity, the officer, speaking in a brusque, barking voice which was unnecessarily loud in the stillness of the night and more suited to the barracks, formally addressed me while reading from his clipboard:

'Under Section 11 of the Emergency Provisions Special Powers Act ... I am arresting you on suspicion of being in possession of arms, ammunition and explosives ... and propose to search the house ... '

A soldier stepped forward and frisked me after ordering me to put up my hands. Two 'Paras' then linked me, yanking me off my feet and declining my request for time to put on my shoes and coat. I was frog-marched down the driveway, while a stream of soldiers filed past me at the double, pouring into the house with a clatter of heavy boots.

As I was bundled into the back of a Saracen, I noticed the curtains parting in the windows of several neighbours' houses. Though I had other things on my mind, I began sadly reflecting on the inevitability of having to leave the neighbourhood I had grown to love, now that suspicion and mistrust had visited me.

The soldier guarding me in the Saracen insisted on me sitting on the rear seat, nearest the back door. I protested at the door being kept open, especially as we were driving at speed along the Antrim Road, which was in complete darkness, blacked out for security reasons.

Not only was I in danger of falling out, but I was fully exposed to any sniper fire or bomb attack as we rumbled past the staunchly republican upper New Lodge area.

It ensued that my destination was a primary school at Glenravel Street, near the city centre, which had been taken over by the 'Paras'. In one of the classrooms, I was made to sit in a chair clearly designed for an infant. It was most uncomfortable, even painful, as I had to wedge my backside into it sideways. In this twisted position, I was told to turn and face a wall that was only inches from my nose. A coloured soldier, guarding me with a rifle, ordered me not to move — as if I could — and not to turn round. Otherwise, he told me that he'd blow my 'bleedin' head off'.

Having taken off my watch earlier, I had no idea of what time it was. Eventually, an officer arrived and ordered me to turn around to face him as he sat in a comfortable man-sized chair. He introduced himself as 'Captain Green', which I assumed was a pseudonym. It was one and the same title used by certain paramilitaries in their press releases.

He was quite an affable man and, in reply to his first question, I most assuredly and emphatically denied being a member in any shape or form of any terrorist organisation whatsoever. His information was, he said, that I was keeping very late hours in these dangerous times and not getting home until early morning. What mischief was I up to, and why was I present at so many IRA funerals, as seen on television news reports?

He seemed taken aback when I informed him I was a journalist and in that capacity I often worked late night shifts. By the same token, I told him that I also attended UFF and UVF funerals. I suggested army intelligence should have done their homework better before acting so precipitously. I also supplied names of some people in high places who could vouch for me.

He left off questioning me abruptly and even mumbled some sort of apology. He asked politely to be excused while he made further inquiries, and left the room.

The coloured soldier, who had been outside the room, returned and offered me the comfortable chair that the officer had just vacated. He also helped to extricate me from the infant's chair. It took some time to get the circulation going again in my numbed backside.

Somewhere in the background a radio was crackling with indistinct voices, but I was able to make out some words that were repeated several times: 'House clean, house clean' and 'suspect clean, suspect clean ... over and out'.

Before my release the interrogating officer returned to announce, in a way that suggested he was not a bit surprised, that I would be allowed to go without charge. He was polite and quietly apologetic to the point of embarrassment. He called me 'old chap' and gratuitously explained his men had been acting on 'information received'. The way he put it was that an informer had 'put two and two together and got five'. This struck me as a rather flippant attempt to justify such a massive search and arrest operation.

He did mark my card, however, about the 'loose tongues' of certain of my neighbours, who had been acting more out of reckless malice than any sense of public duty. In fact, he left me in no doubt as to the identity of one of these neighbours whom I knew personally to be a bigot. 'Watch him, old boy,' he said.

After several hours in custody I thanked the officer for nothing and asked to be ordered a taxi. He would have none of it, insisting the onus was now on the British army to return me home 'safe and sound'. He said this without a trace of cynicism.

Denied a taxi home, I travelled under protest by the same route and in the same hazardous manner in the back of a Saracen. Once again the vehicle rattled along, with its doors left curiously open, through the darkened back streets.

What transpired on my arrival back home ranks as something

unprecedented, given my experience of such events. Over a loud hailer the officer in charge apologised to my neighbours for the army's disruption of their night's sleep. Then, to my astonishment and almost disbelief, he said he wished to make it publicly clear that 'Mr Reynolds' was not guilty of any offence, was totally innocent and he offered my family his apologies. I could see the window curtains in the other houses parting again at his words.

I was relieved to find that, while my family was agog and in a state of shock, the house showed little sign of an all-out raid. In covering stories of other such army swoops, I'd witnessed houses partly wrecked with floorboards torn up, walls and ceilings left with gaping holes and total domestic upheaval. In contrast, the raid on my home had been a relatively genteel affair, though every room, including the attic, was searched. This suggested to me a lack of conviction behind the operation and left me wondering why they'd bothered at all.

My elderly mother-in-law Margaret McAlister, affectionately known as 'Mrs Mac', was particularly bemused by the whole carry on. A native of County Cavan, and then in her eighties with memories of past havoc wreaked by squads of British ex-servicemen in 1920s Ireland, she had asked the soldiers who insisted on looking under her bed, 'Are you the Black and Tans?'

My youngest daughter, Colette, who was then aged five, refused point blank to get out of bed because she was not wearing her pyjama bottoms. At her direction, one of the soldiers fetched the garment and the raiding party were ordered to turn round while she got dressed. The poor child, who hated school, thought we had called in the army to get her to go because she always stubbornly insisted, 'I don't care what you do, I'm not going to school.'

When two of my other daughters, Anne and Pauline, started to cry for their daddy, their younger sister Joanie, seeking to mollify them, counselled: 'It's only a dream, it's only a dream. Close your eyes and go back to sleep.'

As one of the soldiers was looking under Joanie's bed, she told him she had a new dress for her First Holy Communion and asked him if he would like to see it. He took her on his knee and told her he had a daughter just like her who was also making her First Holy Communion, and she had a dress just like it.

By an ironic coincidence, just before my arrest, I had been sitting in my living room and reading a book on the history of the IRA written by my editor in Dublin, Tim Pat Coogan. Tim Pat had sent me a copy to review. The living room was the last to be searched by the soldiers and it was only when the search was underway that Enda spotted the book lying on the settee. My distressed daughters had gathered in the room by this time and Enda, worrying that the book could give the wrong impression given the circumstances, urged Anne to sit on it and not get up.

A quirk of fate also decreed that I should come under suspicion on another occasion, this time underscoring the old adage that looks aren't everything.

An IRA bombing campaign was under way in Britain, and Scotland Yard issued a countrywide television appeal for a 'most wanted' man, complete with photo fit. This man had an Irish accent and was known as 'Paddy the Hat'. It so happened that in some circles, to distinguish me from others called Paddy, I was also known as 'Paddy the Hat'. What's more, friends informed me that the photo fit was a dead ringer for me.

Even my family made a joke of it. But it was no joke when Enda and I were intercepted, while out shopping, by a police Special Branch man who told me I was wanted for questioning. No doubt he would have arrested me on the spot if Enda had not recognised him as a family friend. Both their families were from the same area of County Cavan. At his invitation, we retired to a local pub to renew acquaintances.

He revealed a story that illustrates just how circumstances can sometimes conspire to point the finger of guilt gratuitously at a completely innocent person. He told us about a man who, while being screened after flying to London from Belfast, had told security police the sole purpose of his visit was to attend a relative's funeral. While being questioned about his native stomping ground in republican west Belfast, he was asked if he knew or had ever heard of an Irishman called Paddy the Hat. He replied that he did in fact know of such a person, who was a regular patron of a city centre pub called the Brown Horse. He was, of course, referring to me.

I was aware of the identity of the London visitor my wife's police friend was talking about. This appeared to put me in a spot since it looked like the authorities were now monitoring my travelling friend's every move, believing that he was up to something in London. To avoid the embarrassment of taking me in for questioning there and then, the Special Branch man suggested that I should lie low for a while.

One evening, while watching television, the photo fit that so closely resembled me was flashed on the screen as an introduction to the main news. For a moment my heart stopped. But to my great relief, it was announced that the real Paddy the Hat, whose surname was King, had been arrested on a flight from Dublin to London. I was instantly off the hook.

Reflecting on my experiences at the hands of the security forces, I thought it ironic that, for someone who couldn't recognise a stick of gelignite from a stick of rock, I should have been subjected to such suspicion and interrogation.

However, there was one occasion when it could truthfully be said that I did handle ammunition. This was due to Gerry Fitt, the MP for West Belfast, and later Lord Fitt of Bell's Hill.

Gerry and I were personal friends of long standing and I was a frequent visitor to his Antrim Road home. Shortly after he was issued with a licensed personal protection revolver, my daughter Joanie and I dropped in to see him. Joanie attended the same school as one of Gerry's four daughters, whom he had dubbed the 'Miss Fitts'.

Gerry was without a coat as he opened the door and could be seen to wear his shoulder-strap gun. Even though he represented a staunchly republican area, he was an implacable opponent of the IRA and hated having to carry a gun himself. He said that all he knew about the weapon was that it was supposed to go off when the trigger was pulled. He wasn't even sure if the safety catch was on or off. When he confessed that he would have to take further instruction about using it properly, I was a bit apprehensive as he removed it from the holster for closer inspection.

Now Gerry's eyesight was not the best. He used to joke that one of his spectacle lenses was really the bottom of a jam jar, so when he held the revolver at arm's length to scrutinise it, I was afraid it might go off. Screwing up his eyes he said there was a way of 'breaking' the gun, but he had not yet got the hang of it. Having at last achieved this, he confided that he wasn't sure how to load or unload the weapon.

I suggested that perhaps it would be safest for all concerned if he had no gun at all, as bullets began to pop out in all directions.

'The bloody thing's leaking,' quipped Gerry.

Joanie and I were not amused. The two of us ended up on our hands and knees under a table, retrieving the bullets which Gerry had spilled onto the floor. Gerry put the bullets into his pocket, promising us that he'd take more lessons.

One night shortly afterwards, in August 1976, the same weapon came to his rescue when an angry mob attacked his home and stormed in while his wife and daughters were in bed.

Gerry stood with gun in hand at the top of the stairs and the very sight of the revolver kept the intruders at bay. He threatened that he would shoot the first person to try and get past him. If the gang knew as much as I did about his militant acumen, they might not have been so reticent. As he advanced menacingly, the mob backed away to the front door and finally made off.

But the Fitt family came under constant stone, bottle and missile attack thereafter, although it was not until 3 July 1983 that their now unoccupied house was attacked for the last time and was burned to the ground.

twenty-six

AS NORTHERN EDITOR OF THE *IRISH PRESS*, I fulfilled the dual role of officer-in-charge and private first-class. My brief was to write editorials, news analysis, political commentaries, and carry out other executive functions, as well as slogging it out in the field as a day-to-day routine reporter. The top brass regarded my multi-faceted role as simply being in the scheme of things.

My staff was down to two senior reporters at the best of times: Donal O'Donnell, who was eventually to become editor of the local paper in his native Newry; and Alan Murray, who later became an active all-round freelance in newspapers, radio and television.

Otherwise my team consisted of local freelance correspondents, covering events in the outlying areas of the North.

Despite the paucity of staff, I managed to develop a fail-safe system that ensured we were never scooped on any major news stories. Nor did we miss anything in the broad spectrum of stories across the country.

Over the years, I had built up such a rapport with close contacts in the offices of the regional newspapers that I was able to recruit journalistic moles who would operate for our mutual professional benefit. Whatever the probity of our spy network, it was most efficacious for the *Irish Press* to have paid informers strategically placed in certain local newspapers by day and night. Thus, we availed of full access to the fruits of those newspapers' combined newsgathering, province-wide teams. These moonlighters qualified for both secret retainer fees and lineage payments in return for their services, which included instant tip-offs and full story details.

The eleven years up to my early retirement in 1989 were the most work-intensive of my career, with no let up in the endemic violence of the Troubles. For instance, scarcely a week passed without an interview with the next-of-kin or neighbours of the latest tragic victim of our own parochial holocaust.

This was particularly gruesome when I was working to deadlines. The *Evening Press* was especially demanding. The first country edition, which was sent to the four corners of Ireland, went to bed at around 11am. The city and final editions followed in the late afternoon.

There were occasions when I was compelled, however reluctantly, to operate in conditions bordering on the unethical in order to meet deadlines.

Police Press Office details about the identities of victims were often long delayed and I was under pressure to pad out the facts. The occasional intrusion of privacy, I rationalised, was part of the job and unavoidable. Despite a hard-bitten reputation, this troubled me on occasions as I tried to strike a balance between news desk demands and observing professional standards of conduct.

I recall on one occasion interviewing the distressed members of a family in the immediate aftermath of a particularly vicious sectarian assassination. I had initially mistaken my interviewees to be neighbours of the victim when they were, in fact, next-of-kin. Instead of sending me packing, they co-operated to the extent of supplying photographs of the victim, a teenage boy who had been on crutches all his life, but who had been made to kneel down and then cynically handed a Bible to say his prayers before he was shot. With his mother looking on while he recited the Rosary, he died with a bullet through his head.

In my court reporting days, I once had the novel experience of both covering the news and making it myself. This was a sequel to a clandestine loyalist paramilitary news conference at which guns were produced. Under subpoena I was 'required personally to appear at the Crown Court to be held at the Courthouse at Crumlin Road, Belfast on Monday the 15th day of February 1982 at 9.30 o'clock forenoon to testify and give evidence on behalf of the Queen and to attend the Court regularly from day to day, until discharged'. I was further informed that a refusal to testify 'in the case of the Queen against James Pratt Craig' would be at my 'peril'.

Craig had originally been jointly charged with one Arthur James Bettice, but while awaiting trial, Bettice was shot dead by fellow paramilitaries for being an alleged police informer.

Craig and Bettice were accused of possessing firearms on 2 September 1979. On the same day, they were also alleged to have professed to belonging to a proscribed organisation, namely the UFF.

I had helped arrange a press conference, having received a phone call from a 'facilitator' from the loyalist UDA. The UDA was not legally proscribed at this time despite being the largest paramilitary organisation in the country. The caller requested I contact selected media representatives to attend a secret rendezvous the next day for a big story. The only stipulation was secrecy.

By arrangement, a small party of journalists from both Irish and British newspapers and broadcast organisations waited at the corner of Belfast's Royal Avenue and North Street for a cloak and dagger journey into the unknown. By stealth, we were taken in two cars into a warren of streets in the Shankill area and told to close our eyes and keep our heads down, otherwise we would have to be blindfolded. The passengers in our car included Denis McGrath, *Irish Independent*; Colin Brady, *Daily Telegraph* and John Hicks, *Daily Mirror*. In an attempt at disguise, our driver, in a turned-up collar, had a cap pulled over his eyes, wore dark glasses and appeared to be sporting a wig.

On arrival at our rendezvous, we were ushered into a brick building, which had the trappings of an Orange Hall or loyalist community centre. A dozen members of the UFF, in full paramilitary regalia complete with balaclavas, stood behind a Union

Jack-draped table, each holding a different type of automatic weapon and standing to attention in military-style 'present arms' fashion.

On another table was arranged an awesome display of various weapons. The walls of the room were festooned with Union Jacks and paramilitary pennants. The entire setting was palpably terrifying.

Two spokesmen addressed us. One read a statement, announcing the success of a recent gunrunning operation. The arsenal on show was evidence of it. He claimed innocent Catholics had nothing to fear, but all active republicans were legitimate targets. The other spokesman identified the various modern weapons on display and listed their lethal potential. I shuddered to think what would happen if there was a police or army raid to interrupt the proceedings. In fact, I was driven to ask what they intended to do if the security forces suddenly arrived. 'We would shoot them,' was the reply. 'But we'd shoot you first, Seamus.'

Before dispersing, we were all warned to tell the police nothing. Given the circumstances, there was little of a helpful nature we could tell the detectives anyway after the publication of our reports. But on the strength of photographs, which were published in the newspapers, two men, Craig and Bettice, were arrested.

The original prints of the pictures, seized by police during visits to our offices, were minutely examined. Enlargements of the photos showed that one of the UFF men, holding his gun up for inspection, had allowed the sleeve of his jacket to expose a tattoo near his wrist, which the police claimed identified him. The other suspect was arrested on the strength of a tiny necklace, which his paramilitary regalia failed to conceal.

The court case itself was something of a tragi-comedy in parts. Conscious that there were dangerous characters in the public gallery as paramilitary observers, I sensed a tendency by some journalists to be over-circumspect in giving evidence. After all, one of the defendants in the case had already been murdered for opening his mouth. If the perpetrators would kill one of their own, what then would they do to witnesses?

One photographer in particular, when shown a picture he had

taken at the press conference, was so careful in his choice of words that when the prosecutor asked him to say who was in the photograph he replied, 'People.'

'Were they men or women?' the prosecutor demanded. The photographer didn't know because he couldn't see their faces.

'What were they wearing?'

'Clothes,' he replied.

'Would you describe the clothes as battle dress?' The photographer didn't exactly know what battle dress was.

'What were these people holding?' He didn't know that either.

'Were they not guns?' He didn't know, as he hadn't examined them.

'Did they not look like guns?' Yes, but even if they looked like guns they could have been dummies, for all he knew.

'I am a pacifist,' the photographer urged. 'I am against all guns. Blessed are the peacemakers.'

At this stage the witness, who was on the verge of keeling over, was excused from giving any further evidence and ordered to stand down. Later, he confided to us that perhaps he had taken a drop too much drink to steady his nerves before giving evidence. There was no doubt that he was as scared as the rest of us. It was no surprise, therefore, when the case collapsed due to a lack of real evidence.

It is a grim and salutary footnote to the case that not only was the original defendant, Arthur Bettice, murdered but his comrade-in-arms James Craig was also assassinated in later life by paramilitaries. The judge, too, was to die by an assassin's bullet. William Doyle, who had once been a classmate of mine at the Christian Brothers school in Barrack Street, was gunned down by the IRA one Sunday morning as he was leaving Mass in St Bride's Church on Belfast's Derryvolgie Avenue.

For high drama with multi-ramifications there was nothing to compare, in my newspaper experience, with the seven-month period in 1981 spanning the republican prisoners' hunger strike. It was a nightmare for any news editor to oversee such was the extent and nature of the overpowering turn of events which made Northern Ireland the focus of world media attention.

On 1 March 1981 Bobby Sands, the 27-year-old leader of some three hundred IRA prisoners in the Maze jail, began a lone hunger strike in a bid to secure special category status. The following month, he was elected MP for Fermanagh-South Tyrone and, a month later on 5 May, he died after sixty-six days without food. Nine more prisoners were to die until the hunger strike was eventually called off in October. I covered all ten funerals, which attracted worldwide publicity.

In terms of violence in the aftermath of each death, and the political spin-off, there were widespread repercussions. During the protest, sixty-four people were killed, comprising thirty-four civilians and thirty policemen and soldiers. As an observer, the passions aroused during the dramatic campaign all but defied description.

Of all the sectarian atrocities during the Troubles, the Kingsmills massacre must rank in infamy as one of the most vile. Eleven Protestant workmen were ambushed on their way home at a lonely crossroads in South Armagh. They were all lined up by a ruthless firing squad and gunned down in cold blood. The only survivor later agreed to give his first media interview to the *Irish Press* after months of reluctance to talk publicly to anyone about it. The graphic interview was the result of a chance meeting I had with Alan Black in his native village of Bessbrook.

Greyhounds were the passion of Alan's life and he was out walking two of his dogs when I bumped into him. I was seeking directions, having been sent to Bessbrook to compile a follow-up anniversary story about the massacre. It was part of a series of articles on violence, which the paper was running at the time.

The facts were already well established and I was aware that Alan, who was then forty-two, had previously declined to be interviewed by the press. I had not known him by sight, but when I explained the nature of my mission, he volunteered on the spur of the moment to assist me with his version of the events, saying he had not been able to bring himself until then to talk about what had happened. He had been in hospital recovering from his wounds for a long time and was still undergoing intensive counselling.

His home was on the side of a hill, overlooking a most pleasant valley. After making tea, he went over to the living room window. He pointed to a spot in the far distance where the terrible deed, which would haunt him for the rest of his life, was perpetrated.

'I have only to look through this window and it all comes back to me, over and over again,' he said in his soft, quiet, matter-of-fact voice.

The New Year of 1976 was barely five days old when it happened. Twelve men, aged between twenty and fifty years of age, and including two brothers, had just finished work at 5.30pm in Compton's textile mill in Glenanne, South Armagh. The craic was good as they piled into the minibus for the journey home to Bessbrook. There should have been thirteen passengers, but the odd man out was at a funeral that day, so his life was spared.

Five miles out from Glenanne, the minibus, travelling along the uphill approach to Kingsmills on the Whitecross-Newry Road intersection, was flagged down by someone waving a red lamp in the evening twilight. A man, wearing a mask and brandishing a gun, appeared at the driver's window and ordered everyone out. All twelve workers were then lined up with their hands resting on the side of the bus.

It was then that, out of the shadows, stepped up to a dozen heavily armed men, all wearing masks. Ominously, the gunman in charge asked if there were any Catholics present. The only Catholic worker was urged in a whisper by the two Protestants standing on either side of him to say nothing. They squeezed his hand and tugged his coat by way of tacit reassurance. They assumed that this was a militant loyalist hold-up, as five Catholics had been killed in two recent shootings in the same area, and this was possibly the same gang.

The Catholic worker stepped forward bravely to identify himself and was ordered to lie down in a ditch. Paralysed by fear, he found he couldn't move so he was dragged along and thrown out of the way. Alan felt sorry for his Catholic pal, thinking he was the one being singled out for execution.

Suddenly, however, the command, 'Fire!' rang out and the assassins opened up with a withering hail of bullets from their automatics. As the eleven Protestant workers fell, ten of them mortally wounded, the avenging assassins sought to administer the *coup de grâce*. They riddled the prone bodies on the ground and left them all for dead. The murders were later stated to be in retaliation for the five recent Catholic killings in the area.

Alan reckoned that he was saved as someone had fallen on top of him after he'd been hit in the initial burst of fire. The Catholic survivor in the ditch was ordered by the gunmen not to move for half an hour before raising the alarm.

The massacre was claimed by the South Armagh Republican Action Force, regarded by security forces to be a cover name for the Provisional IRA.

What struck me most perhaps about Alan's horrendous story was the incredibly stoic manner of his relating it and his idiomatic, unassuming descriptive powers. Alan told me that Bessbrook proudly held the accolade of Ulster's model village. The villagers were ideally integrated. There was no bitterness, no bigotry and hardly ever a cross word spoken between them. Catholic and Protestant hearts beat as one. Alan spoke in lyrical terms. Bessbrook was warmly known to everyone as 'the Brook'. Life was once so placid there, he said, that even a stone cast into the stream made a welcome disturbance.

In the aftermath of the massacre, the villagers could only cling to each other in their grief. The once sleepy village had to be lulled to sleep with Valium. Alan concluded that Bessbrook had 'wept its heart out and the terrible ache lingers on'.

In describing his deep personal loss, and pointing to my notebook, he invited me: 'Take your time and write down as slowly as you want the names of ten of your dearest friends, picturing each of them in your mind's eye, savouring the warmth and depth of their closeness. Then, as fast as you can, strike them out one by one and, in an instant, they are all gone, forever, just like that.'

He snapped his fingers and, for a while, was silent. He saw the massacre as an act of the devil, his own survival as an act of God. Then the rhetorical question: 'Why me?'

Alan was almost cut in two as the fusillade of bullets scythed through the victims. To illustrate his brush with death, he rolled up his shirt to reveal a livid jagged scar, extending in an upward curve under the rib cage the entire width of his body.

'The bullet entered here,' he pointed out, tracing the route with his forefinger, 'and came out there, missing my heart by a whisker.' Alan was meant to live.

So too was Gerard McLaverty. He was the final victim on the death list of the notorious Shankill Butchers gang. And it was he who sensationally 'fingered' them, and was later to provide me with an exclusive in-depth interview while he was in hiding.

I was in court when the eleven gang members, the most cold-blooded, anti-Catholic, cut-throat killers in the history of the Troubles, were sentenced on 20 February 1979. What struck me most was the ice cold, passive image which each of the accused projected. The dock could only hold five of them and the other six sat outside, four on one side and two on the other. Without uttering a single word or showing the slightest emotion, they received between them forty-two life sentences and a total of 902 years' imprisonment for nineteen murders and associated UVF crimes.

Slow torture had been their specialty and the weapons they used included meat cleavers, butchers' knives, hatchets and hammers. Their victims included seven Catholics, picked up at random and murdered, as the judge at the trial put it, 'in a manner so cruel and so revolting as to be beyond comprehension'.

Mr Justice O'Donnell, brother of my journalistic colleague Donal, told the two ringleaders, William Moore and Robert Bates: 'I see no reason other than terminal illness that either of you should ever be released. You will serve life in prison, meaning life.'

Subsequently, the judge's edict was to lose its meaning when the powers-that-be in their wisdom overthrew his judgement within twenty years and allowed the release of the entire gang. Life, after all, did not mean life.

Gerard McLaverty recalled how the gang callously left him to bleed slowly to death. But he lived to point them all out, earning him the sobriquet 'the resurrection man'.

Convinced to the point of near paranoia that his life was forfeit if any of the gang's associates ever caught up with him, Gerard fled Belfast to spend the rest of his life looking over his shoulder.

Through an intermediary, I was chosen to 'ghost' his story when he decided to tell all. As the result of information received, I travelled to meet him in hiding, after undertaking not to reveal his whereabouts. In a wide-ranging interview, he related all the harrowing details of his ordeal at the hands of the blood crazed Butchers. He also told of how he helped round up the gang, pointing out his tormentors as he travelled in an unmarked police car around Belfast's trouble spots.

It was during the second loyalist general strike in May 1977 that the Butchers' reign of terror ended. The strike, a successor to the 1974 action which had brought about the collapse of the British Government's power-sharing Executive, saw loyalist paramilitaries manning roadblocks and checkpoints, as well as hijacking cars and intimidating businesses to close in an attempt to bring the province to a standstill. Helping out and providing muscle at the barricades were all the UVF members of the Butchers gang. It was their undoing. One by one, Gerard McLaverty identified them as he cruised around their haunts.

His story made two full pages of our *Sunday Press* and after the interview Gerard arranged to meet me in Dublin for a special assignment. He was planning a new life abroad and wanted to pay a last secretive visit to Belfast. Still fearful that he might be recognised, he asked me to travel with him, but only in the dead of night. There was not a soul in sight as I drove him from Dublin to his old home for a pre-dawn reunion with his family. He also called at a hotel to see his mother, a night shift worker, who had been kept in the dark about his whereabouts for security reasons.

After the fleeting but emotional visit, Gerard insisted on returning to Dublin before daybreak.

twenty-seven

AFTER FORTY YEARS IN JOURNALISM, DIVIDED equally at both English and Irish national newspaper level, it was time to celebrate the joy of leaving. I finally decided to quit at a defining moment in my career, when I found myself lying on the flat of my back, trapped under a pile of bodies like a human haystack, with the sound of concentrated gunfire ringing in my ears.

It was the afternoon of Sunday 12 August 1984. The occasion was the visit to Northern Ireland, at the risk of being arrested on sight, of Martin Galvin, the publicity director of the Northern Irish Aid Committee in America, or Noraid.

Galvin had been banned by the government from setting foot anywhere in the North because of claims that his organisation provided funds for the IRA to buy arms. Three days earlier, he'd slipped through a tight security cordon into Derry to announce to the delight of republicans everywhere that he proposed to attend an anti-internment rally in west Belfast.

When I arrived at the rally, some two thousand vociferous supporters were milling outside Connolly House, the Sinn Féin headquarters in Andersonstown, which was surrounded by barbed wire entanglements in a defence fortress setting. An elevated platform was erected in the front garden for the reception of the would-be hero Galvin.

A one-time New York District attorney, whose parents heralded from Offaly, Galvin had been born in the United States and was a hate figure in unionist eyes. The RUC were under strict orders to arrest him the moment he appeared on the Sinn Féin platform. The only way to accomplish this, of course, was to storm the platform and this was precisely what the police were prepared to do. Thus, the scene was set for mayhem.

As the republican movement's most articulate spokesman in America, Galvin had so far outwitted the RUC and his admirers loved it. Massive numbers of riot squad police were now determined to get him, come what may. They threw a ring of steel around Connolly House, but such was the density of the throng of people blocking the platform, they could not get near it without the use of force.

Suddenly the fanatical crowd burst into a roar of ecstatic approval as their hero, seemingly from nowhere, appeared on stage exulting in triumph and smiling broadly with outstretched arms. A jubilant Sinn Féin president, Gerry Adams, emerged to share centre-stage with Galvin, but the adulation lasted only a few seconds before all hell broke loose. With a powerful forward surge, police batoned their way towards the platform, some trying to scale over the spiked garden railings.

Meanwhile, no time was lost by Galvin's minders who bustled him to safety. He was spirited away, vanishing as quickly as he had appeared. As the crowd battled in hand-to-hand fighting with police, gunshots began to ring out.

I was standing in the crush near the platform and all around me police, who were interspersed through the dense crowd, were opening fire at will. People were fleeing helter-skelter in all directions. Women screamed in terror and, as the shooting became more intense, I feared another Bloody Sunday. Surely to God, I thought, the police could not be firing live ammunition. It was some time before I was convinced that the sounds I was hearing were the discharge of baton rounds, otherwise known as plastic bullets. These bullets, of course, could also be lethal. A short distance from me, a local 22-year-old man, Seán Downes, fell mortally wounded.

He was lying on his back on the ground with his shirt front open, his mouth agape, when I saw him being tended to by friends. I didn't know whether he was dead or dying. His friends said he had been shot at close range.

At the height of the pandemonium which engulfed the sea of people, I was carried on a wave of men, women and children being driven backwards towards a row of shops. The stampede was aggravated by repeated orders shouted by police for everyone to 'Get down! Get down!'

I fell in front of a chemist's shop and people tumbled over me as a policeman, pointing his gun at us while stabbing it in all directions, screamed over and over again for us to get down or he would shoot us. Clearly he had gone berserk. I can still see his bulging apoplectic eyes, flushed face and walrus moustache and hear his high-pitched hysterical voice. The last I saw of him he was backing off, spinning round apparently loading and unloading his gun, and firing at random.

Meanwhile, someone had fallen across my feet. I felt another heavy person lying on my stomach. Someone was sprawled across my chest, so I could hardly breathe.

As I lay trapped under a pile of bodies with only my head visible, the unaccountable thought occurred to me that the new suit I was wearing for the first time would be so begrimed that I could never wear it again. That passing thought was succeeded by an unlikely new terror. A stray dog, a scruffy Alsatian or German Shepherd, had run amok when the commotion began and was now advancing menacingly towards us.

I had noticed the animal earlier, loping aimlessly through the crowd, panting heavily with its mouth wide open, as panic stricken people scattered about. It was either a security guard's dog, which had escaped its minder, or a stray neighbourhood rogue.

In the midst of such pandemonium, I was expecting the animal at any time to start savaging the people who were fleeing all around it. Now it was heading in our direction, showing signs of exhaustion, though still looking decidedly dangerous and drooling copiously. It slumped down, inches from my head. I could feel its breath and almost sense its thumping heartbeat. Then, to compound my terror, it started to sniff my face freely, dispensing its saliva over me. Unable to move a muscle, I dreaded to think I was now at the mercy of a mad dog, liable to turn on me any moment.

The air was still filled with the sounds of concentrated gunfire when the dog made a surprising move. First, it extended a tentative paw over my face. Then, to my astonishment, it started to slowly climb and clamber over the top of our supine bodies. It didn't appear to be demonstrating the aggression I had feared, but seemed to be seeking human comfort and security among the mayhem.

It was only when the shooting finally subsided that our human haystack began to dismantle and I was left aching in every limb. That was when I irrevocably resolved that enough was enough; that there must be a better way of earning a crust and it was time to call it a day.

Unfortunately, circumstances dictated that I was to wait yet another five long years before I could clinch early retirement. However, I can't gripe too much about the extra wait before leaving the rat race as, when I finally did hang up my notebook, I emerged thankfully with my body and mind still intact.

During the Troubles, so many lives were suddenly cut short; so many people died or were maimed for simply being in the wrong place at the wrong time. Those of us who survived unscathed in such a relatively small area, with such a correspondingly small population, can only be regarded as hostages to fate.

For most of the Troubles I lived in north Belfast, which has the worst single death toll of any area in Northern Ireland and where no fewer than 548 men, women and children met a violent end.

A neighbour, who lived three doors up from my house in our quiet leafy suburb in the shadow of Cave Hill, was shot dead in his bedroom. His executioner had been a gunman who had run a ladder up to the bedroom window. Another neighbour, further down the road, was shot five times but escaped with his life in a sectarian attack. Outside the same house on another occasion, a taxi driver, responding to a bogus call, was shot dead as he sat at the steering wheel.

At the lower end of the road, our local pub was bombed on three occasions, having mercifully been given short advance warnings. All patrons managed to be evacuated just in time.

Further down the road again, four people were killed in a bomb attack on a row of shops. It was Bloody Friday, 21 July 1972, when Belfast as a whole sustained twenty-six no-warning bomb explosions in which seven other people were killed and 130 officially injured.

Even our new local Catholic church could not escape the ravages of sectarian hatred. While in its final stages of being built, a bomb was planted inside, completely blowing the roof off.

And just around the corner from my home, a good friend, colleague and leading investigative journalist, Jim Campbell, who was Northern editor of the *Sunday World*, was shot twice in the stomach in the hallway of his home when he answered a call to his front door. Jim, the first and one of only a few frontline journalists to be targeted by the paramilitaries, survived with a bullet still lodged in his body.

It was not always safe, even in the office. Time and again, we were forced to evacuate due to bomb scares. On one occasion, our then Northern editor, Vincent Browne, Declan 'The Digger' Fay, an Australian reporter who had joined our staff, and myself were looking out of the office window, our attention having been drawn to a sudden lull in the busy street activity outside. Traffic was at a standstill and the street was deserted of pedestrians. If this was a bomb scare, then no one had told us. It sometimes happened.

As we watched, a series of explosions ripped through the tall block of shops and offices on the opposite side of the street to our left. Only the corner end of the building directly in front of us remained intact. A man, whom we'd thought had gone berserk, suddenly appeared in the middle of the street. He had seen us from the street below and was gesticulating frantically, punching the air wildly with his fist.

'Would you look at him?' Vincent remarked. 'The poor bugger seems to be enjoying this. I don't believe it, he's actually laughing and pointing up at us.'

The poor bugger was not enjoying it and he wasn't laughing. It was just the expression on his face as he desperately tried to mouth a bomb warning to us, hoping, no doubt, that someone amongst us could read lips.

'Cobblers,' said The Digger as the penny dropped. 'He's not waving. Can't you see he's holding up five fingers? We've five bleedin' minutes to get out.'

Fearfully speculating that there was a bomb ticking away somewhere in the building beneath us, I was transfixed in an instant by a loud explosion, while still standing at the window. The blast was not in our building, but in the one directly across the street and I could scarcely believe my eyes.

The bomb had literally blown up in our faces. Advancing towards us, as if in slow motion, was a huge rolling ball of dense smoke, spanning the entire width of the street until it seemed to gently subside on our very window sills. It had been a massive blast, yet not a single pane of glass in our spacious offices was broken. It was one of those freakish things. All our windows were covered with strips of anti-bomb blast tape, which probably accounted for our general lack of damage. In other explosions during my reporting days, I had seen windows appear actually to bend without breaking, such were the vagaries of the blasts.

There was another scary experience in the same office when someone had carelessly left a large parcel inside our front door, sparking off a bomb alert. It meant that, in evacuating the building, our entire staff had to file past the suspect package, with that being the only exit route, not knowing whether it was a bomb and, if it was a bomb, not knowing when it would go off. The entire area was evacuated but after examination the British army bomb squad declared the parcel harmless.

I had reached the stage in my career, I felt, when I could see the writing was very clearly on the wall. The company was in dire financial trouble and I was convinced it was only a matter of time before the *Irish Press* group, founded by Eamon de Valera, would collapse. Sadly, that was to be its fate.

To mark my farewell, colleagues in Dublin took over a pub in Middle Abbey Street and behind closed doors we had ourselves a ball. It was a joint adieu as our religious correspondent, T P O'Mahony, was also saying goodbye to Dublin and hail to his native Cork.

Now T P was no Pavarotti, but he sang his heart out that night and I thought he would never stop. His swansong was 'The Banks of My Own Lovely Lee', extolling the virtues of his beloved home city. It went on and on, verse after verse, *ad infinitum* and I felt that, when called upon for my own pleasure by raucous acclamation, I should respond in defence of my own lovely Belfast. But for the life of me I couldn't remember the words of 'My Lagan Love', which I considered an appropriate replication.

So it was that I sang the only song that came to mind at that moment, which I knew to be synonymous with my native city, 'The Sash My Father Wore'. This, of course, is the Orangemen's anthem and, while I have no doubt that there were no Orangemen or women present, everyone joined in the chorus and nearly lifted the roof off the pub. What surprised me more than anything was that they all seemed to know the words. Passers-by in Middle Abbey Street must have thought the Twelfth of July, the Orangemen's traditional marching season, had come early to Dublin.

The champagne, whiskey and porter flowed that night and I believe I was the only one not to touch a drop. I had been abstemious for some time and can honestly say I had reached the stage, such was the quality of my contented sobriety, that I no longer regretted not being able to drink again with impunity. Nor did I resent the fact that other people could.

Fifteen years into my early retirement at the time of writing, I can reflect on a total of more than twenty sober years, thanks be to God and with the help of people who were kindred spirits.

Cheers!